ARABIC
FOR BEGINNERS

ARABIC
FOR BEGINNERS

Sarah Risha

TUTTLE Publishing

Tokyo | Rutland, Vermont | Singapore

"Books to Span the East and West"

Tuttle Publishing was founded in 1832 in the small New England town of Rutland, Vermont [USA]. Our core values remain as strong today as they were then—to publish best-in-class books which bring people together one page at a time. In 1948, we established a publishing office in Japan—and Tuttle is now a leader in publishing English-language books about the arts, languages and cultures of Asia. The world has become a much smaller place today and Asia's economic and cultural influence has grown. Yet the need for meaningful dialogue and information about this diverse region has never been greater. Over the past seven decades, Tuttle has published thousands of books on subjects ranging from martial arts and paper crafts to language learning and literature—and our talented authors, illustrators, designers and photographers have won many prestigious awards. We welcome you to explore the wealth of information available on Asia at **www.tuttlepublishing.com**.

Published by Tuttle Publishing, an imprint of Periplus Editions (HK) Ltd.

www.tuttlepublishing.com

Copyright © 2022 Periplus Editions (HK) Ltd.
Illustrations by Scott Larson

Library of Congress Control Number: 2022931197

ISBN 978-0-8048-5258-6

First edition, 2022

Distributed by
North America, Latin America & Europe
Tuttle Publishing
364 Innovation Drive
North Clarendon,
VT 05759-9436 U.S.A.
Tel: 1 (802) 773-8930
Fax: 1 (802) 773-6993
info@tuttlepublishing.com
www.tuttlepublishing.com

Japan
Tuttle Publishing
Yaekari Building, 3rd Floor,
5-4-12 Osaki, Shinagawa-ku,
Tokyo 141 0032
Tel: (81) 3 5437-017
Fax: (81) 3 5437-0755
sales@tuttle.co.jp
www.tuttle.co.jp

Asia Pacific
Berkeley Books Pte. Ltd.
3 Kallang Sector #04-01
Singapore 349278
Tel: (65) 6741-2178
Fax: (65) 6741-2179
inquiries@periplus.com.sg
www.tuttlepublishing.com

26 25 24 23   6 5 4 3 2
Printed in China   2308CM

TUTTLE PUBLISHING® is a registered trademark of Tuttle Publishing, a division of Periplus Editions (HK) Ltd.

Table of Contents

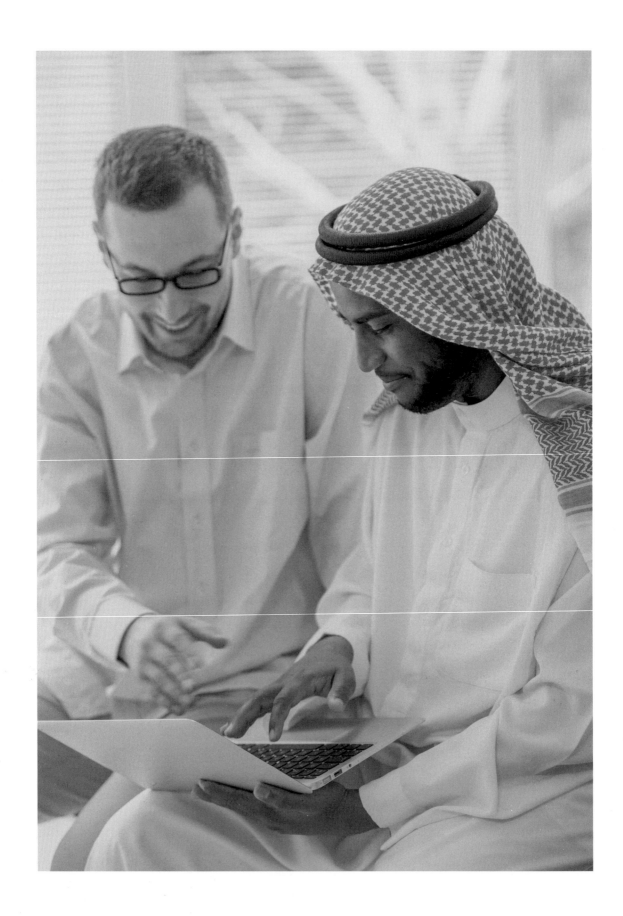

Why Learn Arabic?

There are many good reasons to learn Arabic:
- Arabic is the fifth most widely spoken language in the world.
- Arabic is an official language of the United Nations.
- There is a high demand for speakers of Arabic in the Western world.
- There are financial incentives, as Arabic-speaking nations are fast-growing trade markets.
- Arabic is the liturgical language of Islam.

The Arabic language is strongly connected to Arab culture. Fundamental values and traditions are shared among all Arabs speaker regardless of geographical, historical, social or class differences. However, traditions and practices vary from one country and from one region to another. In 2016, the United Nations calculated the total population of the Arab world at approximately 420 million people spread across a vast area so it is natural for cultural differences to exist. However, there are a few major reasons for these differences. The first is that the Arab world has long been known as the cradle of three major monotheistic religions: Judaism, Christianity and Islam. Although these religions share many common values, each one has its own devotions, tenets and loyalties. Arab culture grew and developed through a combination of the main principles of these three religions; nevertheless, Islam has had the greatest effect on Arab culture. Furthermore, the Arab world was at the crossroads of world trade, which encouraged cultural exchange through commerce among the Persians, Romans, Greeks, Indians, Chinese and Turks. Being the cradle of these three main religions and a center of commerce united Arab societies and cultures and at the same time created cultural differences.

By relating Arab customs to the teaching of Islam, it can be explained how tradition was established and developed or where it came from. This does not mean that all Arabs are familiar with a specific Islamic teaching. This is to say, for example, Islam guides its followers to use their right hand in eating. Therefore, Arabs were directed that it was proper to eat with their right hand. Almost all Arabs use the right hand because it is a part of their culture more than a rule of their religion.

Arabic and the Arab World

There are about seven thousand languages spoken in the world. It is estimated that half of them are spoken by only three thousand people and several languages are expected to become extinct in just a few decades. The most spoken language in the world is Mandarin Chinese with more than one billion speakers. The most commonly used alphabet in the world is the Roman or Latin alphabet used by English speakers and most European languages. However, the Arabic alphabet is the second most used. Arabic alphabets are widespread, used in other languages beside Arabic including Urdu in Pakistan and India, Persian in Iran, Turkish in Turkey and Swahili in Tanzania, Kenya, and other countries in central Africa.

The Arabic language belongs to Semitic family which incudes Arabic, Hebrew, Aramaic, Syriac, Akkadian and Phoenician (Al-Kauther, 2009, p. 7[1]). The 420 million people who speak Arabic are spread throughout the world; however, the nation with the largest Arabic speaking population is Egypt with 82 million and the smallest is in Bahrain with 1.3 million. It is the national language of the twenty-two countries of the Arab world in the Middle East and North Africa—Algeria, Bahrain, the Comoros Islands, Djibouti, Egypt, Iraq, Jordan, Kuwait, Lebanon, Libya, Morocco, Mauritania, Oman, Palestine, Qatar, Saudi Arabia, Somalia, Sudan, Syria, Tunisia, the United Arab Emirates, and Yemen.

One of the most widespread misconceptions about Arabs is that all Arabs are Muslims and all Muslims are Arabs—all Arabic countries have Islam as their main religion but there are Arab Christians and Jews. The word "Arab" is a linguistic term, not a religious one, that refers to a person who speaks Arabic as their first language. There are many non-Arab Muslim countries including Indonesia, with the largest Muslim population, Malaysia, Afghanistan, Bangladesh, Tajikistan and Turkey.

Arab countries enjoy diverse populations with different cultures, politics, history and dialects but formal Arabic plays a major role in connecting Arab cultures, backgrounds and activities. As with any other language, it acts to unite communities with different historical backgrounds, nationalism and ethnicity all over the world.

How to use this book

The most effective way to use this book is to study each part of the lesson alone, as there is more than one point introduced in a chapter. Study the first section carefully and give yourself enough time to understand the information and practice. Later, review what you learned then move to the next section. I encourage you to be dedicated and not to wait too long between tackling sections and lessons. Learning a language is a skill that requires time and practice. All lessons have practice exercises including some which review materials covered earlier to help you practice what you learned. Do not be shy or confused when making mistakes; it is a sign that you are learning and approaching your goal. This book has detailed explanations and exercises on the important topics. All you have to do is work hard.

As you continue, you'll learn that there are three short vowels used in Arabic to make reading easier for the learner. It is important, however, to note that almost all books, magazines or newspapers written in Arabic do not use these vowels. They are only used in elementary classes and in religious works such as the Quran, the Bible and the Torah that are published in Arabic. In order to familiarize you with correct pronunciation and to help make learning and memorizing them easier, you will see vowels incorporated in the new vocabulary of every lesson and in the exercises of the first seven lessons. Beyond that, you will continue without vowels so you will be able to learn to pronounce words without them.

---

1   Al-Kauther. (March/April 2009). *A Rasooli community newsletter*. Retrieved from http://www.nuradeen.com/archives/Al_Kauther_News_Letter.pdf

Each chapter concludes with an opportunity to reflect upon what you have learned so you can better understand the things you need to practice. This will help you measure your progress. There are also opportunities to listen to downloadable audio so you can learn how to properly pronounce Arabic words and to better understand the dialogues presented in the practice lessons.

One of the main objectives of this book is to raise awareness of Modern Standard Arabic. It is my hope that learners of Arabic who use this book will be able to better converse, write, read and otherwise communicate in Arabic and to comprehend what you hear and read in the Arabic language. Additionally, points of Arab culture are introduced in each lesson to present this culture from an Arab's point of view rather than what might be shown in the media.

My advice

- Start by reading, pronouncing and writing the alphabet. Do not move to the next step until you know the alphabet. After this, the following steps will be much easier.

- Read and review each lesson carefully.

- Memorize all the words presented before moving to the next lesson.

- Relate the words you are learning to your daily life. Apply what you learned to your surroundings, friends and family.

- Feel confident when you are speaking Arabic; try not to hesitate or pause between words.

- Try to find a native Arabic speaker in your area and practice speaking with them.

- Consistency is very important, so be dedicated and spend some learning time every day.

- Listen to the new vocabulary as many times as you wish.

- Use flashcards and look at them whenever you have time.

- Work on making your learning experience pleasant and fun.

- The best method to learn a language is practice. Please use the audio to practice as much as possible and compare your pronunciation to the native speaker's pronunciation.

🎧

To access the online audio recordings and printable flash cards for this book:

1. Check that you have an Internet connection.
2. Type the following URL into your web browser.
   https://www.tuttlepublishing.com/arabic-for-beginners

For support, you can email us at info@tuttlepublishing.com.

الوحدة الأولى
The Arabic Language, Alphabet and Writing System
اللغة العربية
Al-logha al-arabiyah

Objectives:

1. Formal vs. Colloquial Arabic
2. The Arabic Writing System
3. Arabic Letters:
   - Consonants with English equivalents
   - Consonants with no English equivalent
4. Special Characteristic: Changing Shapes
5. Table of Arabic Letters

Formal vs. Colloquial Arabic

Arabic is one of the world's oldest languages. The Nabatean people who lived in what is now Jordan and northern Saudi Arabia developed the Arabic alphabet more than two thousand years ago. When the alphabet was first developed it had no dots and by the year 600 dots were added to some letters.

Several forms of Arabic were developed through history. The first, and most historically significant, is Classical Arabic, the language of the Qur'an, the holy book of Islam. All Muslims, whether Arabs or not, must read some verses of the Qur'an in their five daily prayers. This is the main reason Classical Arabic is still a living language fourteen hundred years later. Many non-Arab Muslims teach their children Classical Arabic so that they are able to read the Qur'an and understand its teachings. Additionally, Classical Arabic is the language of the Hadith, the sayings of the Prophet Mohammed. Therefore, learning it helps people understand the teachings of Islam. Classical Arabic was the international language of scientific writing, administration, research and diplomacy throughout Islamic civilization from the seventh to the twelfth centuries (Ryding, 2007, p. 3[1]). Numerous books were translated into Classical Arabic during this era.

---

1   C. Ryding, Karin. (2007). *A Reference Grammar of Modern Standard Arabic.* Language Problems & Language Planning. 31. 10.1075/lplp.31.2.12ton.

During the spread of Islam, Arabic became the major language in several regions. For example, in Spain you will find many areas with Arabic names such as the famous area al-Hamra, meaning "the red." Other languages were influenced by Arabic such as Urdu and Farsi (Persian). As for English, there are many words that are adapted from Arabic such as admiral, alcohol, coffee, balsam, caliph, cipher, giraffe, guitar, lemon, algebra, etc.

Why Modern Standard Arabic

Classical Arabic developed into Modern Standard Arabic (MSA) which is currently used in print, literature, radio and TV shows, books, newspapers, magazines, official documents, businesses, conferences and street signs. Modern Standard Arabic is also the form taught at schools, colleges and universities in all Arab countries. Speaking Modern Standard Arabic makes it easier for people to communicate and avoid misunderstandings caused by differences in dialects. Learning Modern Standard Arabic opens doors throughout the Arab world.

Classical Arabic and Modern Standard Arabic are very similar with very few differences in vocabulary as both represent different cultures. From a linguistic point of view both are similar but not totally. Anyone who knows or speaks Modern Standard Arabic would have no difficulty in reading and comprehending Classical Arabic. This is why in this book we will be learning Modern Standard Arabic.

It is also important to note that Arabic has borrowed words with Latin roots such as "bank" بنك , "telephone" *telefoun* تلفون, "internet" *internet* انترنت , "computers" *combuters* كمبيوتر and others.

The last form of Arabic is colloquial Arabic, which can be called "Spoken Arabic" or the "Dialects of Arabic." As with any dialect, some letters and words are pronounced differently in different countries and regions, as with British and American English, or in different areas within the same country such as in the Southern and Northern United States. In colloquial Arabic the vocabulary and styles are more casual. Like in all parts of the world, there is a difference between city and village dialects. Colloquial Arabic differs between countries, regions and even areas in the same country. However, there are five regional variations of colloquial Arabic. They are:
- Egyptian—spoken in Egypt
- Iraqi—spoken in Iraq
- Levantine—spoken in Lebanon, Jordan, Palestine and Syria
- North African—spoken in Tunisia, Libya, Morocco and Algeria
- Gulf/Arabian—spoken in the Gulf countries of Kuwait, Bahrain, United Arab Emirates, Saudi Arabia, Qatar, Yemen and Oman

Egyptian, Iraqi, Levantine and Arabian Arabic are very similar and the various speakers understand each other very well. However, communicating with speakers of North African dialects can be a challenge. This may be due to the effect that the French occupation of North African Arab countries had on the language (other Arab countries were occupied by the

British). North African dialects are very much affected by the French language. Additionally, while the spread of media like movies, films, television dramas and comedies throughout the Arab world made it easier to communicate, very little media originates from North African Arab countries.

Learning Modern Standard Arabic makes it much easier to communicate in any Arabic dialect as it is the heart and soul of the Arabic language. Therefore, since all native speakers can understand Modern Standard Arabic, most Arabic language programs teach this form. Because of this, the learner will be culturally informed and will be able to communicate with Arabs throughout the Arabic-speaking world.

The Arabic Writing System

There are 28 consonants in the Arabic alphabet and each letter has its own pronunciation. As in English each letter has a name that will be introduced. Our concentration is more on the Transliterations of the letters not on their names. Many Arabic letters have the same Transliteration as they do in English while nine letters do not have equivalency in English.

There are several important distinguishing characteristics in Arabic:
1. Arabic is written from right to left. The same as in Persian (Farsi), Hebrew and Urdu. Therefore, when you write or read Arabic make sure to start from the right.
2. Arabic words always start with a consonant.
3. Vowels do not occur consecutively in a word.
4. The Arabic writing system is phonetic. Words are pronounced as they are written. If you do not hear the Transliteration, do not make up letters. This is different than in English. For example, in English you will find words such as "know," with a silent "k." These silent letters do not exist in Arabic. All the letters shown should be pronounced.
5. Arabic is written in a cursive script. Letters are connected to form words both in print and in handwriting. Unlike Latin writing where alphabets are connected only in cursive, there is no print in Arabic. However, there are six letters that can be connected to other letters from the right side only. That is, they are connected to letters that come before them but not after them. Therefore, they are called one way connecting letters. These letters are:

و	ز	ر	ذ	د	أ	Letter in Arabic
wa	*za*	*ra*	*the*	*da*	*a*	Transliterations

For example (remember to start from the right): (**ba**) با = ا + ب while (**ab**) أب = ب + ا

6. Some letters have the same shape and can be distinguished from each other by a dot over or under them. There are 18 different shapes with 28 different pronunciations. They are like twins or triplets and there are seven twins and two triplets in the Arabic alphabet. For example the letters ب ث and ت may look the same at first glance but they are different in the number and placement of dots that they have. They also have different pronunciations: ث is pronounced "*tha*," ت is pronounced "*ta*," and ب is pronounced "*ba*." As a result of this, it is possible to divide letters into groups according to their shapes. But be careful when you do this. For example, some scholars might add the letter *na* ن to this group; however, if you look at the letter, *na* has a more circular shape than the others and when written falls a little under the line while ت , ب and ث are written on the line.

Here are the triplets and twins of Arabic alphabets:

1.	ث	ت	ب
Transliterations	*Tha*	*ta*	*ba*
2.	خ	ح	ج
Transliterations	*kha*	*ha*	*ja*
3.		ذ	د
Transliterations		*Tha* (as in "the")	*da*
4.		ز	ر
Transliterations		*za*	*ra*
5.		ش	س
Transliterations		*sha*	*sa*
6.		ض	ص
Transliterations		*dh*	Emphatic *sa*
7.		ظ	ط
Transliterations		Emphatic *tha*	Emphatic *ta*
8.		غ	ع
Transliterations		*gh*	*ai*
9.		ق	ف
Transliterations		*qa*	*fa*

Did you notice that the only difference between these letters is the dots they have?

Each letter has its own Transliteration. For example, in English we connect two letters to get a Transliteration as in **th, sh** or **ch**. In Arabic each letter has its own Transliteration and connecting any two letters will not give you a different Transliteration, you just pronounce both. Another note is that **s** in English is pronounced as **s** and sometimes as **z**. In Arabic we have a letter for **s** and a different one for **z** and the pronunciation of a letter does not change.

7. The letter ‎هـ‎ **ha** is the only letter that may be written in five different forms—at the beginning of the word it is ‎هـ‎ , in the middle it may be written as ‎ـهـ‎ or ‎ـﻬـ‎ while at the end it may be as ‎ـه‎ or ‎ه‎ depending on what letter comes before it.

The Arabic Alphabet

Among the 28 Arabic consonants, there are both consonants with an English equivalent and those without. That's why it is very important to be comfortable with Arabic pronunciation before you advance.

The Arabic alphabet is presented below. Study the Arabic letters and repeat the Transliterations a few times until you are comfortable. Mastering the Transliterations is very important as it is a base for learning Arabic. Keep in mind that changing the shape does not mean changing the Transliteration.

Sounds like the first letter in	Transliteration	Name of the letter in Arabic	Letter
Apple	*A*	*Alif*	أ
Bee	*B*	*Ba'a*	ب
Tea	*T*	*Ta'a*	ت
Three	*Th*	*Tha'a*	ث
Jam, judge	*J*	*Jeem*	ج
No equivalence in English	*Hha*	*Ha*	ح
‎خ‎ is pronounced "*ch-ich*" as in the German word "*kochen*" or in the Scottish word "*loch*." It is pronounced when the back of the tongue hits the roof of the mouth. In some cultures, it might be used to say "*yekh*."	No equivalence in English	*Kha'a*	خ
Dad	*D*	*Daal*	د
There	*TH* (that)	*Tha'a*	ذ

Sounds like the first letter in	Transliteration	Name of the letter in Arabic	Letter
Ray (Transliterations as in the Spanish *pero*)	*R*	*Ra'a*	ر
Zoo	*Z*	*Zain*	ز
Sam (Soft *s*)	*S*	*Seen*	س
Shelter	*SH*	*Sheen*	ش
Almost as the Transliteration of *s* in *sod*	Like emphatic *S*	*Saad*	ص
Almost as the Transliteration of the first *D* in *Dumb*	Like emphatic *D*	*Dad*	ض
Almost as the Transliteration of *T* in *Todd*	Like emphatic *T*	*Ta*	ط
No equivalence in English	Like emphatic *th*	*Dha*	ظ
No equivalence in English	No equivalence in English	*Ain*	ع
Pronounced as in the French *Gr* as in *Maigret*, or the German *rot*. The letter غ is similar to the noise you make when you gargle.	No equivalence in English, almost as *gh*	*Ghain*	غ
Fat	*F*	*Fa*	ف
A bit similar to the Transliteration of the *C* in *cot*	No equivalence in English	*Qaf*	ق
Keep	*K*	*Kaf*	ك
Let	*L*	*Lam*	ل
Moon	*M*	*Meem*	م
No	*N*	*Noon*	ن
Hat	*H*	*Ha*	هـ
We	*W*	*Waw*	و
Yam	*Y*	*Ya*	ي

Writing the Arabic Alphabet

In this section, you will be introduced to and practice how to correctly write Arabic letters. Please note that as in all Arabic texts you will be writing from right to left.

As you know by now, there are 28 letters in the Arabic alphabet. Six of these are one-way connectors, that is, they are connected to the letter coming before it but not with the ones after it. Each letter has its own shape at the beginning, middle and end of a word. Some letters have a dot on top or underneath.

So you can become better acquainted with the Arabic alphabet, first write the letters below and then add the dots accordingly.

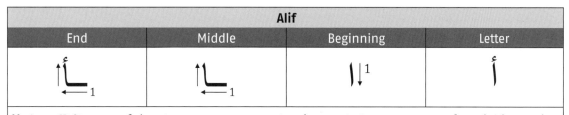

End	Middle	Beginning	Letter
Alif			

Note: *Alif* is one of the six one-way connecting letters; it is not connected to the letter that comes after it.

End	Middle	Beginning	Letter
Ba'a			

Note: *Ba'a* and the following letters *Ta'a* and *Tha'a* are almost the same. The only difference is in the dots. The full form, as seen in the first column, is written when it lies at the end of the word and comes after a one-way connector letter.

End	Middle	Beginning	Letter
Ta'a			

End	Middle	Beginning	Letter
Tha'a			

Jeem			
End	Middle	Beginning	Letter
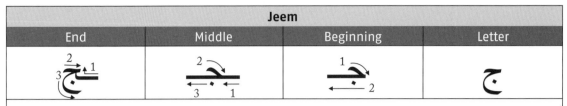			

Note: *Jeem* and the following letters *Ha* and *Kha'a* are almost the same. The only difference is in the dots. The full form, as in the first column, is written when it lies at the end of a word or comes after a one-way connector letter.

Ha			
End	Middle	Beginning	Letter

Kha'a			
End	Middle	Beginning	Letter

Daal			
End	Middle	Beginning	Letter

Note: *Daal* and the next letter, *Thal* are one-way connector letters, the same as *Alif*. They are not connected to the letter that comes after it. They are written on top of the line.

Thal			
End	Middle	Beginning	Letter

Ra'a			
End	Middle	Beginning	Letter

Note: *Ra'a* and the next letter, *Zain*, are one-way connector letters, the same as *Alif*. They are **not** connected to the letter that comes after it. They start at the top of the line and goes under the line.

Zain			
End	Middle	Beginning	Letter
‏ﺰ‎	‏ﺰ‎	‏ﺯ‎	‏ﺯ‎

Seen			
End	Middle	Beginning	Letter
‏ﺲ‎	‏ﺴ‎	‏ﺳ‎	‏ﺱ‎

Note: *Seen* and the next letter *Sheen* are almost the same. The only difference is in the dots. At the beginning and middle of the word, they stay on the line. The full form as in the first column, is written when it lies at the end of a word or comes after a one-way connector letter.

Sheen			
End	Middle	Beginning	Letter
‏ﺶ‎	‏ﺸ‎	‏ﺷ‎	‏ﺵ‎

Saad			
End	Middle	Beginning	Letter
‏ﺺ‎	‏ﺼ‎	‏ﺻ‎	‏ﺹ‎

Note: *Saad* and the next letter, *Dad*, are almost the same. The only difference is the dots. The full form as in the first column, is written when it lies at the end of a word or comes after a one-way connector letter.

Dad			
End	Middle	Beginning	Letter
‏ﺾ‎	‏ﻀ‎	‏ﺿ‎	‏ﺽ‎

Ta			
End	Middle	Beginning	Letter
‏ﻂ‎	‏ﻄ‎	‏ﻃ‎	‏ﻁ‎

Note: *Ta* and the next letter, *Dha* are almost the same. The only difference is the dots. The full form in the first column is written when on the line all the times.

Dha			
End	**Middle**	**Beginning**	**Letter**
ظ	ظ	ظ	ظ

Ain			
End	**Middle**	**Beginning**	**Letter**
ع	ع	ع	ع

Note: *Ain* and and the next letter, *Ghain*, are almost the same. The only difference is the dots. At the beginning and middle of the word, it is written on the line. The full form, as in the first column, is written when it lies at the end of a word or comes after a one-way connector letter.

Ghain			
End	**Middle**	**Beginning**	**Letter**
غ	غ	غ	غ

Fa			
End	**Middle**	**Beginning**	**Letter**
ف	ف	ف	ف

Note: *Fa* and is written on the line all the times.

Qaf			
End	**Middle**	**Beginning**	**Letter**
ق	ق	ق	ق

Note: *Qaf* is written on the line at the beginning and middle of the word. The full form as in the first column is written, when it lies at the end of a word or comes after a one-way connector letter.

Kaf			
End	**Middle**	**Beginning**	**Letter**
			كى

Note: *Kaf* is written on the line all the times.

Lam			
End	**Middle**	**Beginning**	**Letter**
			ل

Note: *Lam* is written on the line at the beginning and middle of the word. The full form as in the first column, is written when it lies at the end of a word or comes after a one-way connector letter. It starts over the line and then goes under it.

Meem			
End	**Middle**	**Beginning**	**Letter**
			م

Note: *Meem* is on the line at the beginning and middle of the word. The full form in the first column is written when it lies at the end of a word or comes after a one-way connector letter. It starts over the line and then goes under it.

Noon			
End	**Middle**	**Beginning**	**Letter**
			ن

Note: *Noon* is written on the line at the beginning and middle of a word. The full form as in the first column, is written when it lies at the end of a word or comes after a one-way connector letter. It starts over the line and then goes under it.

Ha			
End	Middle	Beginning	Letter
ـﻪ	ﻬ	ﻫ	هـ

Note: *Ha* has different shapes. Pay attention to how it is written at the beginning. In the middle of a word it looks like 8 while at the end of a word it looks a little like 9. It stays on the line at the beginning and end of a word.

Waw			
End	Middle	Beginning	Letter
ـﻮ	ـﻮ	ﻭ	و

Note: *Waw* is the last one-way connector letter, the same as in *Alif*. It is **not** connected to the letter that comes after it. It starts at the top of the line and then goes under it.

Ya			
End	Middle	Beginning	Letter
ـﻲ	ـﻴـ	ﻳـ	ي

Note: *Ya* has two forms. At the beginning and middle of the word, it stays on the line, and is the same as *Ba'a* but with two dots underneath it. The full form starts on top of the line, goes under it and then goes back up again. The full form as in the first column is written when it lies at the end of a word or comes after a one-way connector letter.

🔊 **1.1. Practice**

Now repeat the words you hear to practice the letter غ :

Meaning	Transliteration	Word
West	*Gharb*	غرب
Cover	*Ghamara*	غمر
Formed	*Sagha*	صاغ

Meaning	Transliteration	Word
Clouds	*Ghoyoom*	غيوم
Small	*Sagheer*	صغير
Stupid	*Aghbiyaa*	أغبياء

1.2. | **Practice** (see Answer Key)

Circle the words that have the letter ط :

1. دراجة	2. طماطم	3. ذرة
4. طائر	5. تمر	6. طرابلس
7. شيطان	8. تونس	9. طازج
10. تفاح	11. قطر	

1.3. | **Practice**

Read these examples of words with the letter خ :

خبير – خوخ – مخبز – بخيل – خوار – خاوي – خبّاز – تخمة

By now you should have mastered all the twenty-eight letters of the Arabic alphabet.

1.4. | **Practice**

I am sure that you noticed that there are some similarities between Transliterations of letters that might be a little confusing for the non-native speaker of the language at the beginning. To clarify the Transliteration differences between these letters, study the following table.

Read the following letters and make sure you can tell the difference in your pronunciation between each two letters, then listen to see how well you did:

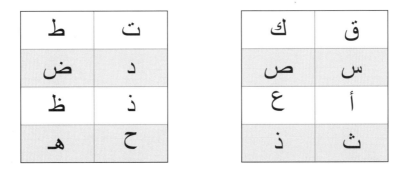

ط	ت
ض	د
ظ	ذ
ه	ح

ك	ق
ص	س
ع	أ
ذ	ث

1.5. | **Practice**

Read the following words and make sure to note the difference in pronunciation of the first letter of the word:

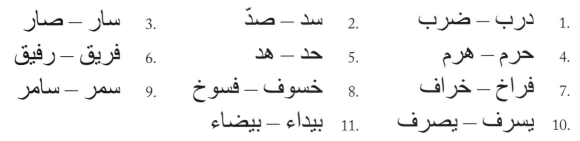

1. درب – ضرب	2. سد – صدّ	3. سار – صار
4. حرم – هرم	5. حد – هد	6. فريق – رفيق
7. فراخ – خراف	8. خسوف – فسوخ	9. سمر – سامر
10. يسرف – يصرف	11. بيداء – بيضاء	

🔊 1.6. Practice

Now listen and circle the letter you hear:

3. ح – هـ		2. ذ – ض		1. د – ذ	
6. كـ - ق		5. ضـ - ظـ		4. س – ص	
		8. ث - ذ		7. عـ – أ	

Special characteristic: Changing shapes

Look at the table to see how the letter changes its shape at the beginning, middle and end of the word:

End	Middle/end Separated	Middle Connected	Beginning	Transliteration	Letter
ـا	ا	ـا	ا	*A*	ا
ـب	ب	ـبـ	بـ	*Ba*	ب
ـت	ت	ـتـ	تـ	*Ta*	ت
ـث	ث	ـثـ	ثـ	*Tha (thin)*	ث
ـج	ج	ـجـ	جـ	*Ja*	ج
ـح	ح	ـحـ	حـ	*Ha*	ح
ـخ	خ	ـخـ	خـ	*Kha*	خ
ـد	د	ـد	د	*Da*	د
ـذ	ذ	ـذ	ذ	*Tha* (the)	ذ
ـر	ر	ـر	ر	*Ra*	ر
ـز	ز	ـز	ز	*Za*	ز
ـس	س	ـسـ	سـ	*Sa*	س
ـش	ش	ـشـ	شـ	*Sha*	ش
ـص	ص	ـصـ	صـ	*Sa (sod)*	ص
ـض	ض	ـضـ	ضـ	*Dha*	ض
ـط	ط	ـطـ	طـ	*Ta*	ط
ـظ	ظ	ـظـ	ظـ	*Tha*	ظ
ـع	ع	ـعـ	عـ	*Ai'*	ع

End	Middle/end Separated	Middle Connected	Beginning	Transliteration	Letter
غ	غ	ـغـ	غـ	*Gha*	غ
ف	ف	ـفـ	فـ	*Fa*	ف
ق	ق	ـقـ	قـ	*Qa*	ق
ك	ك	ـكـ	كـ	*Ka*	ك
ل	ل	ـلـ	لـ	*La*	ل
م	م	ـمـ	مـ	*Ma*	م
ن	ن	ـنـ	نـ	*Na*	ن
ه	ه	ـهـ	هـ	*Ha*	ـهـ
و	و	ـو	و	*Wa*	و
ي	ي	ـيـ	يـ	*Ya*	ي

Note: Each letter has its own shape at the beginning, middle and end of the word. Most letters are recognized very easily in their different forms. Note that the letters غ – ج – ح – خ and ع – ض and ص – ش and س – ق – ل – ن lose their tails at the beginning and middle of the word but they keep it when they fall at the end of the word. Some examples are provided later in this lesson. Each group is written the same and differ in their Transliteration and the dot they have. Note that د and ذ are written on the line while ر and ز fall under the line. The same applies to ف and ق . They look the same especially at the beginning and middle of the word but ق is rounder at the end of the word and it falls below the line.

1.7. Practice

Look at each letter, read it and write it twice:

End	Middle	Beginning	Letter
ـأ	ـا	ا	أ
ـب	ـبـ	بـ	ب

End	Middle	Beginning	Letter
ـت	ـتـ	تـ	ت
ـث	ـثـ	ثـ	ث

End	Middle	Beginning	Letter
جـ	ـجـ	جـ	ج
حـ	ـحـ	حـ	ح
خـ	ـخـ	خـ	خ
ـد	ـد	د	د
ـر	ـر	ر	ر
ـز	ـز	ز	ز
ـس	ـسـ	سـ	س
ـش	ـشـ	شـ	ش
ـص	ـصـ	صـ	ص

End	Middle	Beginning	Letter
ـض	ـضـ	ضـ	ض
ـط	ـطـ	طـ	ط
ـظ	ـظـ	ظـ	ظ
ـع	ـعـ	عـ	ع
ـغ	ـغـ	غـ	غ
ـف	ـفـ	فـ	ف
ـق	ـقـ	قـ	ق
ـك	ـكـ	كـ	ك
ـل	ـلـ	لـ	ل

End	Middle	Beginning	Letter	End	Middle	Beginning	Letter
م	ـمـ	مـ	م	ـو	ـو	و	و
ن	ـنـ	نـ	ن	ـي	ـيـ	يـ	ي
ـه	ـهـ	هـ	هـ				

1.8. **Read then write**

1. سطر : _____

2. طرب : _____

3. خرج : _____

4. أمريكا : _____

5. فيل : _____

6. فراشة : _____

7. أسد : _____

9. السيارة : _____

10. سافر : _____

1.9. Practice (see Answer Key)

Connect the letters to form a word then read it:

1. ر + و + ب + ص = _____
2. ل + ا + ل + ج = _____
3. ن + ا + ك + ر + ب = _____
4. ر + ي + ذ + ب + ت = _____
5. ل + ج + س + م = _____
6. ن + و + م + ل + س + م = _____
7. ة + ب + ل + ا + ط = _____
8. ب + و + ر + ح = _____
9. ر + ي + د + ص + ت = _____
10. ب + ا + ل + ك = _____

1.10. Practice

Listen to the words and repeat, there will be a pause after each word to give you a chance to re-peat. Make sure to differentiate between the similar letters:

1. دال – ضال   2. ضب – دلّ   3. دلال – ضلال
4. رتب – رطب   5. سطر – ستر   6. طيار – تيار
7. يسير – يصير   8. سابح – صابح   9. يحذو – يحظو
10. حضر – حظر   11. أسير – عسير   12. شاء – شاع
13. رعى – رأى   14. فكرة – فقرة   15. قاد – كاد

Reflection:

1. In this Lesson I learned: _____

_____

_____

2. I have some trouble with: _____

_____

_____

3. I need to learn more about: _____

_____

_____

الوحدة الثانية
Arabic Culture
الثقافة العربية

Althaqafa al-Arabiya

Objectives:

1. Long and Short Vowels:
   - *Alif* and *Fat-ha*
   - *Waw* and *Dhamma*
   - *Ya* and *Kasra*

2. Shaddah or Double consonants
3. Culture: Identifying Yourself and Others
4. Shaking Hands

🔊 Vocabulary

Meaning	Transliteration	Word
Peace be upon you	*Assalamu Alaikum*	السَّلامُ عَلَيْكُمْ
And on you be peace	*Wa alikum assalam*	وَ عَلَيْكُمْ السلامْ
Hello	*Marhaba*	مَرْحَباً
Welcome and hi	*Ahlan*	أهْلاً
Good morning	*Sabah al-kair*	صَباحُ الخَيْرِ
Exact meaning: Morning of lights (it means: good morning to you too)	*Sabah anoor*	صَباحُ النور
Good evening	*Masaa alkhair*	مَساءُ الخَيْرِ
Evening of lights (means good evening to you too)	*Masaa anoor*	مَساءُ النور
My name	*Ismee*	إسْمي
Your name	*Ismoka*	إسْمُكَ

Meaning	Transliteration	Word
I am honored – pleased to meet you	*Tasharafna*	تَشَرَّفْنا
What	*Ma*	ما
How	*Kayfa*	كَيْف
Your situation	*Haloka*	حَالَك
Thank God	*Al-hamdulillah*	الحَمْدُلله
I	*Ana*	أنا
You (masculine)	*Anta*	أنْتَ
You (feminine)	*Anti*	أنْتِ
Good	*Bikhair*	بِخَيْر
And	*Wa*	وَ
See you soon – looking forward to seeing you	*Ila aliqa*	إلى اللِقاءْ
Goodbye or go with peace	*Ma'assalama*	مَع السلامة
Pen	*Qalam*	قَلَم
Table	*Tawela*	طاوِلة
City	*Madina*	مَدينَة
Street	*Shari'*	شارِعْ
Teacher	*Ostath*	أُسْتاذْ
Go	*Thahaba*	ذَهَبَ
To	*Fi*	في

Culture: Identifying Yourself and Others
High-context and Low-context Culture

Both Arab and American cultures have their own distinctive features. Although American culture is a melting pot of diverse cultures, with variations across the fifty states, the term "American culture" represents structures acknowledged by intercultural scholars such as Stewart in 1972 and 1989. These characteristics are widespread and prevalent in the media and public communication. In this section, we will examine one main variance between Arab and American cultures in communication and usage of language by discussing the concept of high-context and low-context cultures. The difference between high- and low-context cultures depends on how much meaning is initiated in the context. Hall (1990[1]) states that meaning and context are "inextricably bound up with each other" (p. 18). He added that "most of the information is either in the physical context or internalized in the person, while very little is in the coded, explicit, transmitted part of the message" (p. 18). Arab culture is a high-context culture. This means that the listener must understand contextual indications or signals to comprehend the full message presented. In other words, it is the listeners' job to understand what has been said. Henle (1962) stated that the listener needs to "go to considerable lengths to make sense of an oral message" (p. 371[2]). Consequently, the auditors play a significant role in constructing meaning. Gold (1988) agreed, stating that "the audience cooperates with the speaker by trying to understand the meaning or 'gist' rather than the actual content" (p. 170[3]). Thus, listeners are active partners. Hall summarized the difference between low- and high-context culture when he wrote:

> "People raised in high-context systems expect more from others than do the participants in low-context systems. When talking about something that they have on their minds, a high-context individual will expect his interlocutor to know what's bothering him, so that he doesn't have to be specific. The result is that he will talk around and around the point, in effect putting all the pieces in place except the crucial one. Placing it properly—this keystone—is the role of his interlocutor." (1976, p. 98)

For example, an Arab visitor would say, "I am thirsty," and it is the host's job to get some water for the visitor. Another example is if an Arab needs to borrow money from a friend, he would talk about how difficult life is, describe the situations he faces and gives a few examples of the hardships in his life. It is the listener's job to interpret the message as a loan request or a need for a financial support. Therefore, if the listener has the money, he should offer it to his friend or say, "let me see what I can do." Then he will offer him the money or talk to a mutual friend to support and arrange the amount he needs.

---

[1] Hall, E. T., & Hall, M. R., 1990. *Understanding Cultural Differences: German, French and Americans*, Yarmouth, ME: Intercultural Press.

[2] Henle, M. (1962). On the relations between logic and thinking. *Psychological Review*, 69, 366-378.

[3] Gold, E. (1988). Ronald Reagan and the oral tradition. *Central States Speech Journal*, 39, 159-176.

Another example for high-context culture is when a speaker asks an Arab for help. Instead of saying "No" or "Sorry, I can't help you," the Arab will often say, "I will try" or "Let me look around to see how I can help" regardless of how difficult or even impossible it may be to help. After several times of saying "Not yet" or "I am still checking," the person who asked for help would know that the real response is no. The friendship will remain intact as long as there was not a direct refusal. Additionally, it is also common to respond to yes-and-no questions, such as "Do you understand?" with a yes. Arabs feel it is impolite to say no, which would require the speaker to explain things again or make the speaker feel that he is not being clear. Saying no also could be interpreted as a sign of unhappiness or a desire to end a conversation or relationship.

In contrast, low-context American culture assigns more meaning to the actual words and language used rather than the context. American communication is clear, direct, analytical and to the point (Ting-Toomey[4], 1985). In low-context culture, it is the speaker's role to convey the meaning accurately and methodically with no need of the participation of the listener. Other scholars have used the terms direct versus indirect to distinguish between Arab and American communications to describe this difference. Levine (1985[5]) stated that there are many common expressions used in American culture reflecting direct and clear communication. Some of these expressions include "What do you mean," "Be specific," "Don't beat around the bush," and "Get to the point" (p. 29). Arabs, however, do not have such direct expressions in their communications. For example, criticism of an Arab requires an indirect approach that might include some positive comments in addition to criticism.

On the other hand, Arabs tend to express their feelings and emotions in what might look to the Western eye like a forceful and exaggerated fashion. Arabs in turn often feel that Westerners are cold people. For example, friends may shout and scream at each other when angry, but they also hug and kiss on the cheeks when they miss each other. Likewise, the Arab response to death includes much screaming, weeping and loud wailing. Another example is that when parents are mad at their children, they loudly express their feelings. However, children do not yell back; they just listen and sit still. For Americans, this might be considered abusive. For Arabs it is seen as normal parenting as all parents love their children and work hard to give them everything they can.

So, it is necessary to study the differences between cultures without being judgmental. Nevertheless, many people have an unconscious tendency to view cultural variances as undesirable and negative compared with one's own culture (Zaharna, 2016[6]). We need to absorb differences and deal with them as differences only rather than professing them as right or wrong.

Shaking Hands

The most common greeting in the Arab world is ***Assalamu Alaikum*** meaning "Peace be upon

---

[4] Ting-Toomey, S. (1985). Toward a theory of conflict and culture. In W. Gudykunst, L. Stewart & S. Ting-Toomey (Eds.), *Communication, culture and organizational processes*. Beverly Hills: Sage.

[5] Levine, D. (1985). *The flight from ambiguity*. Chicago: University of Chicago Press.

[6] Zaharna, R. 1995, Bridging Cultural Differences: American Public Relations Practices & Arab Communication Patterns *Public Relation Review*, 21 (1995), P. 241-255

you." The response is *wa Alaikum Assalam* which is "and upon you be peace." When Arabs meet each other, they shake hands using the right hand with a smile and say *Assalamu Alaikum*. Once a relationship is developed, then men would kiss other men on the cheeks while women would kiss other women on the cheeks. Men do not kiss women and vice versa.

In greetings between men and women, a smile and saying *Assalamu Alaikum* is enough. Men do not extend their hands to shake unless the women do it first. Some women do not shake hands with men, so a man should wait and see. If the woman does not extend her hand, then he will bow his head in greeting while putting his right hand on his chest.

Assalamu Alaikum may be used when entering or leaving the house. It might be considered rude not to say it even if it meant to interrupt people's conversation

Another popular greeting that can be used anytime is: *marhaba* مرحبا meaning "Hello," and the response is *ahlan* أهلا meaning "Welcome" it is like Hi and Hello in English.

Both *Assalamu Alaikum* and *Marhaba* can be used for one person or a group of people.

After greeting, it is polite to ask, "how are you" that is "كيف حالك؟." Some people might consider it rude not to ask. The common response is to say *alhamdulillah*, that is "thank God," but the intended meaning is "I am well." Later, after a relation is built, after saying *alhamdulillah* you may talk about your current situation, complain or criticize things.

When entering a social function, the visitor is to start from the person on his/her right and start shaking hands with all attendees and kissing on the cheeks those whom he knew. Just saying Hi or Salam and going inside is considered rude and gives the feeling that you do not care about the people in the room.

In short, when meeting an Arab, it is a good idea to greet, introduce yourself and say goodbye.

Short Vowels

Usually, vowels are not written in Arabic books except for the first few years of elementary schools and in religious book as the Qur'an and Bible. Vowels are important for the first level of Arabic, so students can read better and comprehend words easier. Hence, in this book, all new vocabulary is introduced with short vowels to make it easier to read. Additionally, the first seven lessons have all readings and exercises written with vowels. At this stage, you should be used to reading Arabic words, and therefore the vowels will not be written. The reader must guess the Transliterations while reading and pronouncing words. I am sure, this will be appreciated as you will be able to read words as they appear.

Arabic has three short vowels and they give a Transliteration to the letter. These Transliterations are not considered letters and when written, they appear as signs on or under the letter. They are:

1. *Fat-ha*: has the Transliteration of *a* as in "at." It is written on the top of the letter and looks like � فَ.

2. **Kasra**: has the Transliteration of *e* in the word "bit" and it is written under the letter and looks like ‐ (as in بيَد "bit").

3. **Dhamma**: has the Transliteration of *o* as in "foot." It is written on top of the letter and it looks like ً.

Again, *fat-ha* and *dhamma* are written on top of the letter while *kasra* is written under it.

🔊 **2.1.** | Practice

Read each letter of the alphabets with *fat-ha*, *dhamma* and *kasra*. To make it easier to recognize, here is a table of Arabic alphabets with short vowels with some examples of how they sound in English. They are arranged to have *fat-ha*, *dhamma* and *kasra*:

Example of Arabic words	Sounds like the first letter of	Arabic letters	Example of Arabic words	Sounds like the first letter of	Arabic letters
جَمال *jamal*	jam	جَ	أمل *amal*	at	اَ
جُحا *joha*	job	جُ	أُمي *omee*	on	أُ
جِمال *jimal*	Jesus	جِ	إياد *Iyad*	in	إ
حَمد *hamad*		حَ	باسم *basim*	bat	بَ
حُسين *hoseen*	No equivalent in English	حُ	بُثينة *bothayna*	bush	بُ
حِمار *himar*		حِ	بيَد *biyad*	bit	بِ
خالد *khalid*		خَ	تَيمم *tayamam*	tab	تَ
خلود *kholood*	No equivalent in English	خُ	تونس *toonis*	to	تُ
خِتام *khitam*		خِ	تِلك *tilka*	T-shirt	تِ
دار *dar*	dad	دَ	ثَوب *Thawb*	thank	ثَ
دُنيا *donya*	door	دُ	ثُبوت *thoboot*	thorn	ثُ
ديك *deek*	dip	دِ	ثِمار *thimar*	think	ثِ

Example of Arabic words	Sounds like the first letter of	Arabic letters
ضَار dhar ضُمور dhomoor ضِرار dherar	No equivalent in English	ضَ ضُ ضِ
ظَفَرَ thafara ظُلم tholm ظِباء thiba	No equivalent in English	ظَ ظُ ظِ
عَدَلَ adala عُمَر omar عِماد emad	No equivalent in English	عَ عُ عِ
غادَرَ ghadara غُيوم ghoyoom غِمار ghimar	No equivalent in English	غَ غُ غ
فَتَحَ fataha فُؤاد foad فِريال firyal	fat full feed	فَ فُ ف
قَادر qader قُرون qoroon قِيام qiyam	No equivalent in English	قَ قُ ق

Example of Arabic words	Sounds like the first letter of	Arabic letters
ذَهب thahaba ذُرة thora ذِكر thikr	the though this	ذَ ذُ ذِ
رَوضة rawdha رُبى roba رِهام riham	ran room red	رَ رُ رِ
زَكاة zaka زُهير zoheer زِين zain	Zak zoo zip	زَ زُ زِ
سَمر samar سُهير sohair سِهام siham	Sam so sim	سَ سُ سِ
شَكَرَ shakara شُكرا shokran شِهاب shihab	Shall shore shell	شَ شُ شِ
صَادَ sada صُوَر sowar صِيام siyam	No equivalent in English	صَ صُ صِ

Example of Arabic words	Sounds like the first letter of	Arabic letters
وَلَاء *walaa*	Washington	وَ
وُلَدَ *wolida*	wool	وُ
ولاية *welayah*	went	وِ
هَدية *hadiya*	hat	هَـ
هُدى *hoda*	hood	هُـ
هِيام *hiyam*	him	هِـ
يَدوس *yadoos*	yahoo	يَـ
يُسرى *yosra*	you	يُـ
يليه	yet	يِـ

Example of Arabic words	Sounds like the first letter of	Arabic letters
كَمال *kamal*	cat	كَـ
كُهول *kohool*	cumulative	كُـ
كِفاح *kifah*	keen	كِـ
لَيلى *Layla*	lamp	لَ
لُؤي *loay*	lonely	لُ
لِي *lee*	lentils	لِ
مظاهر *mathaher*	mad	مَـ
مُنير *moneer*	moon	مُـ
مِيعاد *mi-aad*	miss	مِـ
نصَرَ *nasara*	na	نَـ
نون *noon*	nomad	نُـ
نِهاية *nihaya*	near	نِـ

2.2. Practice

Read the following words with their vowels:

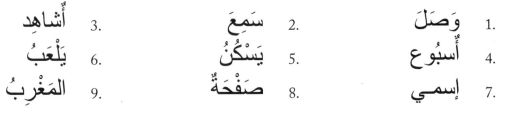

3. أُشاهِد   2. سَمِعَ   1. وَصَلَ

6. يَلْعَبُ   5. يَسْكُنُ   4. أُسبُوع

9. المَغْرِبُ   8. صَفْحَةُ   7. إسمِي

Long Vowels

To make the letter have a long vowel, we add another letter to it. There are three long letters that may be considered as long vowels and they give the letter before them a Transliteration of long vowel. They are:

1. و Transliterations as *oo* in "m**oo**n" and "r**oo**t."
2. ي Transliterations as *ee* in "h**ea**t" and "m**ee**t."
3. ا Transliterations as *a* in "h**a**t" and "c**a**t."

They are a little similar to short vowels but are pronounced with long vowels. The same as in: "**fit**" and "**feet**," "**foot**" and "**food**," "**attorney**" and "**mat**."

🔊 Now listen to the difference between long and short vowels:

Transliteration	Long Vowel	Transliteration	Short Vowel	Letter
baa	با	*ba*	بَ	ب
daa	دا	*da*	دَ	د
zoo	زو	*zo*	زُ	ز
joo	جو	*jo*	جُ	ج
fee	في	*fi*	فِ	ف
see	سي	*si*	سِ	س

The long vowels are also called weak letters because when conjugating a word with one of these letters in the middle, they can be changed to a different letter. For example: when we change كان from past to present tense, it would change to يكون. The other 25 letters would never change so they are called Transliteration letters.

2.3. **Practice**

Read the following words using the vowels shown:

1. بَردْ – بَرِيد   2. زُر – زور

3. دِين – دان   4. نَذَرَ – نَذار

5. يَزِدْ – يزيد

🔊 **Double consonants or Shaddah**

In Arabic, doubling a letter is indicated by writing a *shaddah* شَدّة on top of it. *Shaddah* is not a letter, it is only a symbol written on the letter. This means letters with *shaddah* on top of them should be pronounced with a stress. The *fat-ha* and *dhamma* are written on top of the *shaddah* while the *kasra* is written under the *shaddah*. They would look like this: ـّ and ـِّ, ـُّ.

Meaning	Transliteration	Word
Announce something via media	*Bath-tha*	بَثَّ
Teacher	*Moddaris*	مُدَّرِس
School	*Kottab*	كُتَّاب
To return something	*Rajja'a*	رَجَّع
Got married	*Tazzawaja*	تَزَوَّجَ

2.4. **Practice**

Each of the following words have either *shaddah* or long vowel. Read carefully and notice the difference:

1. زَوَّجَ – زَوَاجٌ.
2. رَاجَعَ – رَجَّعَ.
3. حَدَّدَ – حِدَادٌ.
4. ثَابِتٌ – ثَبتَ.
5. دَرَّسَ – دَارِسٌ.
6. صَابَحَ - صَبَّحَ.

Nunation

Another characteristic of Arabic letters is that sometimes the letter has double *dhammas*, double *fat-ha* or double *kasra*. Doubling short vowels is called *tanween* تنوين in Arabic or nunation in English. From the name: *tanween* you might guess that is has a relation with the letter *N*. Yes, you are right.

Tanween is used only at the last letter of the word and it gives these three Transliterations:
a) With double *fat-ha* it is pronounced as *an*
b) With double *dhamma* it is pronounced as *on*
c) With double *kasra* it is pronounced as *in*

Look at these examples:
رَ With *fat-ha* is pronounced as *ra* while with *tanween fat-h* رأ it is pronounced as *ran*
سُ With *dhamma* is pronounced as *son* while with *tanween dhamma* سٌ it is pronounced as *soon*
سِ With *kasra* is pronounced as *sip* while with *tanween kasr* سٍ it is pronounced as *sin*

Note that the *N* is not written but is pronounced as long as we have the short vowel doubled.

To summarize what we learned. Arabic has:

- 3 short vowels *fat-ha*, *dhamma* and *kasra*
- 3 long vowels: اـ و and ي
- 3 nunations tanween *fat-ha*, *tanween dhamma* and *tanween kasra*
- Consonants may be doubled by putting *shaddah* on or under it

2.5. Practice (see Answer Key)

Connect to form a word:

_____ =	ك + ش + ف	1.
_____ =	ش + ك + ر	2.
_____ =	د + ج + ا + ج	3.
_____ =	ض + ح + ك	4.
_____ =	س + ك + و + ن	5.
_____ =	ي + ب + ح + ث	6.
_____ =	ب + ا + ر + د	7.
_____ =	ت + أ + ث + ي + ر	8.
_____ =	و + ر + و + د	9.
_____ =	إ + ث + ب + ا + ت	10.

2.6. Practice (see Answer Key)

Read the following words and pay attention to the difference between ح and هـ:

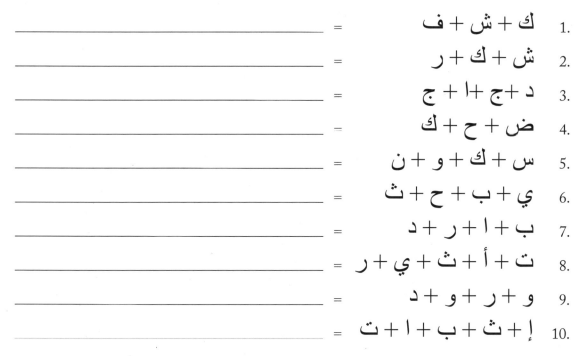

1. أَحْرُقُ - أُرْهِقُ.
2. حَامِدٌ - هَامِدٌ.
3. فَهْمٌ - فَحْمٌ.
4. سهْم - شَهْمٌ.
5. جَاحِدٌ - جَاهَدَ.
6. حَمَّامٌ - هَمَّامٌ.

2.7. Practice (see Answer Key)

Listen to the words and write the missing letter:

1. بـ___ور
2. با___د
3. تأ___ير
4. ___رز
5. ___زواج
6. ___ديد

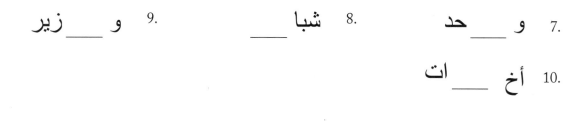

7. و ____ حد   8. شبا ____   9. و ____ زير

10. أخ ____ ات

2.8. Practice (see Answer Key)

Translate to Arabic using *tanween* when applicable:

1. The teacher: _____

2. Pen: _____

3. The street: _____

4. Table: _____

5. The city: _____

Read the following conversation between Amal and Hind (two female names), listen to compare your reading, then practice it with your partner:

marhaba. Hello.	أَمَلُ: مَرْحَبًا.
ahlan. Hi – welcome.	هَنَّدَ: أَهْلًا.
kayfa haloki? How are you?	أَمَلُ: كَيْفَ حَالُكَ؟
alhamdulillah, ana bekhayr wa anti kayfa haloki? Thank God, I am doing well. And you? How are you?	هَنَّدَ: الحَمْدُلِلهِ! أَنَا بِخَيرٍ وَ أَنْتَ؟ كَيْفَ حَالُكَ؟
alhamdulillah ana bekhayr. Thank God, I am good.	أَمَلُ: الحَمْدُلِلهِ أَنَا بِخَيرٍ.
men ayna anti? Where are you from?	هَنَّدَ: مِنْ أَيْنَ أَنْتِ؟
ana men sorya wa anti? I am from Syria, how about you?	أ مل: أَنَا مِنْ سُورِيَا وَ أَنْتِ؟
ana men al-iraq. I am from Iraq.	هَنَّدَ: أَنَا مِنْ العِرَاقِ.
ila alliqa. Until we meet.	أ مل: إِلَى اللِّقَاءِ.
ma'a assalamah. Go with peace.	هَنَّدَ: مَعَ السَّلَامَةِ

Now read this conversation between Ali and Ahmed who met for the first time, then practice it with a partner:

Assalamu Alaikum Peace be upon you.	عَلِي: السَّلَامُ عَلَيْكُمْ.
wa alaikum assalam And on you be peace.	أَحْمَدُ: وَ عَلَيْكُمْ السَّلَامُ.
ismee Ali My name is Ali.	عَلِي: اِسْمِي عَلِيٌّ.
tasharrafna, ismee ahmad I am honored, my name is Ahmad.	أَحْمَدُ: تَشَرَّفْنَا! أَنَا اِسْمِي أَحْمَدُ.
ahlan wa sahlan. Kayfa haloka? You are welcome. How are you?	عَلِي: أَهْلًا وَ سَهْلًا كَيْفَ حَالُكَ؟
Alhamdulillah, ana bekhayr wa anta? Thank God, I am good. How about you?	أَحْمَدُ: الحَمْدُ لله أَنَا بِخَيْرٍ وَ أَنْتَ؟ كَيْفَ حَالُكَ؟
Alhamdulillah, ana bekhayr Thank God, I am good.	عَلِي: الحَمْدُ لله أَنَا بِخَيْرٍ.

2.9. **Practice**   (see Answer Key)

Connect words from the right column with the suitable response from the left (See Answer Key):

الحمدلله أنا بخير ( )	1. مرحبا
الى اللقاء ( )	2. كيف الحال ؟
أهلا ( )	3. السلام عليكم
و عليكم السلام ( )	4. اسمي خالد
تشرفنا . اسمي أحمد ( )	5. مع السلامة

Reflection

1. In this Lesson I learned: _____

2. I have some trouble with: _____

3. I need to learn more about: _____

الوحدة الثالثة
The Classroom
غرفة الفصل

Gorfat al-fasel

Objectives:

1. Gender in the Arabic Language
2. Ta Marbuta
3. Numerals:
   - 0–9
   - 10–100
   - Tens in Arabic
   - 100
   - More than 100
4. Culture: Introducing Someone and Forms of Address
5. Reading

 Vocabulary

Meaning	Transliteration	Plural	Transliteration	Word
Hey (Oh you)	–	–	Ya	يَا
Notebook	*Dafater*	دَفَاتِرْ	*Daftar*	دَفْتَرْ
Boy	*Awlad*	أوْلادْ	*Walad*	وَلَدْ
Girl	*Banat*	بَنَاتْ	*Bent*	بِنْتْ
Book	*Kotob*	كُتُبْ	*Kitab*	كِتَابْ
Pen	*Aqlam*	أقْلامْ	*Qalam*	قَلَمْ
Picture	*Sowar*	صوَرْ	*Soura*	صورَة
Room	*Ghoraf*	غُرَفْ	*Ghorfa*	غُرْفَة

Meaning	Transliteration	Plural	Transliteration	Word
Board	Alwah	أَلْواحْ	Law-h	لَوْحْ
Chair	Karasi	كَراسِي	Korsee	كُرْسِيْ
Bag/suitcase	Haqa'eb	حَقائِبْ	Haqeeba	حَقَيبَة
Recorder	Mosajelat	مُسَجِّلات	Mosajela	مُسَجِّلة
Key	Mafateeh	مَفاتِيح	Mof-tah	مُفْتاح
House	Beyoot	بُيوت	Bayt	بَيْت
Eraser	–	–	Memhah	مِمْحاة
Desk	Adraj	أَدْراج	Dorj	دُرْج
Paper	Awraq	أَوْراق	Waraqa	وَرَقة
Mr.	Sadah	سادة	Sayyed	سَيِّد
Mrs.	Sayyedat	سَيِّدات	Sayyedah	سَيِّدة
Father	Abaa'	آباء	Ab	أَب
Mother	Omahat	أَمَّهات	Om	أُمْ
Tired	–	–	Ta'aban	تَعْبان
Good	–	–	Jayed	جَيِّد
He	–	–	Howa	هوَ
She	–	–	Hiya	هيَ
From	–	–	Min	مِن
Where	–	–	Ayna	أَيْن
Thank you	–	–	Shokran	شُكْراً
You're welcome	–	–	A'fwan	عَفْواً

Culture: Introducing Someone & Forms of Address

Speaking politely is important in Arabic culture. To address people, there are various titles that are used. For example, in formal situation for people who have professional title, Arabs will address them with their titles as doctor, engineer or teacher.

For people with no professional title, we address them by saying: "Mr" سيد *sayyed* followed by his name and "Mrs." سيدة *sayyeda* or "Miss" آنسة *anisa* for unmarried or younger age girls followed by her name.

For informal situations, usually you call a person who is older than you saying *amee* عمي meaning "uncle" for males and خالتي *khalatee* "aunt," for females. The older person does not have to be a relative to call him/her uncle/aunt. It might be a person you just met for the first time and wanted to talk to him/her or ask about something.

Usually titles are followed by the person's first name not his last and are proceeded by the word *ya* يَا . The closest meaning for يَا is: "Oh You." يَا is used when addressing someone in front of you or directly to attract his/her attention.

If you know the family, then it is also very common to call a person by using the word أبو *abo* for father meaning "the father of," and أم *om* for the mother meaning "the mother of," followed by the name of their oldest son. For example, when the oldest son's name in the family is Ahmed, then you call the "father" أبو أحمد *abu ahmad* and the "mother" is *om ahmad* أم أحمد .

There is no need to use titles to call friends, just say their names.

It is not very common for men and women to greet each other in public.

Additionally, it is very rude to leave someone's house, a group gathering and friends without "saying goodbye" or "see you later" الى اللقاء *ila aliqaa* & مع السلامة *ma'assalamah*.

Gender in Arabic

Words in Arabic are considered either masculine or feminine. When a word refers to a masculine human then it is masculine and when it refers to female human then it is feminine. The tricky part is that some words have no gender, but they are defined as masculine or feminine. Some examples are: *nar* نار "fire," *riyah* رياح "wind," *yad* يد "hand," are considered feminine while اصبع *isba'* "finger," رأس *ra's* "head," or باب *bab* "door" are considered masculine. Additionally, most towns, cities and countries are considered feminine words as in America, Britain and Saudi Arabia. What makes it easier is to remember that words ending in *ta marbuta* (ة - ﺔ) are feminine as will be explained.

It is very important to know the gender of the nouns because the verbs and adjectives are conjugated accordingly. The proper way to do is by memorization. Just memorize words with their gender.

Ta Marbuta

Words in Arabic are considered either masculine or feminine. When a word refers to a masculine human then it is masculine and when it refers to female human then it is feminine. The tricky part is that some words have no gender, but they are defined as masculine or feminine.

As explained, words in Arabic have gender. Most feminine nouns and adjectives end in *ta marbuta* التاء المربوطة represented as (ة - ـة). التاء المربوطة is not a new letter. It is as you noticed a combination of ـه and ت. When it is accompanied with any short vowel or *tanween* it is pronounced as *ta*, but when it is silent or comes at the end of the sentence it is pronounced as *ha*. Examples of words end in *ta marbuta* are as in:

Meaning	Transliteration	Word
Cat	*Qittah*	قطة
Room	*Ghorfah*	غرفة
Car	*Sayarah*	سيارة

Meaning	Transliteration	Word
Tent	*Khaymah*	خيمة
Beautiful	*Jameelah*	جميلة

In most cases *ta marbuta* is silent unless it is followed by a possessive noun or pronoun then it should be pronounced as *ta*. 🔊

Meaning	Transliteration	Word
A big school	*Madrasaton kabeerah*	مَدْرَسَةٌ كَبِيرَةٌ.
A beautiful student	*Talibaton jameelah*	طَالِبَةٌ جَمِيلَةٌ.
My sister's story	*Qisato okhtee*	قِصَّةُ أُخْتِي

Most of the times when we change nouns and adjectives related to living creatures from masculine to feminine, we just add *ta marbuta*. Here are some examples of feminine and masculine nouns:

Meaning	Transliteration	Feminine	Transliteration	Masculine
Cat	*Qittah*	قطة	*Qit*	قط
Dog	*Kalbah*	كلبة	*Kalb*	كلب
Prince	*Ameerah*	أميرة	*Ameer*	أمير
Teacher	*Ostathah*	أستاذة	*Ostath*	أستاذ
Hero	*Batalah*	بطلة	*Batal*	بطل
Beautiful	*Jameelah*	جميلة	*Jameel*	جميل
Big	*Kabeerah*	كبيرة	*Kabeer*	كبير

Meaning	Transliteration	Feminine	Transliteration	Masculine
Small	*Sagheerah*	صغيرة	*Sagheer*	صغير
Tall	*Taweelah*	طويلة	*Taweel*	طويل
Short	*Qaseerah*	قصيرة	*Qaseer*	قصير
Happy	*Sa`eedah*	سعيدة	*Sa`eed*	سعيد

3.1. **Practice** (see Answer Key)

Read these words and circle the feminine words. If you do not know the word, then you follow the rule of *ta marbuta*:

1. خَيْمَةٌ – بِنْتٌ – بيتٌ.

2. دَجَاجَةٌ – لَوْحٌ – جَرِيدَةٌ.

3. زُجَاجَةٌ – حِمَارٌ – نَهْرٌ.

4. طَاوِلَةٌ – زَوْجَةٌ – كُرْسِيٌّ.

5. سَعيدَةٌ – قَصِّيرُ – طَوِيلٌ.

6. كِتَابٌ – دَفْتَرٌ – مَجَلَّةٌ.

7. بَطَّةٌ – غُرْفَةٌ – كَوْكَبٌ.

8. طَبِيبٌ – كَاتِبٌ – كَاتِبَةٌ.

9. أَثَاثٌ – كُلِّيَّةٌ – جَامِعَةٌ.

10. أَمْرِيكَا – قَطَرُ – جَامِعَةٌ.

Numerals

Arabic numbers were developed in the Middle ages and they are the ones used in European languages replacing the Roman numbers.

Here are numbers from 0-10 in Arabic: 🔊

English number	Transliteration	Name	Arabic number	English number	Transliteration	Name	Arabic number
Number	*Raqam*	رقم/أرقام		5	*Khamsa*	خمسة	٥
0	*Sifr*	صفر	٠	6	*Sitah*	ستة	٦
1	*Wahed*	واحد	١	7	*Sab`ah*	سبعة	٧
2	*Ithnan*	اثنان	٢	8	*Thamaniyah*	ثمانية	٨
3	*Thalatha*	ثلاثة	٣	9	*Tesa`ah*	تسعة	٩
4	*Arba`ah*	أربعة	٤	10	*A`sharah*	عشرة	١٠

Please note that numbers 1 and 2 match in gender with the word following it. If there is two of anything, we use the dual form and there is no need to use the word 2 (اثنان). Numbers 3–9 are the opposite in gender.

As in many other words, the number can be changed into feminine by adding *ta marbuta* at the end of it.

Meaning	Transliteration	Feminine Number	Transliteration	Masculine Number
One	*Wahedah*	واحدة	*Wahed*	واحد
Two	*Ithnatan*	اثنتين	*Ithnan*	اثنين
Three	*Thalatha*	ثلاثة	*Thalath*	ثلاث
Four	*Arba`ah*	أربعة	*Arba`*	أربع
Five	*Khamsa*	خمسة	*Khams*	خمس
Six	*Sitah*	ستة	*Sit*	ست
Seven	*Sab`ah*	سبعة	*Sab`a*	سبع
Eight	*Thamaniyah*	ثمانية	*Thaman*	ثمان
Nine	*Tesa`ah*	تسعة	*Tesa`*	تسع
Ten	*A`sharah*	عشرة	*A`shar*	عشر

3.2. **Practice**   (see Answer Key)

Identify each of the Arabic numbers below by writing the question number next to the correct translation:

17 ( )	أربعة	4.	13 ( )	عشرة	1.
4 ( )	ثلاث عشر	5.	15 ( )	سبعة عشر	2.
9 ( )	خمسة عشر	6.	10 ( )	تسعة	3.

The tens

Numbers 20–90 are conjugated as the Transliteration masculine plural. You just add "*een*" when accusative or "*oon*" when nominative to the end. The same situation applies to regular plurals. There is no masculine or plural form in the tens. They are as follows:

English	Arabic	Transliteration	Number in accusative	Transliteration	Number in genitive
20	٢٠	*Eshroon*	عشرون	*Eshreen*	عشرين
30	٣٠	*Thalathoon*	ثلاثون	*Thalatheen*	ثلاثين
40	٤٠	*Arba`oon*	أربعون	*Arba`een*	أربعين
50	٥٠	*Khamsoon*	خمسون	*Khamseen*	خمسين
60	٦٠	*Sitoon*	ستون	*Siteen*	ستين
70	٧٠	*Sab`oon*	سبعون	*Sab`een*	سبعين
80	٨٠	*Thamanoon*	ثمانون	*Thamaneen*	ثمانين
90	٩٠	*Tes`oon*	تسعون	*Tes`een*	تسعين

100- مائة *h`am*

100- مائة is a noun and may end with *fat-ha*, *dhamma* or *kasra* as any other noun according to its position in the sentence. The noun it is counting comes after it and it should be singular and indefinite all the times. It is considered as the second noun in *idafa*, as would be explained in detail in next lessons. This means the noun should always have *kasra*. مائة كتابٍ—*mi'a say-yarah* مائة سيارةٍ *mi'a kitab*.

1,000- Thousand

الف *alf*- thousand also forms *idafa* with its noun where the noun should be singular, indefinite and genitive since it is idafa.

To read numbers in Arabic we follow the same procedure as in English. You start with the highest category while inserting (و) meaning a comma before each category. For example, the number 6,457 is read as: ست آلاف و أربع مائة و سبعة و خمسين.

It is very important to keep in mind that numbers in Arabic are written in the same order as English numbers. They are written from left to right. Look at the table to compare the equivalence between Arab and English numbers

Numbers in English	Transliteration	Numbers in Arabic
1,957	*Alf wa tes'm`ah wa sab`a wa khamseen*	١٩٥٧
20,345	*Eshroon alf wa thalath me`ah wa khamsa wa arb`oon*	٢٠٣٤٥
325	*Thalathm`ah wa khamsa wa e`shreen*	٣٢٥
98	*Thamaniya wat es`oon*	٩٨
100	*Ma`ah*	١٠٠

3.3. **Practice**   (see Answer Key)

Now write the following numbers in figures:

2. سبعة عشر   : _____   1. خمسة و ثلاثين : _____

4. سبعة و خمسين : _____   3. ثمانية   : _____

6. أربعة و عشرين: _____   5. ستة و سبعين : _____

8. عشرين   : _____   7. خمسة عشر : _____

10. تسعة و ستين : _____   9. احدى عشرة : _____

3.4. **Practice**   (see Answer Key)

Write the following numbers using letters. Don't forget to follow the rule of masculine and feminine:

1. 11 books   _____   6. 50 tables   _____
2. 14 pens   _____   7. 22 keys   _____
3. 65 chairs   _____   8. 384 erasers _____
4. 76 girls   _____   9. 104 rooms   _____
5. 289 houses _____   10. 563 papers _____

3.5. **Practice**   (see Answer Key)

To review your writing skills: Match the same words then write the word on the line beside it:

_____   ن س ك   ضرب   1.

_____   ك س ب   صرخ   2.

_____   ض ر ب   نسك   3.

_____   ص ر خ   كشف   4.

_____   ع م ل   كسب   5.

_____	ع د ل	٦. كتب
_____	ك ت ب	٧. علم
_____	ع ل م	٨. عمل
_____	ك ش ف	٩. عدل
_____	غ س ق	١٠. قمر
_____	ق ر أ	١١. غسق
_____	غ ر ق	١٢. قرأ
_____	ق م ر	١٣. غرق

3.6 | Practice   (see Answer Key)

Read and respond to the following:

أمل : من أين أنت؟		أمل : مرحبا !	
هدى : _____		هدى : _____	
أمل : من أين أنت؟		أمل : ما اسمك ؟	
هدى : _____		هدى : _____	
أمل : الى اللقاء		هدى : و انت؟ ما اسمك؟	
هدى : _____		أمل : _____	
		أمل : كيف حالك؟	
		هدى : _____	

3.7. | Practice

To review your reading skills, read the following and pay attention to the difference in pronunciation of letters:

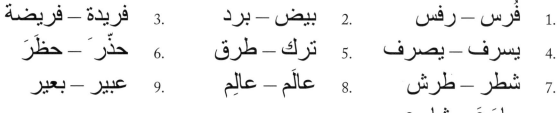

١. فُرس – رفس   ٢. بيض – برد   ٣. فريدة – فريضة

٤. يسرف – يصرف   ٥. ترك – طرق   ٦. حذَّرَ – حظَرَ

٧. شطر – طرش   ٨. عالَم – عالِم   ٩. عبير – بعير

١٠. سارَعَ – شارِع

3.8. Practice   (see Answer Key)

This is your final review for the alphabet. Please circle the word/words that have the letter mentioned at the beginning in it:

يهدي	كتيب	مكتبة	هدى	هـ : وردة	1.
لعب	طائر	سبيكة	سكن	ك : كتب	2.
سمر	حرف	مثال	اسمي	م : لعبة	3.
سمر	حرف	منال	نلعب	ن : لعبة	4.
يبحث	أستاذ	ادريس	جديد	ي : جنسية	5.
	ذكر	تعليم	حديث	ت : جانب	6.
	تمثيل	خطوط	جنوب	ج : تعليم	7.
	مشرك	شارك	رضى	ش : سالم	8.
	طبيب	طريقة	غروب	غ : عرفات	9.
	طبيب	صخرة	فاز	ف : زفاف	10.

Reflection

1. In this Lesson I learned: _____

2. I have some trouble with: _____

3. I need to learn more about: _____

الوحدة الرابعة
Arab Hospitality
الضيافة و الكرم العربي

Al-deyafa wa al-karam al-arabi

Objectives:

1. The Definite Article and its uses
2. *Alif Mad* and *Hamza*
3. *Alif Maqsoora*
4. *Dagger Alif*
5. The particle *ya*
6. Culture: Arab Hospitality: Visiting Friends and Family
7. Reading

🔊 **Vocabulary**

Meaning	Transliteration	Plural	Transliteration	Words–(verbs are past tense followed by present tense)
Reside	–	–	*Sakana-yaskon*	سَكَنَ / يَسْكُنْ
Enter	–	–	*Dakhala-yadkhol*	دَخَلَ / يَدْخُلْ
Entrance	–	–	*madkhal*	مَدْخَلْ
Go out	–	–	*Kharaja-yakhroj*	خَرَجَ / يَخْرُجْ
Exit	–	–	*Makhraj*	مَخْرَجْ
Wash	–	–	*Ghasala-yaghsel*	غَسَلَ / يَغْسِلْ
Travel	–	–	*Saafara-yosaafer*	سافَرَ / يُسافِرْ
Talk to	–	–	*Hadatha-yahdoth*	حَدَّثَ / يُحَدِّثْ

Meaning	Transliteration	Plural	Transliteration	Words–(verbs are past tense followed by present tense)
Come	–	–	*Hadara-yahdor*	حَضَرَ / يَحْضُرْ
Study	–	–	*Darasa-yadros*	دَرَسَ / يَدْرُسْ
Learn	–	–	*Ta`lamma-yata`lam*	تَعلَّمْ / يَتَعَلَّمْ
Pray	–	–	*Salla-yosali*	صَلَّى / يُصَلِّي
School	*Madares*	مَدارِسْ	*Madrasa*	مَدْرَسة
University	*Jame`at*	جامِعاتْ	*Jame`a*	جامِعة
College	*Koliyyat*	كُلِّياتْ	*Koliyyah*	كُلِّية
Library	*Maktabat*	مَكْتَباتْ	*Maktabah*	مَكْتَبة
Office	*Makateb*	مَكاتِبْ	*Maktab*	مَكْتَبْ
Street	*Shaware`*	شَوارِعْ	*Share`*	شارِعْ
Museum	*Matahef*	مَتاحِفْ	*Mathaf*	مَتْحَفْ
Mosque	*Masajid*	مَساجِدْ	*Masjid*	مَسْجِدْ
Here	–	–	*Hona*	هُنا
There	–	–	*Honak*	هُناكْ
Many	–	–	*Katheerah*	كَثيرة
Engineering	–	–	*Handasah*	هَنْدَسة
Business	–	–	*Tejarah*	تِجَارة
Literature	–	–	*Al-adab*	الآدابْ
Sciences	–	–	*Oloom*	عُلومْ

Meaning	Transliteration	Plural	Transliteration	Words–(verbs are past tense followed by present tense)
Mathematics	–	–	*Riyadiyat*	رِياضِيّاتْ
Computer	–	–	*Hasoob*	حاسوبْ
Computer	–	–	*Kombuter* *hasoob*	كُمْبُيوتَر (more commonly used than حاسوبْ)
Door	–	–	*Bab*	بابْ
Window	–	–	*Shobbak*	شُبّاكْ
Car	*Sayyarat*	سَيّارات	*Sayyarah*	سَيّارة
Bicycle	*Darrajat*	دَرّاجاتْ	*Darraja*	دَرّاجَة
Get angry	–	–	*Ghadeba-yaghdab*	غَضَبْ / يَغْضَبْ
Be happy	–	–	*Fareha-yafrah*	فَرحَ / يَفْرَحْ
I want	–	–	*Oreed*	أريد
Beside	–	–	*Bejaneb*	بجانب
I have	–	–	*Endee*	عندي

Hospitality and Food

A hallmark of Arab cultural practice is hospitality and generosity. As an example, when someone praises an object, be it a picture frame on the wall, a watch, a purse or item of clothing, an Arab may give it to the admirer and insist that he takes it. They would say, "Since you like it so much, it is yours." As long as it is something they can live without, it will be generously offered. In terms of hospitality toward guests, in regular visits (not an invitation for a meal), when Arabs have a visitor, they start by offering juice or soda, followed by hot tea with assorted sweets such as cakes, cookies and other popular local confections. Nuts such as pistachios, almonds, peanuts, cashews and seeds are presented after the refreshments and kept on the table so the visitor may enjoy them during the visit. At the end of the visit, the host presents coffee accompanied with chocolates or dates, as is common in Gulf countries. Arab hospitality requires that when presenting something, the host should offer it at least three times and insist on the guest tasting what is on offer before finally accepting a guest's negative response. It is not considered polite to ask a guest whether he prefers tea or soda, for example, but rather to present a beverage and allow the guests to either drink it all or have a sip of it.

Lunch is the main meal in Arab countries. Government jobs start at about seven in the morning and conclude at one or two o'clock in the afternoon, thus allowing Arab families to share lunch and spend quality time together. Some private-sector companies have a long lunch break for three to four hours, after which employees might go back to work in the afternoon until seven or eight o'clock in the evening. Those with a long lunch break may take a nap, spend time with friends or, in the case of students, finish schoolwork. Lunch is also the main meal to which guests are invited, and if a friend, neighbor or family member knocks at the door during lunch time, an Arab usually insists that the visitor come in and have lunch with them.

Although, using the right hand is an Islamic custom rather than simply an Arab custom, however, using the right hand while eating and drinking is the cultural norm. Muslims believe that Islam organizes all aspects of life, with verses from the Qur'an or sayings of the Prophet directing Muslims what to do and not to do. Among the directions for acts of worship, morals, manners, interactions with others and private affairs are customs for eating and drinking. The Prophet said, in teaching a companion eating with his left hand, "Oh young man, say the name of Allah, eat with your right hand and eat from what is nearest to you" (*Al-Bukhari*, Vol 7, Book 65, # 288). This **hadith**, or utterance of the Prophet, also directs Muslims to begin eating by saying "**bismillah**" or "in the name of Allah" while using the right hand and to eat what is front of him if the food is presented on one communal tray. Today most Arabs provide individual plates for each guest, so they can choose what they wish to eat. Use of the left hand to eat is only acceptable if one is unable to use the right hand for medical reasons.

It is customary practice for a guest to taste everything offered on the table. When served something unfamiliar, guests may ask about the dish and how it was prepared. Hosts usually invite guests to take a second and third serving. It is recommended to take a second serving, even if it is very small, to show appreciation to the host. After the meal, fruits, sweets, hot tea and coffee are served. Throughout the meal, the guests usually praise the food and compliment the host. It is impolite and may be considered shameful for a guest to criticize the food presented. This also goes back to the teachings of the Prophet, as noted in Sahih Al-Bukhari that "The Messenger of Allah has never criticized any food. If he liked it, he would eat it, if not he would leave it" (*Sahih al-Bukhari*, Vol. 4, Hadith 764). When they are done eating, guests usually wish the host a full table all the time. It is customary for guests to reciprocate by inviting the host to a meal.

Dates are very popular, especially in Gulf countries, and are often served with hot coffee. In addition to coffee, hot tea, especially with mint, is popular with many Arabs. Although alcoholic drinks are forbidden by Islam and are not served or used in cooking, alcohol is sold in some Arab countries to tourists or non-Muslims.

Islam, like Judaism, demands a clear dietary code, and these dietary codes apply equally when dining in someone's home or at a restaurant. Muslims dining out in a western country often ask if the food they are served contains any pork.

Definite Article or Al-ashamsiyah and Al-alqamariyah

To define a noun or adjective in Arabic, we add *al* ال at the beginning of it. *Al* ال is equivalent to "the" in English. ال is connected to the word and is NOT used as a separate word.

As in English, *al* is added to nouns and adjectives but never to verbs. When we add *al* ال, the noun or adjective may have a vowel but never **tanween** or double vowel. You can say:

الكبير & *kabeerin* بيتٌ *bayton* – كتاباً *kitaban* & كبيرٍ and البيتُ *albayt* – الكتابَ *alkitab* & الكبير *alkabeer* ِ

There is no equivalent to "a" in Arabic, so we just use ال .

Please keep in mind that proper nouns are definite whether we add al to them or not. When adding *al* ال to nouns and adjectives there are two cases:

1. Pronouncing both letters, *a* and *l* very clearly as in: القمر & الغرفة. The letters following this pattern are called moon letters and they are: أ, ب, ج, ح, خ, ع, غ, ف, ق, ك, م, و, ي, هـ

2. Pronouncing only the *a* and not the *l* while putting more stress on the letter that comes after it as if it has **shaddah**. It is like the letter is assimilating to the *l*. These are called the sun letters and they are: ت, ث, د, ذ, ر, ز, س, ش, ص, ض, ط, ظ, ل, ن

Look at the table of moon and sun letters. Listen to the words, the moon letter words are read first followed by the sun letter words: 🔊

Transliteration	Sun letters with examples	Transliteration	Moon letters with examples
Attamr	ت التمر	*Alamal*	ا الأمل
Ath-thawb	ث الثوب	*Albab*	ب الباب
Addokkan	د الدكان	*Aljar*	ج الجار
Ath-thakee	ذ الذكي	*Alhoot*	ح الحوت
Arra'i	ر الراعي	*Alkhabar*	خ الخبر
Azzeen	ز الزين	*Ala'yn*	ع العين
Assa'ah	س الساعة	*Alghobar*	غ الغبار
Ashams	ش الشمس	*Alfat-h*	ف الفتح
Assayad	ص الصياد	*Alqamar*	ق القمر
Adofda'	ض الضفدع	*Alkalb*	ك الكلب
Atamatem	ط الطماطم	*Almanzil*	م المنزل
Ath-thil	ظ الظل	*Alhoda*	هـ الهدى
Alayl	ل الليل	*Alwalad*	و الولد
Annoor	ن النور	*Alyawm*	ي اليوم

Some examples on definite article:

Meaning	Transliteration	Word
The girl is beautiful	*albent jameela*	البنت جميلة
The dates are on the table	*attamr a'la attawelah*	التمر على الطاولة
The room is small	*Alghorfah sagheerah*	الغرفة صغيرة
The dress is short	*ath-thawb qaseer*	الثوب قصير

4.1 Practice (see Answer Key)

Circle the words in which the *al* is NOT pronounced:

الشارع – المدينة – القرآن – الصف – الكرسي – النهاية – البيت

4.2 Practice (see Answer Key)

Underline the correct form:

مسجداً – الشارعاً – مكتبةٌ – الساعة – شجرةً – كتابٍ – شمساً – الولد – الطالباً

Alif and Hamza

There are three ways to pronounce alif, the first letter of the alphabet, and several ways to be written which makes it a unique letter. *Alif* may be pronounced as a as in apple. This form of *alif* is when it has *hamza* over or under it. We add the short vowel, that is *fat-ha* or *dhamma* on top of *hamza* while we add the *kasra* under the *hamza* and both are written under the *alif*. When the *alif* has *hamza* it is pronounced as with a sudden stop or as it called in linguistics a glottal stop.

As you remember, when the أ has *fat-ha* on it, it is pronounced as "an," when it has *dhamma* on it, it is pronounced as in "on" and when it has *kasra* it is pronounced as "in." *Alif* with *hamza* may be at the beginning, middle or end of a word. When a word begins with *hamza*, it is always written on the *alif* and it might be accompanied with any of the three vowels. *Dhamma* may be added or it will be written on a *waw* ؤ . However with *kasra* it changes its shape to be written as: ـئـ . At the end of the word and after a long vowel, the *hamza* is written by itself as in: ء . Some examples of *hamza* at the end of the word are: شفاء – ضوء – سماء

Some examples of *alif* and *hamza* with different vowels are: 🔊

Meaning	Transliteration	Word
Father	*ab*	أَب
Mother	*Um*	أُم
Permission	*ithn*	إذن
Thing	*shay'*	شيئ
Family	*A'ilah*	عائلة
Question	*so'al*	سؤال

Meaning	Transliteration	Word
Woman	*imra'ah*	إمراة
Monday	*al-ithnayn*	الإثنين
Bird	*ta'er*	طائر
Kind/caring	*ra'oof*	رؤف
Responsible	*mas'ool*	مسؤول

The second form of *alif* is when it is used as a long vowel *aa* as in rat or at. It was introduced in Lesson 2.

The third form of *alif* is when it is used as a very long *aa*, there is no equivalent to it in English. It is written as آ. Examples of آ are as in: 🔊

Meaning	Transliteration	Word
I am sorry	*Aasif*	آسف
The Qur'an	*Alqura'an*	القرآن

Meaning	Transliteration	Word
I eat	*Aakol*	آكل
Now	*Alaan*	الآن

Alif Maqsoura- Broken Alif

Alif maqsoura is a form of *alif* that comes at the end of the word only. It is pronounced as *alif* and written as ى. This is why its name is *alif maqsoura*, meaning *broken*. Some examples of *alif maqsoura* are in words such as: 🔊

Meaning	Transliteration	Example
Moses	*Musa*	موسى
Isa/Jesus	*Eesa*	عيسى
Accept	*Yardda*	يرضى
Strive	*yas'aa*	يسعى
Walk	*Masha*	مشى

Meaning	Transliteration	Example
Female name	*Layla*	ليلى
Female name	*Najwa*	نجوى
Female name	*Mona*	منى
Female name	*Salma*	سلمى

Notice it looks the same as *ya* at the end of the word, but it has no dots under it. If it has two dots, then it is *ya* and pronounced as *ya*.

Dagger Alif

The last type of *alif* is called *dagger alif*. It has its name because it looks like a small dagger on top of the letter. It represents the old spelling of *alif* in Classical Arabic. It is still used on few words and names. It is pronounced as long *alif*. The most common words using *dagger alif* are: 🔊

Meaning	Transliteration	Word
This (masculine)	*Hatha*	هذا
This (feminine)	*Hathihi*	هذه
These	*Ha'olaa*	هؤلاء

Meaning	Transliteration	Word
But	*Lakenna*	لكن
That (masculine)	*Thalika*	ذلك

The particle ya يا

The particle يا is called vocative because it is only used to call attention of someone who can hear you. It is used before the names, titles and terms of address. It is never used by itself. It is very close to the meaning of "hey, you" and it is used as a respected form of calling attention of someone. Some examples are: يا أستاذ – يا أُخت – يا أُمي

4.3 **Practice** (see Answer Key)

Circle the word that does not belong:

1. كِتَابٌ ـ دَفْتَرٌ ـ وَاحِدٌ ـ قَلَمٌ.

2. دَرَّاجَةٌ ـ سَيَّارَةٌ ـ غُرْفَةٌ.

3. تلفاز ـ مُسَجِّلَةٌ ـ مَدِينَة ـ حَاسُوبٌ.

4. مَدْرَسَةٌ ـ كُلِّيَّةٌ ـ بَابٌ ـ جَامِعَةٌ.

5. طَاوِلَةٌ ـ كُرْسِيٌّ ـ كِتَابٌ ـ أَنَا

4.4 **Practice** (see Answer Key)

Read the following conversation between Ahmad and Khaled. After you finish reading please respond to the following questions:

Masa alkhair Good evening.	خَالِدُ: مَسَاءُ الخَيْرِ.
Masa anoor Good evening to you too.	أَحْمَدُ: مَسَاءُ النُورِ.
Ana ismee khalid My name is Khalid.	خَالِدُ: أَنَا اسِمِي خَالِدُ.
Tasharafna. Ana ismee ahmad I am honored, my name is Ahmad.	أَحْمَدُ: تَشَرُّفِنَا. أَنَا اسِمِي أَحْمَدُ.
Ahlan wa sahlan You are welcome.	خَالِدُ: أَهْلًا وَ سَهْلًا.
Men ayna anta Where are you from?	أَحْمَدُ: مِنْ أَيْنَ أَنْتَ؟
Ana men dimashq I am from Damascus.	خَالِدُ: أَنَا مِنْ دِمَشْقَ.

Conversation *(continued)*

Ayna Dimashq? Where is Damascus?	أَحْمَدُ: أَيْنَ دِمَشْقُ؟
Dimashq fee Soorya. Men ayna anta? Damascus is in Syria. Where are you from?	خَالِدُ: دِمَشْقُ فِي سُورِيَا. مِنْ أَيْنَ أَنْتَ؟
Ana men tempi. I am from Tempi.	أَحْمَدُ: أَنَا مِنْ تمبي.
Ayna tempi? Where is Tempi?	خَالِدُ: أَيْنَ تمبي؟
Tempi fee Arizona. Tcmpe is in Arizona.	أَحْمَدُ: تمبي فِي أريزونا.
Matha ta'lamta alyawm? What did you learn today?	خَالِدُ: مَاذَا تَعَلَّمْتَ الْيَوْمَ؟
Ta'lamto asma al-ashyaa almawjooda fi alghorfa. I learned the names of things in the room.	أَحْمَدُ: تَعَلَّمْتْ أَسْمَاءُ الأَشْيَاءَ الْمَوْجُودَةَ فِي الْغُرْفَةِ
Mithla matha?s Like what?	خَالِدُ: مِثْلَ مَاذَا!
Tawela wa korsi wa shobbak. Table, chair and window.	أَحْمَدُ: طَاوِلَةٌ وَ كُرْسِيٌّ وَ شُبّاك .
Shokran lak ila aliqa. Thank you, see you soon.	خَالِدُ: شُكْرًا لَكَ. إِلَى اللِّقَاءِ
Ma'assalama. Go with peace/goodbye.	أَحْمَدُ: مَعَ السَلَامَةِ

After you finish reading please respond to the following questions:

1. مِنْ أَيْنَ أَحْمَدُ؟ _____

2. أَيْنَ دِمَشْقُ؟ _____

3. مَاذَا تَعَلَّمَ أَحْمَدُ الْيَوْمَ؟ _____

4. مَا هِيَ الأَشْيَاءُ الْمَوْجُودَةُ فِي الْغُرْفَةِ؟ _____

5. أَكْتُبُ ثَلَاثَةَ أَشْيَاءٍ مَوْجُودَةٍ فِي غُرْفَتِكَ؟ _____

4.5. Practice   (see Answer Key)

Fill in the blanks with a word from the list:

أُرِيدُ ـ بِجَانِبِ ـ سَافَرَ ـ الطَّاوِلَةُ ـ الحَقِيبَةُ ـ أَيْنَ

1.   دَفْتَرُكَ مَعِي فِي _____.

2.   الحَاسُوبُ عَلَى _____.

3.   أَنْتِ تَسْكُنُ _____ المَكْتَبَةِ.

4.   _____ أَبُو أَحْمَدُ إِلَى أَمْرِيكَا.

5.   _____ مِفْتَاحُكَ؟

6.   _____ أَنْ أُدَرِّسَ الرِّيَاضِيَّاتِ فِي الجَامِعَةِ

4.6. Practice

To make sure you know your numbers, contact five of your friends and fill in their names, date and place of birth:

مكان الميلاد *Makan almeelad* Place of birth	تاريخ الميلاد *Tareekh almeelad* Date of birth	الاسم *Al-ism* Name

4.7. Practice   (see Answer Key)

By now you should be familiar with connecting letters. Please connect the following:

1.   ن + ظ + ا + ر + ة   = _____.

2.   ب + ع + ي + د   = _____.

3.   أ + م + ا + ل   = _____.

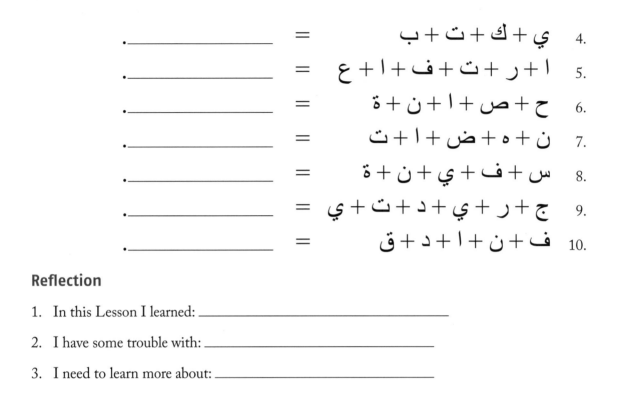

4. ي + ك + ت + ب   =   ــــــــــــــــــ .

5. ا + ر + ت + ف + ا + ع   =   ــــــــــــــــــ .

6. ح + ص + ا + ن + ة   =   ــــــــــــــــــ .

7. ن + ه + ض + ا + ت   =   ــــــــــــــــــ .

8. س + ف + ي + ن + ة   =   ــــــــــــــــــ .

9. ج + ر + ي + د + ت + ي   =   ــــــــــــــــــ .

10. ف + ن + ا + د + ق   =   ــــــــــــــــــ .

Reflection

1. In this Lesson I learned: _____

2. I have some trouble with: _____

3. I need to learn more about: _____

الوحدة الخامسة
Tea and Arabic Coffee
الشاي و القهوة العربية
Ashay wa alqahwa al-arabuyah

Objectives:

In this Lesson you will be introduced to:

1. Days of the Week
2. Academic Fields of Study (Academic Subjects)
3. Grammar: Singular, Dual and Plural Forms (Regular and Irregular)
4. Culture: Coffee and Tea
5. Expression of Courtesy

Vocabulary

Meaning	Transliteration	Plural	Transliteration	Word in singular
Student	*Tollab*	طُلَّاب	*Taleb*	طَالِبْ
Teacher	*Mo'alemeen*	مُعَلِّمِينْ	*Moa'lem*	مُعَلِّمْ
Subject	*Mawad*	مَوَاد	*Maddah*	مادّة
History	–	–	*Tareekh*	تَارِيخْ
Geography	–	–	*Joghrafya*	جُغْرَافِيا
Chemistry	–	–	*Keemya'*	كِيمْيَاءْ
Science	*Oloom*	عُلُومْ	*Ilm*	عِلْمْ
Art	–	–	*Rasm*	رَسْمْ

Meaning	Transliteration	Plural	Transliteration	Word in singular
Sport	*Riyadat*	رِياضات	*Riyadah*	رِياضة
Music	–	–	*Moseeqa*	موسيقى
Photography	–	–	*Attasweer*	التصْوير
Language	*Loghat*	لُغات	*Logha*	لُغة
Arabic Language	–	–	*Allogha al-arabiyah*	اللُغة العَرَبِيّة
English Language	–	–	*Allogha al-ingleeziah*	اللُغة الإنْجِليزِيّة
Religion	–	–	*Attarbiyah addeeniyah*	التربِية الدينِيّة
Medicine	–	–	*Attib*	الطِبّ
Before	–	–	*Qabl*	قَبْلْ
After	–	–	*Ba'ad*	بَعْدْ
From	–	–	*Min*	مِنْ
Until	–	–	*Hatta*	حَتَّى
In front of	–	–	*Amam*	أَمامْ
Behind	–	–	*Khalf*	خَلْفْ
Phone	*Hawatif*	هواتف	*Hatif*	هاتِفْ
Eye-glasses	*Nath-tharat*	نَظّارات	*Nath-tharah*	نَظّارة
Pictures	*Sowar*	صوَرْ	*Sourah*	صورة
Classroom / class	*Fosool*	فُصولْ	*Fasl*	فَصْلْ
Question	*As'elah*	أَسْئِلة	*So'al*	سُؤالْ
Several	–	–	*Eddah*	عِدّة

Meaning	Transliteration	Plural	Transliteration	Word in singular
There is/are	–	–	*Honak*	هُنَاكْ
Most	–	–	*Mo'th-tham*	مُعْظَمْ
Some	–	–	*Ba'ad*	بَعْضْ
All	–	–	*Kol*	كُلْ
Help	–	–	*Sa'ad- yosa'ed*	ساعَدَ / يُساعِدْ
Want	–	–	*Arada- yoreed*	أرادَ / يُريدْ

Coffee and Tea

Coffee قهوة and tea شاي are very important drinks in the Arab world. While Arabs started to drink coffee during the 1200s, Europeans started their coffee drinking habits in the 1600s. Coffee and tea are usually served hot during all day as in with breakfast, after lunch and after dinner. When visitors come tea and coffee are served. They are also served at business meetings and social events. Additionally, they are served during card games, football or just watching movies.

For social gatherings, tea is usually served with cake, cookies or any type of sweets. Later and before the end of the event coffee is served with dates or chocolate.

A fun fact that I read recently is that and according to the International Coffee Organization (ICO) report, the consumption of coffee in the Arab world is estimated to be 1.4 billion cups of coffee daily.

It is very popular to see people selling hot tea and coffee in the *souks*, *bazara* and streets. They do have stores such as Starbucks or Coffee Rush, and they may have a small table and move around people selling their hot drinks. Men selling coffee are called *kah-waji* قهوجي meaning coffee seller and those selling tea are called *Sababeen elshay* صبابين الشاي which literally means the tea pourers. Tea is mostly flavored with mint or with sage in some areas.

Days of the week

Meaning	Transliteration	Arabic	Meaning	Transliteration	Arabic
Saturday	*Assabt*	السبت	Friday	*Aljoma'a*	الجمعة
Sunday	*Al-ahad*	الأحد	Day	*Yawm- ayyam*	يوم / ايام
Monday	*Al-ithnayn*	الاثنين	Today	*Alyawm*	اليوم
Tuesday	*Ath-tholatha*	الثلاثاء	Week	*Osboo'*	أسبوع / أسابيع
Wednesday	*Al-arbia'a*	الأربعاء			
Thursday	*Alkhamees*	الخميس	Month	*Asabee'*	شهر / أشهر

Weekdays in Arab countries start with Sunday as the first day of the week. The weekend is Friday and Saturday.

Please note that يوم *yawm* means "day" while اليوم *alyawm* means "today."

Grammar: Singular, Dual and Plural Forms (regular and irregular)

There are three states for words in Arabic. They are singular, dual and plural. As you know singular refers to a single person or thing, dual refers to two while plural refers to more than two.

Dual forms

Dual is the easiest form and it is used with nouns, verbs, adjectives and pronouns. Dual forms can be created just by adding ان or ين at the end of the word depending on its case:

a) When the word is nominative, as when referring to the subject, the doer of the action or the first noun in a sentence, we add ان as in:

Transliteration	Dual	Transliteration	Word in Singular
Kitaban	كتابان	*Kitab*	كتاب
Yal'aban	يلعبان	*Yala'ab*	يلعب
Taweelatan	طويلتان	*Taweelah*	طويلة
Ghorfatan	غرفتان	*Ghorfa*	غرفة

b) when the word is accusative, as when it is the direct object of a verb or proceeded by a preposition, then you add ين as in:

Transliteration	Dual	Transliteration	Word in Singular
Kitabayn	كتابين	*Kitab*	كتاب
Taweelatayn	طويلتين	*Taweelah*	طويلة
Ghorfatayn	غرفتين	*Ghorfah*	غرفة

As you noticed:

1. When the word ends in **ta marbuata**, then you change it into the letter **ta** and add the ين or ان to it.
2. The dual form is used with definite and indefinite nouns
3. In verbs, we use only ان as verbs cannot be objects or come after a preposition

Plural forms

There are different forms of plurals that we are going to introduce for you today:

1. **Transliteration Masculine plural:** it is the form that deals with nouns referring to male humans. It is an easy form, all what you do is add ون – ين at the end of the word. When the word is accusative, as when it is the direct object of a verb or proceeded by a preposition, then you add ين . However, when the word is nominative, as when referring to the subject, doer of the action or the first noun in a sentence, then we add ون. Some examples are:

Meaning	Transliteration	Plural	Transliteration	Word
Engineer	*Mohandiseen/ mohandisoon*	مهندسين / مهندسون	*Mohandis*	مهندس
Teacher	*Mo'alimeen / Mo'alimoon*	معلمين / معلمون	*Mo'alim*	معلم
Writer	*Katibeen/ katiboon*	كاتبين / كاتبون	*Katib*	كاتب
Farmer	*Fellaheen/ fallahoon*	فلاحين / فلاحون	*Fallah*	فلاح
Employee	*Mowath-thafeen/ Mowath-thafoon*	موظفين / موظفون	*Mowath-thaf*	موظف
Egyptian	*Mesriyeen/ mesriyoon*	مصريين / مصريون	*Mesriyy*	مصري
Translator	*Motarjimeen/ motarjimoon*	مترجمين / مترجمون	*Motarjim*	مترجم

2. **Transliteration Feminine Plurals:** It is the form that is used with feminine plural nouns ending in ta marbuta. All what you have to do is: remove the ta marbuta and add ات at the end of the word. Some examples are:

Meaning	Transliteration	Plural	Transliteration	Word
Female teacher	*Ostathat*	أستاذات	*Ostatha*	أستاذة
Female student	*Talibat*	طالبات	*Taliba*	طالبة
Car	*Sayyarat*	سيارات	*Sayyarah*	سيارة
Library	*Maktabat*	مكتبات	*Maktabah*	مكتبة
Aunt	*Khalat*	خالات	*Khalah*	خالة
Busy	*Mash-gholat*	مشغولات	*Mash-ghoolah*	مشغولة
State	*Wilayat*	ولايات	*Wilayah*	ولاية
Building	*Benayat*	بنايات	*Benayah*	بناية

3. **Broken plurals:** These plurals earned their names because they break the letters of the word or change their order in it. There are different forms in plurals that follow different patterns. The best way to learn these plurals for now is whenever you use flashcards, write the word and its plural beside it and memorize both together. This type of plural is called broken plurals as they keep the root/original letters of the word and add few other letters in between. Some examples are:

Meaning	Transliteration	Plural	Transliteration	Word
Color	*Alwan*	ألوان	*Lawn*	لون
Shape	*Ash-kal*	أشكال	*Shakl*	شكل
Pen	*Aqlam*	أقلام	*Qalam*	قلم
Book	*Kotob*	كُتُب	*Kitab*	كتاب
Film	*Aflam*	أفلام	*Film*	فيلم
Name	*Asma'*	أسماء	*Esm*	اسم
City	*Modon*	مدن	*Madinah*	مدينة
Mr.	*Sadah*	سادة	*Sayyed*	سيّد

Meaning	Transliteration	Plural	Transliteration	Word
Brother	*Okhwah*	اخوة	*Akh*	أخ
Street	*Shaware'*	شوارع	*Share'*	شارع
Office	*Makateb*	مكاتب	*Maktab*	مكتب

In short, to learn plurals you need to master the agreement rules and you can also memorize the plurals.

5.1. **Practice** (see Answer Key)

Fill in the blanks with the suitable word:

لُغَتَيْنِ ـ مَادَّةٌ ـ أَيَّامٌ ـ الجَامِعَةُ ـ نَظَّارَاتٌ ـ بَعْدُ ـ قَبْلَ ـ أَسَابِيعُ

1. يَوْمَ الاِثْنَيْنِ يَأْتِي ــــــــــــــــ يوم الثُّلَاثَاءِ.

2. السَّبْتَ يَأْتِي ــــــــــــــــ يَوْمَ الجُمْعَةِ.

3. هناك سَبْعَةٌ ــــــــــــــــ فِي الأُسْبُوعِ.

4. فِي الشَّهْرِ أَرْبَعَةٌ ــــــــــــــــ

5. أتكلم ــــــــــــــــ اللُّغَةُ العَرَبِيَّةُ وَ الإِنْجِلِيزِيَّةُ.

6. أَذْهَبُ إِلَى ــــــــــــــــ كُلَّ يَوْمٍ.

7. عِنْدِي ثَلَاثَ ــــــــــــــــ

8. أَنَا لَا أُحِبُّ ــــــــــــــــ الجُغْرَافِيَا

Read:

Hathihi eman ali This is Eman Ali.	هَذِهِ إِيمَانُ عَلِي.
Tadros eman alhandasa fi jame'a oxford fe breetanya. Eiman is studying Engineering in Oxford University in Britain.	تَدْرُسُ إِيمَانُ الهَنْدَسَةَ فِي فِي جَامِعَةِ أُوكْسْفُورْد فِي بِرِيطَانِيَا.
Fee hatha alfasl tadros al/oloom wa al-kee-mya' wa almoseeka. In this semester, she is studying Science, Chemistry and Music.	فِي هَذَا الفَصْلُ تُدَرِّسُ مَادَّةُ العُلُومِ وَ الكِيمِيَاءُ وَ المُوسِيقَى.
Um eman wa abooha yskonan fee Madinat amman fe al-ordon wa yaskon ma'homa ikhwat eman ath-thalatha. Eman's father and mother live in Amman in Jordan and her three brothers live with them.	أُمُّ إِيمَانَ وَ أَبُوهَا يَسْكُنَانِ فِي مَدِينَةِ عُمَانَ فِي الأُرْدُنِّ وَ يَسْكُنُ مَعَهُمَا إِخْوَةُ إِيمَانَ الثَّلَاثَةِ.
Eman taskon fe shaqqa sagheera bejaneb aljame'a. Eman lives in a small apartment beside the university.	إِيمَانُ الآنَ تَسْكُنُ فِي شِقَّةٍ صَغِيرَةٍ بِجَانِبِ الجَامِعَةِ.
Taskon ma'ha fe alshaqqa taliba arabiyya men falstine ismoha amal mohammad. An Arab student from Palestine lives with her in the apartment. Her name is Amal Mohammad.	تَسْكُنُ مَعَها فِي الشَّقَّةِ طَالِبَةٌ عَرَبِيَّةٌ مِنْ فِلَسْطِينَ اِسْمُهَا أَمَلُ مُحَمَّدٌ.
Tadros amal alhandasa Aydan. Amal is studying Engineering too.	تَدْرُسُ أَمَلُ الهَنْدَسَةَ أَيْضًا.
Fee hatha alfasl tadros amal arriyadhiyat wa allogha al-ingleezia. In this semester, Amal is studying Mathematics and English Language.	فِي هَذَا الفَصْلُ تَدْرُسُ أَمَلُ الرِّيَاضِيَّاتِ وَ اللُّغَةَ الإِنْجِلِيزِيَّةَ.

5.2 **Practice**   (see Answer Key)

Translate the following sentences into Arabic:

1. Students sit in front of the teacher in the classroom. _____

2. Each student sits on a chair with his pen and notebook on the desk.
   _____

3. There are two teachers for this class. _____

4. The teacher is standing in front of his 23 students. _____

5. How many subjects do you study? _____

5.3. **Practice**   (see Answer Key)

Change into plural:

1. تَسْكُنُ الطَّالِبَةُ فِي غُرْفَةٍ صَغِيرَةٍ. _____

2. ذَهَبَ الطَّالِبُ إِلَى الكُلِّيَّةِ. _____

3. أُدَرِّسُ لُغَةً وَاحِدَةً. _____

4. هُنَاكَ مَعْلَمٌ فِي المَكْتَبَةِ. _____

5. كَتَبَ الطَّالِبُ عَلَى اللَّوْحِ. _____

5.4. **Practice**   (see Answer Key)

Write the plural of the following words:

2. كلمة _____   1. ورقة _____

4. سوري _____   3. لغة _____

5. كويتي _____

5.5. **Practice**   (see Answer Key)

Answer the following questions:

2. كَمْ شَهْرًا فِي السَّنَةِ؟   1. كَمْ يَوْمًا فِي الأُسْبُوعِ؟

4. كَمْ طَالِبًا فِي صَفِّكَ؟   3. كَمْ فَصْلًا فِي السَّنَةِ؟

6. كَمْ عُمْرُكَ؟   5. كَمْ عَدَدُ إِخْوَتِكَ؟

8. كَمْ سَاعَةً فِي اليَوْمِ؟   7. مَتَى عِيدُ مِيلَادِكَ؟

10. مَا هُوَ آخِرُ شَهْرٍ فِي السَّنَةِ؟   9. مَا اليَوْمَ بَعْدَ الثَّلَاثَاءِ؟

5.6. Practice (see Answer Key)

Rearrange the following sentences in order to form a story. Order the sentences by writing the number of the sentence in the brackets:

( ). أخذ كتاب مادة التاريخ

( ). قرأ عادل الكتاب .

( ). ذهب عادل الى المكتبة .

( ). لم يجد عادل الكتاب في البيت .

( ). أجاب على كل الأسئلة .

( ). كتب معلم التاريخ الأسئلة على اللوح .

( ). في الصباح ذهب عادل الى فصل التاريخ .

Reading

Read the following conversation between Mohammad and Ayman:

Masa' alkhair. Good evening.	مُحَمَّدٌ: مَسَاءُ الخَيْرِ.
Ahlan masaa annor. Welcome, good evening.	أَيْمَنْ: أَهْلًا! مَسَاءُ النُورِ.
Ana Mohamad sadiq fu'ad. I'm Mohammad, Fouad's friend.	مُحَمَّدٌ: أَنَا مُحَمَّدٌ. صَدِيقُ فُؤَادَ.
Ahlan wa sahlan! You are welcome!	أَيْمَنْ: أَهْلًا وَ سَهْلًا!
Wa anta ma ismoka? What's your name?	مُحَمَّدٌ: وَ أَنْتَ؟ مَا اِسْمُكَ ؟
Ana ayman. My name is Ayman.	أَيْمَنْ: أَنَا أَيْمَنْ.
Tasharafna, ayna fou'ad? I am honored, where is Fouad?	مُحَمَّدٌ: تَشَرُّفِنَا!
Howa fii almaktaba. He's at the library.	أَيْمَنْ: أَيْنَ فُؤَادٌ؟
Kam omroka? How old are you?	مُحَمَّدٌ: هُوَ فِي المَكْتَبَةِ.

Conversation *(continued)*

Omree thalath ashrata sana wa anta? I am thirteen years old. How about you?	مُحَمَّدٌ: عُمْرِي ثلاث عشرة سنة. وَ أَنْتَ؟
Ana omree arba'a wa eshroon sana. I am twenty-four years old.	مُحَمَّدٌ: أَنَا عُمْرِي أَرْبَعٌ و عشرون سَنَةً.
Hal anta talib fee almadrasah? Are you a student at school?	هل أَنْتَ طَالِبٌ فِي المَدْرَسَةِ؟
Na'am ana fee assaf attase.' Yes, I am in the ninth grade.	أَيْمَنْ: نَعَمْ. أَنَا فِي الصَّفِّ التَّاسِعُ.
A hiya madatoka almofaddalah? What is your favorite subject?	مُحَمَّدٌ: مَا هِيَ مَادَّتُكَ المُفَضَّلَةُ؟
Ana ohibo arriyadhiyat wa almoseeqa kateeran. I love mathematics and Music a lot.	أَيْمَنْ: أَنَا أُحِبُّ الرِّيَاضِيَّاتِ وَ المُوسِيقَى كَثِيرًا.
Matha toreed an tadros fee aljame'a? What do you want to study at the university?	مُحَمَّدٌ: مَاذَا تُرِيدُ أَنْ تَدْرُسَ فِي الجَامِعَةِ؟
Lam oqarrer ba'd. I did not decide yet.	أَيْمَنْ: لَمْ أُقَرِّرْ.
Sa'th-hab ila almaktaba e'nda fuad. I will go to the library to see Fouad.	مُحَمَّدٌ: سَأَذْهَبُ إِلَى المَكْتَبَةِ عِنْدَ فُؤَادَ.
Hasana ila aliqa.' OK, goodbye.	أَيْمَنْ: حَسَنًا. إِلَى اللِّقَاءِ.
Ma' assalamah. Go with peace.	مُحَمَّدٌ: مَعَ السَلَامَةِ.

5.7. **Practice** (see Answer Key)

Now answer the following questions:

2. أين فؤاد؟   1. من هو محمد؟

4. في أي صف أيمن؟   3. كم عمر أيمن؟

5. أين سيذهب محمد؟

5.8. Practice   (see Answer Key)

Change the following to feminine:

2. طالب   _____

1. معلّم   _____

4. ولد   _____

3. أمير   _____

6. تعبان   _____

5. سيّد   _____

8. كثير   _____

7. هو   _____

10. حضر   _____

9. قط   _____

5.9. Practice   (see Answer Key)

Circle the word that does not belong:

1. مدرسة – كلية – جامعة – أنا

2. خرج – دخل – حضر – مكتبة

3. أنا – أنت – كتاب – هي

4. مكتبة – مسجد – يلعب – متحف

5. سيارة – آداب – تجارة – علوم

Reflection

1. In this Lesson I learned: _____

2. I have some trouble with: _____

3. I need to learn more about: _____

الوحدة السادسة
Social Life and Visits
الزيارات و العلاقات الاجتماعية
Azziyarat wa al-ilaqat al-ijtima'yah

Objectives:
1. Months and Seasons Vocabulary
2. Grammar
   • Verbs
   • Nouns
   • Prepositions
   • Question Words
3. Culture: Greetings and Visits
4. Reading

 Vocabulary

Meaning	Transliteration	Plural	Transliteration	Word
Month	*Ash-hor*	أَشْهُرْ	*Shahr*	شَهْرْ
Season	*Fosool*	فُصول	*Fasl*	فَصْلْ
Summer	–	–	*Sayf*	صَيْفْ
Fall	–	–	*Khareef*	خَرِيفْ
Winter	–	–	*Shita'*	شِتاءْ
Spring	–	–	*Rabee'*	ربيع
Year	*Sanawat*	سَنَواتْ	*Sanah*	سَنة
Weather	–	–	*Taqs*	طَقْسْ
Trees	*Ashjar*	أَشْجارْ	*Shajarah*	شَجَرة

Meaning	Transliteration	Plural	Transliteration	Word
Flower	*Azhar*	أَزْهارْ	*Zahrah*	زَهْرة
Wind	*Riyah*	رِياحْ	*Reeh*	ريحْ
Rain	*Amtar*	أَمْطارْ	*Matar*	مَطَرْ
Snow	*Tholooj*	ثُلُوج	*Thalj*	ثَلْجْ
Sky	–	–	*Sama'*	سَماءْ
Cold	–	–	*Bared*	بَارِدْ
Hot	–	–	*Har*	حارْ
Very	–	–	*Jedan*	جِدّاً
Mountains	*Jibal*	جِبالْ	*Jabal*	جَبَلْ
Beautiful	–	–	*Jameel*	جَميلْ
Suit	*Bedal*	بدل	*Badlah*	بَدْلة
Coat	–	–	*Balto*	بالْطو
Jacket	*Jaketat*	جاكيتات	*Jakeet*	جاكيت
T-shirt	*Balayez*	بلايز	*Bloozah*	بْلوزة
Skirt	*Tananeer*	تنانير	*Tanoorah*	تَنّورة
Clothes	*Malabis*	مَلابِسْ	*Malbas*	ملبس
Uniform	–	–	*Zey*	زِيّ
Specify	–	–	*Yohadid*	يُحَدِّدْ
To fall	–	–	*Yasqot*	يَسْقُطْ
Travel	–	–	*Yosafer*	يُسافِرْ
Traveling	–	–	*Assafar*	السَّفَرْ

Meaning	Transliteration	Plural	Transliteration	Word
Daily	–	–	*Yawmay*	يَوْميْ
Weekly	–	–	*Osboo'ee*	أُسْبوعيْ
Monthly	–	–	*Shahree*	شَهريْ
Annually	–	–	*Sanawee*	سَنَويْ
Old	–	–	*Qadeem*	قَديْمٌ
New	–	–	*Jadeed*	جديد
Tall & long	–	–	*Taweel*	طَويْلٌ
Short	–	–	*Qaseer*	قَصيْرٌ
Fast	–	–	*Saree'*	سَريْعٌ

Greetings and Visits

One very important factor constituting to a person's character is good manners, which starts with greetings. Arabs shake hands using only the right hand when they meet and say goodbye. Sometimes failure to shake hands might be considered rude, especially among older generations. Close friends and people whom one has not seen for a while may hug and kiss on both cheeks when greeting. Arab men kiss other men and women kiss other women. However, women and men do not kiss, as this is considered immodest and shameful unless they are close family members such as brothers and sisters, daughters and fathers or nieces and uncles. When meeting older family members such as parents, uncles or grandparents, it is customary to kiss either forehead, nose, or right hand of that person, depending on family's tradition, to show admiration and respect.

Shaking Hands

When a guest arrives, all people sitting in the room stand up to greet the newcomer, who shakes hands and kisses all attendees starting with those on his right side. Some Arabs, among them those from the Gulf countries, place their right hand on their heart after shaking hands as a sign of respect and love. Sometimes, when an Arab woman is introduced to a man who is not a family member, it is the woman's choice to shake hands or not. Some Arab women might initiate the handshake while others do not, depending on their background and family rules.

It is common to have separate seating for men and women. Usually, when entering a house as a guest, males and females are directed to different rooms. In the Gulf countries, most houses have separate entrances for men and women.

During visits, one sits properly without drooping, wiggling or sliding down in one's seat, especially in a gathering among different age groups. While seated, Arabs do not put their feet or shoes facing one another or pointing at someone's face, as it is considered disrespectful; visitors usually keep both feet on the floor. These seating traditions are required particularly when older people are in the room; however, friends of the same age may sit however they feel comfortable. In conversation, between different generations, it is disrespectful to lean against the wall or put one's hands in one's pockets, as it reflects tiredness, boredom or lack of enthusiasm for the conversation.

The origins of greeting with a smile and showing feelings are rooted in Islamic teachings, as the religion encourages its followers to greet each other and all people they meet to spread love, peace and friendship. The Prophet said, "You will never enter Paradise until you believe, and you will never believe fully until you love each other. Shall I not lead you to something that if you do it, you will love each other? Spread the greetings of 'Salaam' amongst yourselves" (*Muslim*, Vol. 1, # 68). Additionally, when someone greets you, it is your obligation to respond to his greetings as Allah says in the Qur'an: "When you are greeted with a greeting, greet in return with what is better than it, or (at least) return it equally" (4:86). The teachings of the Prophet clarified who should initiate the greeting, as he said, "A rider should greet a pedestrian, a pedestrian should greet one who is seated, and a smaller group of people should greet a larger" (*Muslim*, Vol. 1, # 857).

When saying goodbye, guests and hosts shake hands again and sometimes kiss. It is very common to see Arabs standing and talking at the door, where they might start another conversation and spend few more minutes talking. The host usually accompanies his guests to the door and to their cars if they are the last to leave.

Months and Seasons

As you know, Gregorian calendars are accepted and used all over the world. Some Arab countries, such as Syria and Lebanon, use Aramaic names based on the Babylonian calendar. The dates do not change except for the name of the month. For example the Aramaic name for May is *Ayar* أيار. Other Arab countries use the an Arabized name of the months, as in: May would be *Mayo* مايو and September would stay the same *Sebtember* سبتمبر.

Here are the names of the Gregorian Arabic months.

English	Transliteration	Arabic
July	*Yolyo*	يوليو
August	*Oghostos*	أغسطس
September	*Sebtember*	سبتمبر
October	*October*	أكتوبر
November	*November*	نوفمبر
December	*December*	ديسمبر

English	Transliteration	Arabic
January	*Yanayer*	يناير
February	*Febrayer*	فبراير
March	*Maris*	مارس
April	*Ibreel*	ابريل
May	*Mayo*	مايو
June	*Yonyo*	يونيو

However, Saudi Arabia uses the Islamic calendar as its main calendar. The Islamic calendar is based on the lunar cycle. It started in 638 CE using the date of migration of the Prophet Mohammed from Mecca to Medina. Months in the Islamic/lunar calendar are either 29 or 30 days which differs from the Gregorian calendar by ten to eleven days each year. Almost all other Arab countries use both calendars and write both dates in their official letters and communication. The current Islamic year is 1440 and in August 19 the year 1441 would start. The Islamic calendar is important because it is used to determine the proper days for Islamic rituals and holidays as in the month of Ramadan and the month of pilgrimage to Mecca. Here is a list of the twelve months of the Lunar Calendar:

Month	Transliteration	Islamic Month
7	*Rajab*	رَجَبُ
8	*Sha'ban*	شَعْبَانُ
9	*Ramadan*	رَمَضَانُ
10	*Shawwal*	شَوَّالُ
11	*The alqe'dah*	ذِي القَعْدَةِ
12	*The alhijjah*	ذِي الحُجَّةِ

Month	Transliteration	Islamic Month
1	*Moharram*	مُحَرَّمٌ
2	*Safar*	صَفَرٌ
3	*Rabee'awal*	رَبِيعٌ أَوَّلُ
4	*Rabee'thani*	رَبِيعٌ ثَانِي
5	*Jamadi alawal*	جمادي الأَوَّلُ
6	*Jamadi athanni*	جمادي الثَّانِي

Grammar
Verbs
In Arabic, verbs do change their forms according to tense, gender and number as the verb reflects whom or what we are talking about. We add a prefix, suffix or both to indicate the

person/persons or thing we are talking about. Now, we will learn about verbs in the present tense. Verbs in present tense may refer to present tense as in "he drinks" or to continuous tense as in "he is drinking" depending on the context.

The following table shows the forms of present tense verbs conjugated according to the person we are talking about. Please note: the prefixes, suffixes or both added to the verbs. When you know the stem of the verb, you may conjugate any verb very easily.

When you look carefully at the table, you will notice that verbs keep a base of letters that keep repeated in each conjugation. This base is called the root of the verb. Arab language cites verbs in the third person masculine singular past tense. What we do is add a prefix, suffix or both. Look at the verb سكن for example and note what we add to indicate "I," you masculine, you feminine...etc.

There are some verbs with double consonant as in: أحبّ (love, (think) ظنّ & ضمّ)(hug). Double consonant verbs occur with verbs in the past as well as in Present tense when talking about the third person but not with the first or second person. For some more explanation look at the table below:

Transliteration	Past Tense	Transliteration	Present Tense	Transliteration	Pronoun
Ahbabto	أحببت	*Ohib*	أحبّ	*Ana*	أنا
Ahbabna	أحببنا	*Nohib*	نحب	*Nahno*	نحن
Ahbabta	أحببت	*Tohib*	تحب	*anta*	أنتَ
Ahbabti	أحببت	*Tohibeen*	تحبين	*Anti*	أنتِ
Ahbabtoma	أحببتما	*Tohiban*	تحبان	*Antoma*	أنتما
Ahbabtom	أحببتم	*Tohiboon*	تحبون	*Antom*	أنتم
Ahbabtonna	أحببتن	*Tohbibna*	تحببن	*Antenna*	أنتن
Ahaba	أحب	*Yohib*	يحب	*Howa*	هو
Ahabat	أحبت	*Tohib*	تحب	*Hiya*	هي
Ahabba	أحبا	*Yohiban*	يحبان	*Homa*	هما
Ahabata	أحبتا	*Tohiban*	تحبان	*Homa*	هما
Ahaboo	أحبوا	*Yohiboon*	يحبون	*Hom*	هم
Ahbabna	أحببن	*Yohbibna*	يحببن	*Honna*	هن

Verb	أنا	نحن	أنتَ	أنتِ	أنتما	هو	هي	هما	هم
سكن *sakana*	اسكن *askon*	نسكن *naskon*	تسكن *taskon*	تسكنين *taskoneen*	تسكنان *taskonan*	يسكن *yaskon*	تسكن *taskon*	يسكنان *yaskonan*	يسكنون *yaskonoon*
كتب *kataba*	اكتب *Aktob*	نكتب *Naktob*	تكتب *Taktob*	تكتبين *Taktobeen*	تكتبان *Taktoban*	يكتب *Yaktob*	تكتب *Taktob*	يكتبان *Yaktoban*	يكتبون *yaktoboon*
قرأ *Qara'*	اقرأ *Aqra'*	نقرأ *naqra'*	تقرأ *Taqra'*	تقرأين *Taqra'een*	تقرآن *Taqra'an*	يقرأ *yaqra'*	تقرأ *Taqra'*	يقرآن *Yaqra'an*	يقرأون *Yaqra'oon*
فعل *Fa'ala*	افعل *Afa'l*	نفعل *Nafa'l*	تفعل *Tafa'l*	تفعلين *Tafa'leen*	تفعلان *Tafa'lan*	يفعل *Yafa'l*	تفعل *Tafa'l*	يفعلان *Yafa'lan*	يفعلون *Yafa'loon*
ذهب *Thahaba*	اذهب *Ath-hab*	نذهب *Nath-hab*	تذهب *That-hab*	تذهبين *That-habeen*	تذهبان *Thath-aban*	يذهب *Yath-hab*	تذهب *That-hab*	يذهبان *Yath-haban*	يذهبون *yath-haboon*
شرب *Shariba*	اشرب *Ashrab*	نشرب *Nashrab*	تشرب *Tashrab*	تشربين *Tashrabeen*	تشربان *tashraban*	يشرب *Yashrab*	تشرب *Tashrab*	يشربان *Yashraban*	يشربون *yashraboon*

Note how the double consonant in the third person, did not use the *shaddah* but used the double letter be instead.

6.1. **Practice**   (see Answer Key)

Apply the rules you learned to conjugate the following verbs:

هم	هما	هما	نحن	هي	هو	أنتِ	أنتَ	أنا	Verb	Meaning
									حدّد	Assign
									حفظ	Keep
									درس	Study
									رسم	Draw
									شاهد	Watch
									أكل	Eat
									سمع	Hear
									خرج	Go out
									فتح	Open

6.2. Practice   (see Answer Key)

Conjugate the verbs into the present tense:

1.   ماذا (رسم) يا أمل؟   ـــــــــــــــ

2.   هم (سكن) في بيت كبير.   ـــــــــــــــ

3.   أحمد و هدى (ذهب) الى لندن.   ـــــــــــــــ

4.   الاستاذ (تكلم) أربع لغات.   ـــــــــــــــ

5.   أنا (درس) في الجامعة.   ـــــــــــــــ

6.   هما (شاهد) التلفزيون في المساء.   ـــــــــــــــ

7.   هي (كتب) الواجب.   ـــــــــــــــ

8.   اخوته (تكلم) اللغة الايطالية.   ـــــــــــــــ

9.   أنا (أحب) القهوة مع السكر.   ـــــــــــــــ

10.   نحن (سمع) الموسيقى .   ـــــــــــــــ

6.3. Practice   (see Answer Key)

Translate into Arabic

1. I am studying Chemistry and Literature.

2. Monday is the first day of the week.

3. You look tired, are you OK?

4 Where is your back bag?

5. I like Art but hate Science.

6.4. Practice   (see Answer Key)

Conjugate the verb عرف in the following sentences:

1.   أنا لا ـــــــــــــــ اسمه.

2.   نحن ـــــــــــــــ الى أين أنت ذاهب.

3.   هل ـــــــــــــــ اسم الكتاب الذي أقرأه يا هدى؟

4.   هم ـــــــــــــــ أين أسكن.

5.   السيدة هدى ـــــــــــــــ أسماء كل أقاربي.

Nouns

As explained earlier in Lesson 3, words in Arabic have a gender as they are either masculine or feminine. Masculine words refer to masculine humans or objects and feminine refer to female humans or objects. If a word ends in *ta marbuta* (ة ـة) then it is feminine.

It is very important to know the gender of the nouns because the verbs and adjectives should agree with gender to be conjugated correctly.

6.5. Practice   (see Answer Key)

When the sentence refers to a feminine subject, change into masculine and if it refers to a masculine subject change into feminine:

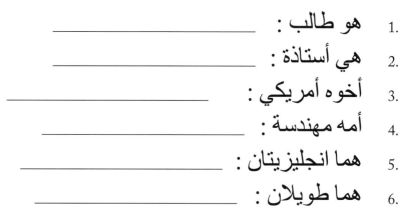

1. هو طالب : _____

2. هي أستاذة : _____

3. أخوه أمريكي : _____

4. أمه مهندسة : _____

5. هما انجليزيتان : _____

6. هما طويلان : _____

Prepositions:

The prepositions we have in Arabic are:

English Meaning	Transliteration	Preposition in Arabic	English Meaning	Transliteration	Preposition in Arabic
In	*Fee*	في	Over	*Fawqa*	فوق
On	*A'la*	على	Under	*Tahta*	تحت
Beside	*Bejanib*	بجانب	In front of	*Amam*	أمام
Between	*Bayna*	بين	Behind	*Khalfa*	خلف

All words after a preposition should be genitive, that is, to have *kasra*.

When definite nouns come after a preposition, they always have *kasra* but when an indefinite noun comes after a preposition, then it should have *tanween kasra* or double *kasra*.

Some examples are provided for you:

Meaning	Transliteration	Example
My book is on the table	*kitabi ala attawelati*	كتابي على الطاولةِ
The pen is on the book	*alqalam fawqa alkitabi*	القلم فوق الكتابِ
The teacher is in class	*Alostath fee assaffi*	الاستاذ في الصفِ

If a noun is dual or plural, then we use the *een* ين suffix to both definite and indefinite

Question Words

Here is a list of question words used in Arabic:

Meaning	Transliteration	Question word in Arabic
Do/Does/Did/Is/Are	*Hal*	هل
Where	*Ayna*	أين
When	*Mata*	متى
What (always followed by a noun)	*Ma*	ما
What (always followed by a verb)	*Matha*	ماذا
How many/how much	*Kam*	كم
Do/Does/Did/Is/Are	*A*	أ
Who	*Man*	مَن
How	*Kayfa*	كيف
Why	*Limatha*	لماذا

Please note:

For *kam* كم:
- كم is always used to ask about numbers
- كم is always followed by a singular indefinite noun. The noun is in the singular form and should have *tanween* as in:

Meaning	Transliteration	Example
How many books did you read?	*Kam kitaban qarata?*	كم كتابا قرأت؟
How many students are there in class?	*Kam Taliban fee assaf?*	كم طالبا في الصف؟
How many rooms are there in your house?	*Kam ghorfatan fee baytika?*	كم غرفةً في بيتك؟

For *hal* هل:

- As in English, the answer for هل should start by yes نعم or no لا
- The noun after هل is always definite, that it should have possessive letter added to it or you add ال to it as in:

Meaning	Transliteration	Example
Is my book with you?	*Hal kitabi ma'ak*	هل كتابي معك؟
Is the book with you?	*Hal alkitab ma'ak?*	هل الكتاب معك؟

For *a* أ:

أ is the same as هل in that the response should always be yes نعم or no لا. أ is added to the first word of the sentence. When it is used, it changes the statement into a yes/no question. It is prefixed to nouns, verbs, adjectives, particles or pronouns. Some examples are:

Meaning	Transliteration	Example
Is he your friend?	*Ahowa sadeeqok?*	أهو صديقك؟
Do you have a car?	*A'endoka sayyarah?*	أعندك سيارة؟
Do you want to eat?	*Atoreed an ta'kol?*	أتريد أن تأكل؟
Didn't you know?	*Alam ta'rif?*	ألم تعرف ؟
Is this your house?	*Ahatha baytoka?*	أهذا بيتك؟

For *man* مَن and *ayna* أين :

Please note that مَن and أين may be followed by a noun, verb or pronoun ٥

Meaning	Transliteration	Example
Who is he?	*Man howa*	من هو؟
Where is she?	*Ayna hiya*	أين هي؟
What is this?	*Ma hatha*	ما هذا؟
Where is Tunisia?	*Ayna Toonis*	أين تونس؟
Where do you live?	*Ayna taskon*	أين تسكن؟

All question words do no change the word order or the form of words coming after it

For *ma* "ما" and *matha* "ماذا":

"ما" and "ماذا" as you noticed have the same meaning. The only difference is that ما is followed by nouns while ماذا is followed by verbs. For example:

Meaning	Transliteration	Example
What do you study?	*Matha tadros*	ماذا تدرس؟
What do you do?	*Matha ta'mal*	ماذا تعمل؟
What is your name?	*Ma ismoka*	ما اسمك؟
What is your phone number?	*Ma raqam talefonak*	ما رقم تلفونك؟

For لماذا: as in English, when you respond use: "because" لأن or بسبب "because it is" followed by complete sentences. However, sometimes the nominal sentences start with a pronoun. So, when this happens, we need to use the attached pronouns as they will be explained with more details in Lesson 7. Now to learn how لأن would look like with attached pronouns, look at the following table:

Transliteration	Conjugation of لأن	Transliteration	Pronoun
li-annanee	لأنني	*Ana*	أنا
li-annana	لأننا	*Nahno*	نحن
li-annaka	لأنكَ	*Anta*	أنتَ

Transliteration	Conjugation of لأَن	Transliteration	Pronoun
li-annaki	لأَنكِ	*Anti*	انتِ
li-anakoma	لأَنكما	*Antoma*	أنتما
li-annaho	لأَنه	*Howa*	هو
li-annaha	لأَنها	*Hiya*	هي
li-annahoma	لأَنهما	*Homa*	هما
li-annahom	لأَنهم	*Hom*	هم
li-annahonna	لأَنهن	*Honna*	هن

Some examples are:

Meaning	Transliteration	Example
I don't like winter because the weather is cold.	*la ohibo ashitaa' li-anna attaqs barid.*	لا أحب الشتاء لأن الطقس بارد.
I want to eat because I am hungry.	*oreed an aakol li'anee ja'ea.*	أريد أن آكل لأنني جائعة.

6.6. Practice   (see Answer Key)

Use the proper question word to fill in the blanks:

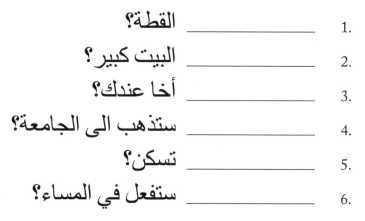

1. _____ القطة؟

2. _____ البيت كبير؟

3. _____ أخا عندك؟

4. _____ ستذهب الى الجامعة؟

5. _____ تسكن؟

6. _____ ستفعل في المساء؟

6.7. Practice   (see Answer Key)

Write questions in Arabic to your friend to find the answers to the following:

1. Location of the library. _____

2. Number of rooms in her house. _____

3. His telephone number. _____

4. The name of her Arabic teacher. _____

5. Does he have a car? _____

6. Whether he goes to college by bus or car. _____

7. The meaning of desk in Arabic. _____

8. Where did she come from? _____

9. How many brothers and sisters does she have? _____

10. How do they come to school? _____

6.8. Practice   (see Answer Key)

Use the correct form of لان:

1. نذهب الى الصف (لأن + نحن) نريد أن نتعلم. ـــــــــــــــــــ

2. هو تعبان ـــــــــــــــــــ يعمل كثيرا.

3. هي في المكتبة ـــــــــــــــــــ تريد أن تدرس للامتحان.

4. أنتم تحبون اللغة العربية ـــــــــــــــــــ لغة سهلة.

5. لا أسكن مع عائلتي ـــــــــــــــــــ يسكنون بعيدا عن الجامعة.

6.9. Practice   (see Answer Key)

Form into questions using the interrogative words that you learned:

1. سنذهب الى المكتبة يوم الخميس القادم.

2. أحمد يدرس التاريخ.

3. أول يوم في الأسبوع هو الاثنين.

4. عندي ثلاثة اخوة.

5. لا عائلتي صغيرة جدا.

6.10. Practice (see Answer Key)

Read the following paragraph:

Fee asana arba'to fosool: arrabee' wa ashitta wa alkhareef wa assayf. There are four seasons in a year: spring, winter, autumn and summer.	فِي السَّنَةِ أَرْبَعَةُ فُصُولٍ: الرَّبِيعُ وَ الشِّتَاءُ وَ الخَرِيفُ وَ الصَّيْفُ.
Ajmal alfossol howa fasl arrabee'. The most beautiful season is spring.	أَجْمَلُ الفُصُولِ هُوَ فَصْلُ الرَّبِيعِ
Takoon fehi al-ashjar khadra' wa alazhar katheera. In spring trees are green and have beautiful flowers.	تَكُونُ فيه الأَشْجَارُ خَضْرَاءَ وَ الأَزْهَارُ كَثِيرَةٌ
Wa taqs Jameel jidan laysa barid wala har. The weather is very beautiful, it's not cold or hot.	وَ الطَّقْسُ جَمِيلٌ جِدًّا لَيْسَ بَارِدٌ وَ لَا حَارَ.
Ya'tee fasl assayf ba'da arrabee' wa yakoon attaqs har jidan. Summer comes after spring and the weather becomes very hot.	يَأْتِي فَصْلُ الصَّيْفِ بَعْدَ الرَّبِيعِ وَ يَكُونُ الطَّقْسَ حَارٌّ جِدًّا.
Fee assayf yath-hab annas ila albahr wa yasbahoon honak. In summer, people go the beach and swim there.	فِي الصَّيْفِ يَذْهَبُ النَّاسُ إِلَى البَحْرِ وَ يسبحون هُنَاكَ
Fasl ashita' bared jidan wa yasqot feehi almatar wa athalj ala aljibal. Winter is very cold and has a lot of rain and it snows on the mountains.	فَصْلُ الشِّتَاءِ بَارِدٌ جِدًّا وَ يَسْقُطُ فِيهِ المَطَرُ وَ الثَّلْجُ عَلَى الجِبَالِ.
Amma fasl alkhareef, yakoon feehi riyah katheera wa tasqot awraq alashjar. As for autumn, it has a lot of wind and tree leaves fall.	أَمَّا فَصْلُ الخَرِيفِ يَكُونُ فِيهِ رِيَاحٌ كَثِيرَةٌ وَ تُسْقِطُ أَوْرَاقَ الأَشْجَارِ.
Ana ohib fasl arrabee' katheeran thomma fasl ashitta'. I love spring season first, then winter.	أَنَا أُحِبُّ فَصْلَ الرَّبِيعِ كَثِيرًا ثُمَّ فَصْلُ الشِّتَاءِ

Answer the following questions:

2. مَا هُوَ أَجْمَلُ الفُصُولِ؟   1. كَمْ فَصْلًا فِي السَّنَةِ؟

4. مَتَى يَكُونُ الطَّقْسُ حَارٌّ؟   3. مَتَى يُنَزِّلُ المطرُ والثلج؟

5. أَيَّ فَصْلٍ تُحِبّ؟

6.11. **Practice** (see Answer Key)

Connect the related words by writing their numbers in the brackets:

حار ( )   1. ربيع

أزهار ( )   2. خريف

أخضر ( )   3. شتاء

مطر و ثلج ( )   4. صيف

رياح ( )   5. شجر

Reflection

1. In this Lesson I learned: _____

2. I have some trouble with: _____

3. I need to learn more about: _____

الوحدة السابعة
Arabic Calligraphy
الخط العربي
Alkhat al-arabi

Objectives:

1. Colors (masculine & feminine)
3. Culture: Greetings and Visits
4. Reading

2. Grammar
   • Singular Pronouns (I, he, she)
   • Plural Personal Pronouns (we, they)
   • Possessive Pronouns (my, his, her)
   • Plural Possessive Pronouns (your, their, our)
   • Attached Pronouns
   • Demonstrative Pronouns

🔊 Vocabulary

Meaning	Transliteration	Plural	Transliteration	Word
This	Ha'ola'	هؤلاء	Hatha/hathihi	هذا / هذه
What is this?	–	–	Ma hatha	ما هذا؟
I do not know	–	–	La a'ref	لا أَعْرِفْ
Of course.	–	–	Tab'an	طَبْعاً
Doctor	–	–	Doctor/ doctoora	دكْتورْ/ دكتورة
Hospital	Mostashfayat	مُسْتَشْفيات	Mostashfa	مُسْتَشْفى
Early	–	–	Mobakir	مُبَكِّرْ
Late	–	–	Mota'khir	مُتَأَخِّرْ

Meaning	Transliteration	Plural	Transliteration	Word
How much/ how many	–	–	Kam a'dad	كَمْ عَدَدْ
Room	Ghoraf	غُرَف	Ghorfah	غُرْفَةُ
Bedroom	Ghoraf nawm	غُرَف نوم	Ghorfat nawm	غُرْفَةُ نَوْم
Living room	Ghoraf joloos	غُرَف جُلوسْ	Ghorfat joloos	غُرْفَةُ جُلوسْ
Guest room	Ghoraf istiqbal	غُرَف إِسْتِقْبال	Ghorfat istiqbal	غُرْفَةُ إِسْتِقْبالْ
Dining room	Ghoraf safrah	غُرَف سُفْرة	Ghorfat sofra	غُرْفَةُ سُفْرة
Kitchen	Matabekh	مَطابخ	Matbakh	مَطْبَخْ
Bathroom	Hammamat	حَمّاماتْ	Hammam	حَمّامْ
Swimming pool	Hammamat sebaha	حَمّاماتْ سِباحة	Hammam sebaha	حَمّامْ سِباحة
Apartment	Shoqaq	شُقَق	Shaqa	شَقّة
Nature	–	–	Tabee'ah	طَبيعة
There is	–	–	Uwjad	يوجَدْ
Breakfast	–	–	Aliftar	الإفْطارْ
Lunch	–	–	Alghada	الغِداءْ
Dinner	–	–	Alasha'	العَشاءْ
Restaurant	Mata'em	مطاعم	Mat'am	مَطْعَمْ
Hotel	Fanadeq	فَنادق	Findoq	فُنْدُقْ
Stadium	Mala'eb	ملاعب	Mal'ab	مَلْعَبْ
Shopping center	Aswaq	أسْواق	Sooq	سوقْ
Thing	Ashya'	أشياء	Shay'	شَيءْ

Meaning	Transliteration	Plural	Transliteration	Word
Please	–	–	*Law samaht*	لَو سَمَحْتْ
Cup	*Fanajeen*	فناجين	*Fenjan*	فِنْجانْ
Glass	*Ko'oos*	كؤوس	*Ka's*	كَأْس
Sugar	–	–	*Sokkar*	سُكَّرْ
Salt	–	–	*Milh*	مِلْحْ
Milk	–	–	*Haleeb*	حَليبْ
Tea	–	–	*Shay*	شايْ
Coffee	–	–	*Qahwah*	قَهْوة
Water	–	–	*Maa'*	ماءْ
Ready	–	–	*Jahizah*	جاهِزة
Café	*Maqahi*	مَقاهي	*Maqha*	مَقْهى
Wait	–	–	*Yantathir*	يَنْتَظِرْ
Bakery	*Makhabiz*	مَخابز	*Makhbaz*	مَخْبَزْ
Chocolate	–	–	*Shokolatah*	شوكولاتة

Culture

Calligraphy الـخـط الـعـربـي *alkhat alarabi*

Calligraphy is an art form that has been highly developed through the centuries. Handwritten with pen or brush and ink, calligraphy is highly appreciated in Arab and Islamic culture because it is connected with writing the Qur'an, the holy book of Muslims. It is regarded as an art form like painting. It is a primary form of art for Islamic expression and creativity and represents beauty, creativity and power.

Arabic script can be written in various cursive styles such as Naskh, Thuluth and Kufi. On traditional buildings such as mosques, companies and even homes, different writing styles would be designed on the walls, windows, or minarets. Most of the inscriptions are not only from the Qur'an but also the Hadith (the Prophet's words).

Artists have continuously created new styles and designs of calligraphy since the time of the earliest scripts: the Kufic writing in the eighth century A.D. Kufic writing has beautiful geometrical measurement that are known to the writers. It is mostly used with Qur'anic verses, poetry and proverbs which are used to decorate building entrances, offices, houses and monuments. One will find the word الله *Allah* (God), محمد *Mohammed* (Prophet of Islam), بسم الله (in the name of God), or ما شاء الله (may God Bless Our Home) written with very different beautiful artistic styles and displayed on walls.

There are several forms of calligraphy. For example, the name of the prophet Mohammed can be written in many different ways:

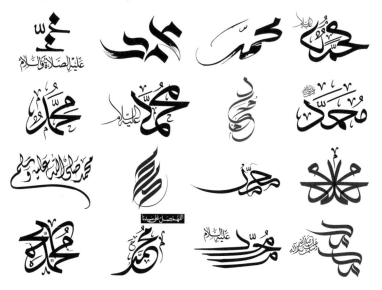

Colors

Colors have their own masculine and feminine rules. The easiest way to learn them is to relate the color to something you are familiar with as in "my car is black," "my cat/dog is white," etc. Here is the table of colors. 🔊

Color in English	Transliteration	Masculine form	Transliteration	Feminine Form
White	*Abyadh*	أبيض	*Baydhaa'*	بيضاء
Black	*Aswad*	أسود	*Sawdaa'*	سوداء
Blue	*Azraq*	أزرق	*Zarqaa'*	زرقاء
Yellow	*Asfar*	أصفر	*Safraa'*	صفراء
Green	*Akhdar*	أخضر	*Khadraa'*	خضراء

Color in English	Transliteration	Masculine form	Transliteration	Feminine Form
Red	*Ahmar*	أحمر	*Hamraa'*	حمراء
Brown	*Bonni*	بنّي	*Bonniyah*	بنيّة
Orange	*Bortoqali*	برتقالي	*Bortoqaliyyah*	برتقالية

Read:

Ba'd albihar wa almanatiq yojad fee ismoha lawn. Some seas and areas have a color in their name.	بَعْضُ البِحَارِ وَ المَنَاطِقِ يُوجَدُ فِي اسْمِهَا لَوْنٍ.
Mathalan albahr al-ahmar bayn mesr wa assa'oodiya wa alyaman. For example the Red Sea between Egypt, Saudi Arabia and Yemen.	مَثَلًا: البَحْرُ الأَحْمَرُ بَيْنَ مِصْرَ وَ السَّعُودِيَّةِ وَ اليَمَنِ.
Albar al-abyadh almotawaset bayn afreeqia wa asya. The Mediterranean White Sea between Africa and Asia.	البَحْرُ الأَبْيَضُ المُتَوَسِّطُ بَيْنَ افرِيقِيَا وَ آسِيَا.
Albahr al-aswad fee asya. The Black Sea in Asia.	البَحْرُ الأَسْوَدُ فِي آسِيَا.
Amma benesbah lilmodon, fa honak Madinat addar al baydha fee almaghrib wa tosama toonis bi toonis alkhadra li-anna feeha ashjar khadhraa katheera. As for cities, there is the city of White House in Morocco. Tunis is called the "Green Tunisia" because it has so many green trees.	أَمَّا بِالنِّسْبَةِ للمُدُنِ فَهُنَاكَ:. مَدِينَةُ الدَّارِ البَيْضَاءُ فِي المَغْرِبَ. تُسَمَّى تُونِس بِ "تُونِس الخَضْرَاءُ" لِأَنَّ فِيهَا أَشْجَارُ خَضْرَاءُ كَثِيرَةً
Tosama marakish be-ism marakish alhamra lekathrat albeyoot wa al-ammarat alhamraa almawjooda feeha. Marrakesh is called the red Marrakesh because it has so many red buildings and houses.	تُسَمَّى مَرَّاكِش بِاسْمِ "مَرَّاكِش الحَمْرَاءُ" لِكَثْرَةِ البُيُوتِ وَ العمارات الحَمْرَاءُ المَوْجُودَةُ فِيهَا

7.1. Practice (see Answer Key)

Write the following in Arabic:

1. The sky is blue. (sky is feminine word in Arabic) _____

2. My car is brown _____

3. I like the red color _____

4. Trees are green in spring (trees are feminine) _____

5. Our door is black (door is masculine) _____

Pronouns (Singular, dual and Plural)

There are two types of pronouns:

The first type is called independent pronouns: ضمائر منفصلة (*dhama'er monfasela*) and as in their name, they stand alone. They are the same as the possessive pronouns in English. If a group has feminine and masculine names, things or people, then we use the masculine pronouns. Note that feminine plural هن *honna* is not used a lot as all group members should be feminine. Additionally, pronouns should agree with the number and gender with the person or object we are referring to.

Independent pronouns are:

Transliteration	Example	Transliteration	Independent pronoun	English pronoun
Ana talib	أنا طالب	*Ana*	أنا	I
Nahno tollab	نحن طلاب	*Nahno*	نحن	We
Anta talib	أنتَ طالب	*Anta*	أنتَ	You (masculine)
Anti talibah	أنت طالبة	*Anti*	أنتِ	You (feminine)
Antoma Taliban/ talibatan	أنتما طالبان / طالبتان	*Antoma*	أنتما	Dual (m. & f.)
Antom tollab	أنتم طلاب	*Antom*	أنتم	You (plural)
Howa talib	هو طالب	*Howa*	هو	He
Hiya talibah	هي طالبة	*Hiya*	هي	she

Transliteration	Example	Transliteration	Independent pronoun	English pronoun
Homa Taliban/ talibatan	هما طالبان/ طالبتان	*Homa*	هما	Dual (m. & f.)
Hom tollab	هم طلاب	*Hom*	هم	They-Masculine
Honna talibat	هن طالبات	*Honna*	هن	They-Feminine

7.2. **Practice** (see Answer Key)

Underline the suitable pronoun:

١. (هو – هي – هما) يدرسان في الكلية.

٢. (هو – هي – هم) أستاذي.

٣. هل (أنت – هم – نحن) عربية.

٤. من أين (أنتما – هم – أنت) يا أحمد.

٥. هما أوقفا (سيارتك – سيارتهم – سيارتهما) بجانب المكتبة.

7.3. **Practice** (see Answer Key)

Fill in the blanks with the appropriate pronoun:

هو – هي – هما – هم – أنا – أنت – أنتما – أنتم – نحن

١. هل _____ أمريكي ؟ لا _____ عربي.

٢. أين _____ يا أولاد؟ _____ في الغرفة يا أمي.

٣. أين يعمل أخوك؟ _____ يعمل في البنك.

٤. _____ يجلسان بجانب المكتبة كل يوم.

٥. _____ تنامون مبكرين كل يوم.

The second type is called **attached pronouns** or **possessive pronouns** ضمائر متصلة. They are called this because they are added as a suffix to the noun. For example, to say "from me," we would use مني. We just added *ya* to the preposition من.

Look at the table and note what we attached for the preposition depending on the person being talked about. Here is the conjugation of the word book (*kitab*) كتاب :

Transliteration	Example	Transliteration / Attached pronouns	Transliteration / pronoun	English pronoun
Kitabee	كتابي	Ee ـي	Ana أنا	mine
Kitabona	كتابنا	Na نا	Nahno نحن	our
Kitaboka	كتابكَ	Ka كَ	Anta أنتَ	Your (masculine)
Kitaboki	كتابكِ	Ki كِ	Anti أنتِ	Your (feminine)
Kitabakoma	كتابكما	Koma كما	Antoma انتما	Yours -dual (m. & f.)
Kitabokom	كتابكم	Kom كم	Antom انتم	his
Kitaboho	كتابه	Ho ـه	Howa هو	hers
Kitaboha	كتابها	Ha ـها	Hiya هي	Dual (m. & f.)
Kitabahoma	كتابهما	Homa ـهما	Homa هما	
Kitabohom	كتابهم	Hom ـهم	Hom هم	Their–masculine
Kitabohonna	كتابهن	Honna ـهن	Honna هن	Their–feminine

As you noticed, most possessive endings are easy to remember because they are the same as the pronoun.

7.4.　Practice　(see Answer Key)

Fill in the blanks in the schedule below to practice conjugation of possessive pronouns. The first one is done for you:

أنتن	أنتم	نحن	أنتما	انتِ	انتَ	أنا	الكلمة
دفتركن	دفتركم	دفترنا	دفتركما	دفترك	دفترك	دفتري	دفتر
							فستان
							مكتب
							جامعة
							اسم

أنتن	أنتم	نحن	أنتما	انتِ	انتَ	أنا	الكلمة
							أم
							ولد
							أخت
							بيت
							سيارة
							غرفة

7.5. **Practice** (see Answer Key)

Fill in the blanks using the right form of attached preposition. As an example the first one is done for you:

Preposition would be	preposition	pronoun
عليها	على	هي
	فوق	نحن
	تحت	أنتَ
	يمين	انتِ
	يسار	أنتم
	على	هو
	أمام	هي
	بجانب	هما
	بين	هم

7.6. **Practice** (see Answer Key)

Fill in the blank with the correct form of possessive pronoun:

1. (اسم + أنا) _____ سارة.

2. (والدة + هي) _____ تعمل دكتورة في المستشفى.

3. (بيت + نحن) _____ في مدينة بغداد.

4. ما هو _____ (عنوان + أنتم) الجديد؟

5. تسكن (خاله + هو) _____ في (بيت + أنا).

6. (جامعة _ هم) _____ من أكبر الجامعات.

7. (كتاب + هما) _____ على الطاولة.

8. ابن (عم + هي) _____ سافر الى البحرين أمس.

Demonstrative Pronouns

"This" in Arabic هذه *hathihi* & *hatha* هذا:

In English we use demonstrative pronouns to identify entities by making a reference to them as in: this and that (for singular) and these and those (for plural). This is the same as in Arabic. In Arabic there are two types of demonstrative pronouns.

1. Used for near or close objects.

Transliteration	Example	Transliteration	Feminine Demonstrative Pronoun	Transliteration	Masculine Demonstrative Pronoun
Hatha dafar/ hatha abee/ hathihi talibah	هذا دفتر / هذه غرفة هذا أبي ـ هذه طالبة	*Hathihi*	هذه	*Hatha*	هذا
Hathan kitaban/ hatan ghorfatan	هذان كتابان / هاتان غرفتان	*Hatan*	هاتان	*Hathan*	هذان

Transliteration	Example	Transliteration	Feminine Demonstrative Pronoun	Transliteration	Masculine Demonstrative Pronoun
Ha'ola'ash-abee/ Ha'ola' sadeeqati / Ha'ola'attol-lab	هؤلاء أصحابي / هؤلاء صديقاتي / هؤلاء الطلاب	*Ha'ola'*	هؤلاء	*Ha'ola'*	هؤلاء

2. Used for far or distant objects.

Transliteration / Example	Transliteration	Feminine	Transliteration	Masculine	Demonstrative Pronoun
Thalika maktabi/ tilka okhtee ذلك مكتبي / تلك أختي	*tilka*	تلك	*Thalika*	ذلك	That is
Ola-ika ahlee أولئك أهلي	*Ola-ika*	أولئك	*Ola-ika*	أولئك	These are

As you have probably noticed, demonstrative pronouns agree with number and gender.
With non-human plurals we use هذه *hathihi* as in:

Meaning	Transliteration	Example
These are books	*Hathihi kotob*	هذه كتب
These are cars	*Hathihi sayyarat*	هذه سيارات
These are universities	*Hathihi jame'at*	هذه جامعات

هذا is considered as a noun and functions as a noun. This means that هذا might:
a) Be the subject in a nominal sentence as in: هذا كتابي *hatha kitabi* (this is my book)
b) Come after a preposition as in: اسقني من هذا العصير *isqini hatha al-asse* (give me some of this juice)

c) Be the object of a verb as in: اعطني هذا الكتاب *A'tini hatha alkitab* (give me this book)

d) Be part of idafa structure as in: هذا الأستاذ *hatha alostath* (this teacher)

7.7. | Practice | (see Answer Key)

Fill in the blanks using *hathihi* هذه or *hatha* هذا:

2. _____غرفة.   1. _____ قلم.

4. _____كأس.   3. _____ أستاذة.

5. _____ فاطمة.

7.8. | Practice | (see Answer Key)

Write the following in Arabic using demonstrative pronouns:

1. This is his office. _____

2. These are my friends. _____

3. This is her grandmother. _____

4. These two notebooks are yours. _____

5. This is his dog. _____

6. This is the college of literature. _____

7. These girls are in my classroom. _____

8. This is an Arabic name. _____

9. These are new houses. _____

10. These two girls are my new friends. _____

7.9. | Practice | (see Answer Key)

Underline the suitable word from the three in the parenthesis:

1. (هي – هو – هما) طالبة في كلية الهندسة.

2. كتبت كل (الكلمة – الكلمات – الطاولة) و درستها.

3. (هذه – هذا – هما) البيوت جميلة و كبيرة.

4. الشجرة (لونها – لونه – لونهم) أخضر.

5. قالت أمل (كليتها – كليتهم – كليتهما) هي أكبر كلية في الجامعة.

7.10. Practice (see Answer Key)

Rearrange the words to form meaningful sentences:

1. سبع – الصف – طالبات – في – يوجد.

2. في – المكتبة – الطابق – الرابع.

3. الغداء – طعام – المطعم – في – آكل.

4. تذهب – المخبز – هل – معي – الى؟

5. الأصدقاء – يلعب – السلة – كرة – الملعب – في.

6. عادل – أخو – السوق – في – يعمل.

7. بيتي – غرف – في – أربع – و ثلاثة – حمامات.

7.11. Practice (see Answer Key)

Read the following conversation between Ahmad and his wife Amal:

Ayna anti ya amal? Where are you Amal?	أَحْمَدُ: أَيْنَ أَنْتَ يَا أَمَلُ؟
Ana fee almatbakh. Hal toreed shay'an? I am at the kitchen do you want anything?	أَمَلُ: أَنَا فِي المَطْبَخِ. هَلْ تُرِيدُ شَيْئًا؟
Na'am, oreed finjanan men alqahwa law samahti. Yes, I want a cup of coffee please.	أَحْمَدُ: نَعَمْ أُرِيدُ فِنْجَانًا مِنْ القَهْوَةِ لَوْ سَمَحْتِ.
Hasanan sa'mal laka qahwa. Hal toreed sokkar ma'alqahwa? OK, I will do you some coffee. Do you want sugar with it?	أَمَلُ: حَسَنًا. سَأَعْمَلُ لَكَ قَهْوَةً. هَلْ تُرِيدُ سُكَّرَ مَعَ القَهْوَةِ؟
Mil'aka wahida. Yes, one spoon.	أَحْمَدُ: مِلْعَقَةٌ وَاحِدَةٌ.
Hal toreed haleeban ma'qahwatik? Do you want milk with your coffee?	أَمَلُ: هَلْ تُرِيدُ حَلِيبًا مَعَ قَهْوَتِكَ؟
La shokran! No, thank you!	أَحْمَدُ: لَا شُكْرًا.
Intather khams daqa'ik wa satakoon alqahqa jahiza. It will be ready in five minutes.	أَمَلُ: انْتَظَرْ خَمْسُ دَقَائِقَ وَ سَتَكُونُ القَهْوَةُ جَاهِزَةٌ

Conversation *(continued)*

Hal toreedeen an tashrabi qahwa ma'ee? Do you want to drink some coffee with me?	أَحْمَدُ: هَلْ تُرِيدِينَ أَنْ تَشْرَبِي قَهْوَةً مَعِي؟
Na'am hathihi fekrah jayyedah. Yes, this is a good idea.	أَمَلُ: نَعَمْ. هَذِهِ فِكْرَةٌ جَيِّدَةٌ.
Hasanan sa'antathiroki. Great, I will be waiting for you.	أَحْمَدُ: حَسَنًا. سَأَنْتَظِرُكَ!
Hathihi hiya alqahwa tafadhal. Here is the coffee, please take it.	أَمَلُ: هَذِهِ هِيَ القَهْوَةُ. تَفَضَّلْ.
Hal toreedeen shokolata ma' alqahwa? Do you want chocolate with your coffee?	أَحْمَدُ: هَلْ تُرِيدِينَ شُوكُولَاتَةً مَعَ القَهْوَةِ؟
Na'am ana ohibu alqahwa ma'a shokolata. Yes, I love chocolate with coffee.	أَمَلُ: نَعَمْ. أَنَا أُحِبُّ القَهْوَةَ مَعَ الشُّوكُولَاتَةِ.
Tafadali wa haya najlis fee ghorfat aljoloos. Here it is. Let's sit in the living room.	أَحْمَدُ: تَفَضَّلِي! وَ هَيَّا نَجْلِسُ فِي غُرْفَةِ الجُلُوسِ

Now answer the following questions:

1. أين أمل؟

2. ماذا يريد أحمد؟

3. كيف يشرب أحمد قهوته؟

4. ماذا ستأكل أمل مع قهوتها؟

Reflection

1. In this Lesson I learned: _____

2. I have some trouble with: _____

3. I need to learn more about: _____

الوحدة الثامنة
The Arab Family
العائلة العربية
Al-a'ilah al'rabiyyah

Objectives:

In this lesson you will be introduced to:

1. Vocabulary of Family Structure
2. Identifying Family Members
3. Grammar: Comparatives
4. Culture: Most Popular Arabic Names
5. Reading

 ## Vocabulary

Meaning	Transliteration	Plural	Transliteration	Family member
Family	*A'ilat*	عائلاتْ	*A'ilah*	عائِلة
Father	*Aabaa*	آباء	*Ab*	أَبْ
Mother	*Omahat*	أُمَّهاتْ	*Om*	أُمْ
Brother	*Ikhwah*	أُخْوة	*Akh*	أَخْ
Sister	*Akhawat*	أَخَواتْ	*Okht*	أُخْتْ
Son	*Abna'*	أَبْناءْ	*Ibn*	إبْنْ
Daughter	*Banat*	بَناتْ	*Bent*	بِنْتْ
Paternal uncle	*A'mam*	أَعْمامْ	*Amm*	عَمْ
Paternal aunt	*Ammat*	عَمَّاتْ	*Ammah*	عَمَّة

Meaning	Transliteration	Plural	Transliteration	Family member
Maternal uncle	*Akhwal*	أَخْوال	*Khal*	خالْ
Maternal aunt	*Khalat*	خالاتْ	*Khalah*	خالة
Grandfather	*Ajdad*	أَجْداد	*Jed*	جَدّ
Grandmother	*Jaddat*	جَدّاتْ	*Jedda*	جَدّة
The son of paternal uncle	–	–	*Ibn a'm*	إِبْنُ عَمْ
The son of paternal aunt	–	–	*Ibn a'mmah*	إِبْنُ عَمّة
The son of maternal uncle	–	–	*Ibn khal*	إِبْنُ خالْ
The son of maternal aunt	–	–	*Ibn khalah*	إِبْنُ خالة
The daughter of paternal uncle	–	–	*Bent a'm*	بِنْتُ عَمْ
The daughter of paternal aunt	–	–	*Bent a'mmah*	بِنْتُ عَمّة
The daughter of maternal uncle	–	–	*Bent khal*	بِنْتُ خالْ
The daughter of maternal aunt	–	–	*Bent khalah*	بِنْتُ خالة
Husband	*Azwaj*	أَزْواج	*Zawj*	زَوْج
Wife	*Zawjat*	زَوْجاتْ	*Zawjah*	زَوْجة
Member	*Afrad*	أَفْراد	*Fard*	فَرْد
Housewife	*Rabbat beyoot*	رَبّات بيوت	*Rabbat bayt*	رَبّةُ بَيْتْ
Night	–	–	*Layl*	لَيْل
Day	–	–	*Nahar*	نَهار
Land – floor	*Aradi*	أَراضي	*Arddq*	أَرْضْ

Meaning	Transliteration	Plural	Transliteration	Family member
Date of	–	–	*Tareekh*	تاريخْ
Sea	*Bihar*	بحارْ	*Bahr*	بَحْرْ
Late	–	–	*Ta'khara/ yata'khar*	تأخّرْ/ يتأخر
Change	–	–	*Ghayyara/ yoghayyer*	غَيَّرْ / يُغَير
Gift	*Hadaya*	هَدايا	*Hadiyyah*	هَديّة
Active	–	–	*Nasheet*	نَشيطْ
Lazy	–	–	*Kaslan*	كَسْلانْ
Now	–	–	*Alaan*	الآنْ
Since	–	–	*Montho*	مُنْذْ
Birth	–	–	*Meelad*	ميلادْ
Death	–	–	*Wafat*	وَفاةْ
Residence	*Iqamat*	إقامات	*Iqamah*	إقامة
Work-job	*A'mal*	أعمال	*Amal*	عَمَلْ
Place	*Amakin*	أماكن	*Makan*	مَكانْ

Arabic Names:

In Arab countries, names are composed of 4 names, not two as here in the US. The name includes the person's name, his father, grandfather and then family name. Some countries as in Saudi Arabia and Yemen include the word ابن / بن meaning the son of, after each name. Most of the time, the last name represents a place of origin or attribution of profession. For example, the family name Nabulsi, refers to the city of Nablus in Palestine; the name *Sayegh* الصايغ meaning "goldsmith" represents that the family ancestors used to work with gold and الصبّاغ reflects that the family used to have a business of painting houses.

Almost all Arabic names have pleasant meaning as in: *Amal* means "hope;" *Khalid* means "eternal," *Tahani* means "congratulation," *Salam* means "peace" and *Mohammed* means "a person with many virtues." Mohammed is the most popular male name after the Prophet of Islam may be to inspire people to follow the Prophet's path. As for girls, the most popular female name is Fatima after the Prophet's daughter and Maryam, the mother of Prophet Jesus. Arabs tend to name their children after prophets, so you would find ***Ibraheem*** (Abraham), ***Issa*** (Jusus), ***Moosa*** (Moses), ***Dawood*** (David), ***Yousef*** (Joseph) and ***Sulaiman*** (Solomon). Christian Arabs would call their children ***Bulus*** (Paul), ***Butrus*** (Peter).

There are also compound names as in عبد الرحمن & عبدالله , the first part عبد means the servant of, and the second part is a name of God. There is a common mistake in a west which is calling a person Abdul, it is a mistake because it does not mean anything, and it combines عبد with *al*.

Family Structure

Western media often portray Arab families as Bedouins, tribal societies or other nomadic groups. However, the Bedouin way of life has almost disappeared in nearly all Arab countries beyond the Gulf states and Morocco. What is more accurate is that religious affiliation, place of birth, occupation and ethnicity are now more important than one's tribe. Almost every Arab can classify himself by his original clan or tribe, yet he will not employ this allegiance for any social purpose as used to be the case.

For Arabs, the center of obligation and loyalty is the family. Arabs have close relationships with their relatives but even tighter relationships with their own immediate families. The most authoritative social obligation is the family, rather than friends, jobs or any other social affiliation. Arabs take more pride in the accomplishments of their family than in their own personal accomplishments, as is often the case in the West. Individuality is not encouraged and is not considered as important as family association. People hold profound respect for the familial expectations and integrity upon which they base their actions and decisions. They pay great heed to their family's reputation as well, because social approval is usually gained through good relations with one's own family. Any member's accomplishment advances the entire family's reputation, while his mischievous actions can harm the whole family. Because negative actions by one family member affect the entire family, not just the individual, such actions result in increased shame. The feeling of kinship and association with one's family is so strong, in fact, that the easiest way to insult an Arab is to curse one of his relatives.

Maintaining the family's name applies to men as well as women. Even after marriage, a woman keeps her family name and does not change it to her husband's family name, as is often the

case in the United States. In addition, when a married couple has their first child, people stop referring to the parents by their first names. They are called by the name of their first child with a prefix to indicate "father of" or "mother of." For example, if a couple named their first child Ahmad, the father is called *Abu* Ahmad and the mother is called *Um* Ahmad. Furthermore, parents typically name their first male child after the paternal grandfather to show admiration and love for parents.

In the past, Arab families were large and had profound influence on their members' lives, as several generations often lived together in the same house. Once married, children continued to live in a parent's home. However, this is not the situation anymore. Recently, families have become smaller and have less influence on individuals, with married children moving to their own homes. Nevertheless, even today most Arabs live with their parents until they get married, regardless of their age at marriage. Those who do not marry remain in the home of their parents.

It is worthy to note, there are four categories of family units. The highest and most important is the nuclear unit represented by the father, mother, brothers and sisters. It is called *usrah* أسرة, in Arabic. The father is the head of the family, the supporter who is respected and obeyed by all. Arab societies are hierarchal and patriarchal, as fathers and male elders in the family have the final say. Yet Arab families are also considered partnerships in which the husband and wife are assigned to complimentary duties and responsibilities. The husband supports the family financially, while the wife takes care of children and the household. The wife is not expected to have a job to support the family. If she does, then it is not her responsibility to pay for family's expenses. It is the father's full responsibility. In real life and in many situations, the working mother is a partner and participates with her family's expenses.

The second category is the extended family, or *ayla* عائلة in Arabic, consisting of sons' wives, their children, aunts and uncles; in other words, blood relatives and the women who marry into the family. All people in this unit look to the grandfather or eldest male in the family for guidance. The importance of extended family should not be underestimated. Usually, the extended family resides in the same area and supports each other. It is common for Arabs to ask the opinion or advice of older males in the family before making a decision. The elders enjoy obedience and respect from all family members and at the same time are expected to guide and discuss family matters wisely. For Westerners, this might be considered meddling or a constraint on individuality, but Arabs accept this structure as part of their culture. If a family member does not agree with an elder's advice or opinion, he usually does not announce his disagreement but instead feigns agreement and then does what he wants or has decided for himself.

Growing up in Kuwait, my father was the eldest of his brothers and cousins. Although every family lived in a different area, I remember how respectfully everyone treated my father.

They consulted with him about personal matters and followed his suggestions, and when he spoke, everyone would stop talking and give him their full attention.

The third category is the clan, or *hammula* in Arabic, which is a combination of joint families. Members of the clan are related through a male ancestor. The importance of clans varies from one Arab country to another. In some areas, the clan may seem to surpass the extended family unit in influence, while in other areas the clan may not have any obvious role in societal structure. Members of the clan know each other very well and know the exact descendants and relatives of other members. They relate themselves to one another systematically, referring to each other. Interestingly, there are different words to distinguish paternal uncles from maternal uncles, which reflects the importance of family structure and knowing how people are related to each other. For example, the paternal uncle is called *amm* عم, while the maternal uncle is called *khala* خالة Similarly, the paternal aunt is called *amma* عمة, while the maternal aunt is called *khaala* خالة. However, these names are not exclusively used for family members. It is very common to call older people *amm* عم (for males) or *khaala* خالة (for females) because it is not polite to call older people by their first names when they are not relatives. Another example is with the terms *ibn 'amm* ابن عم, meaning paternal first cousin for males, and *bint 'amm* بنت عم, for a paternal female cousin. Such identifications reflect how each clan member is connected and is part of a larger family beyond his closer biological one.

The fourth and last category is the tribe, which consists of several clans. Tribes may vary in size, with some numbering a few hundred people and others ranging in the thousands. Many villages have three to four tribes. Tribes do not convey inheritance rights, as members might not be related. Each tribe has a leader called a *sheikh* شيخ. When the sheikh dies, the tribal council meets and decides who is most fit to be the new leader. The sheikh is very well respected and loved by his tribe as he governs through affection and respect and acts according to his tribal interests and needs. The sheikh represents his tribe, maintains the tribe's status in the neighborhood and strives to exceed in generosity, hospitality and strength. As explained earlier, the tribes are not popular now in most Arab countries.

Reading:
Fatima wrote this to introduce herself in class.

A'alitee kabeerah. I have a big family.	عَائِلَتِي كَبِيرَةٌ.
Endee sab'ato a'mam wa laken laysa endee amat. I have seven uncles, but I do not have any paternal aunts.	عِنْدَي سَبْعَةُ أَعْمَامٍ وَ لَكِنَّ لَيْسَ عِنْدَي عَمَّاتٍ.
Wa endee sit khalat wa khalayn ithnayn. I have six maternal aunts and two maternal uncles.	وَ عِنْدَي سِتُّ خَالَاتٍ وَ خَالَيْنِ اثْنَيْنِ.

Conversation (continued)

English	Arabic
Amee ali endaho sitato abnaa thalath banat wa thalath abnaa'. My uncle Ali has six children, three boys and three girls.	عَمِّي عَلَى عِنْدَهُ سِتَّةُ أَبْنَاءٍ ثَلَاثُ بَنَاتٍ وَ ثَلَاثَةُ أَولَادٍ.
Khalee ahmad endaho nafs al'adad thalath banat wa thalathato abnaa. My uncle Ahmad had the same number, three boys and three girls.	خَالِي أَحْمَدُ عَنْدَةُ نَفْسُ العَدَدِ ثَلَاثُ بَنَاتٍ وَ ثَلَاثَةُ أَبْنَاءٍ.
Khalee mohammad indaho sit banat wa walad wahid. My uncle Mohammad has six girls and one son.	خَالِي مُحَمَّدٌ عَنْدَةُ سِتُّ بَنَاتٍ وَ وَلَدٍ وَاحِدٌ.
Ibnoho yadros fee jami'at alazhar fee mesr. His son is studying at Al-Azhar University in Egypt.	ابْنَةُ يَدْرُسُ فِي جَامِعَةِ الأَزْهَرِ فِي مِصْرَ.
Ana endee akhayn wa okhtayn. I have two sisters and two brothers.	أَنَا عِنْدِي أَخِينَ وَ أُخْتَيْنِ.
Lee okht ta'eesh fee alordon wa okht fee al-imarat wa akh fee asaoodiya wa ikh fee alkowayt. I have a sister who lives in Jordan, and a sister who lives in Emirate, a brother in Saudi Arabia and a brother in Kuwait.	لِي أُخْتٌ تَعِيشُ فِي الأُرْدُنِّ وَ أُخْتٌ فِي الإِمَارَاتِ وَ أَخٍ فِي السَّعُودِيَّةِ وَ أَخٍ فِي الكويت.

Comparatives:

When we compare between things in English we add *-er* or *-est* at the end of the adjective as in cheaper, slower, happiest or funniest. Sometimes we add the word "more" or "most" depending on what we are expressing as in: more suitable or most agreeable.

In Arabic, the adjective should rhyme with the pattern: أفعل and it does not change whether I am comparing between singular, dual, plural, masculine or feminine. It is always followed by the word مِن The same as in English, it should be followed by "than."

The superlative is the same, as it is to rhyme with the pattern أفعل however, it is not followed by مِن and it should be followed by a noun as in English. We would say: "the tallest man" أطول رجل or "the highest mountain" أعلى جبل.

However, there are few important things to notice:

1. When the second or third letter of the adjective are the same, we combine them and use *shaddah* for example:

Transliteration	Changes to	Transliteration	word	Meaning
Akhaff	أخف	*Khafeef*	خفيف	Light- not heavy
Ajadd	أجدّ	*Jaded*	جديد	New
Allath	ألذ	*Latheeth*	لذيذ	Delicious

2. When the last letter is a *waw* (و) or *ya* (ي) then we change it to *alif maqsoura* ى , as in:

Meaning	Transliteration	Comparative	Transliteration	Word
Sweet- beautiful	*Ahla*	أحلى	*Hilo*	حلو
smart	*Athka*	أذكى	*Thaki*	ذكي

3. When the word has ya as the third letter, then we remove it as in:

Meaning	Transliteration	Comparative	Transliteration	Word
Old	*Aqdam*	أقدم	*Qadeem*	قديم
Tall	*Atwal*	أطول	*Taweel*	طويل
Short	*Aqsar*	أقصر	*Qaseer*	قصير
Fast	*Asra'*	أسرع	*Saree'*	سريع

4. Sometimes we add al as a prefix to mean the superlative, as in English we add "*the*" as in: "the highest" الأعلى *al-a'la*, "the smallest" الأصغر *alasghar* or "the best" الأفضل *alafdal*

5. Both superlatives and comparatives are always considered as nouns

6. The superlative should agree with gender which rhymes with the pattern فُعلى as in "the youngest" الصُغرى or "the biggest" الكُبرى.

8.1. Practice (see Answer Key)

Change the following adjectives into comparisons by filling in the blanks. The first one is done for you:

Comparisons	Adjective	Romanization
أقدم	قديم	*Qadeem*
	كثير	*Katheer*

Comparisons	Adjective	Romanization
	كبير	*Kabeer*
	شديد	*Shaded*

Comparisons	Adjective	Romanization
	هام	*Ham*
	فقير	*Faqeer*
	غني	*Ghaniy*
	رخيص	*Rakhees*

Comparisons	Adjective	Romanization
	غالي	*Ghalee*
	حسن	*Hasan*
	رحيم	*Raheem*

8.2. **Practice** (see Answer Key)

Derive the comparative or superlative from the words in parentheses in the sentences below:

1. ما هي (صغير) دولة عربية؟ _____

2. اشترى سامي كتبا (قليل) من أحمد. _____

3. ما هو (لذيذ) طعام أكلته في هذا المطعم؟ _____

4. سيارتي (جديد) من سيارتك. _____

5. ما هو (طويل) مبنى في العالم؟ _____

6. هدى تحب البيتزا (كثير) من اللحم. _____

7. شارع الحمراء هو (نظيف) شارع في المدينة. _____

8. سيارتي هي (سريع) سيارة في البلد. _____

9. ايمان هي (نشيط) بنت في الصف. _____

10. (جميل) هدية هي التي اشترتها أمي. _____

8.3. **Practice** (see Answer Key)

Rearrange the order of sentences to form a meaningful paragraph by writing order in the parentheses:

( ) فرح الأولاد بها كثيرا.

( ) اشترى الأب علبة شوكولاتة.

( ) فتحت الأم العلبة.

( ) في العلبة اثنتا عشرة قطعة.

( ) أعطت الأم كل واحد أربع قطع .

8.4. Practice (see Answer Key)

To review your colors, please fill in the spaces using masculine or feminine forms of the colors. By the way, these are very commonly used in Arab countries:

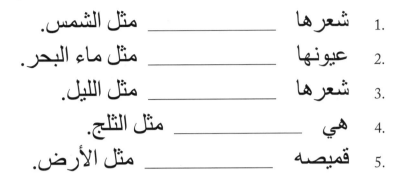

1. شعرها _____ مثل الشمس.
2. عيونها _____ مثل ماء البحر.
3. شعرها _____ مثل الليل.
4. هي _____ مثل الثلج.
5. قميصه _____ مثل الأرض.

8.5. Practice (see Answer Key)

Provide questions for the following responses:

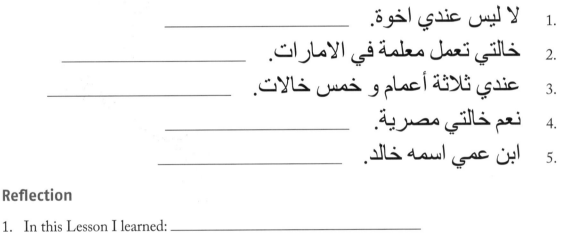

1. لا ليس عندي اخوة. _____
2. خالتي تعمل معلمة في الامارات. _____
3. عندي ثلاثة أعمام و خمس خالات. _____
4. نعم خالتي مصرية. _____
5. ابن عمي اسمه خالد. _____

Reflection

1. In this Lesson I learned: _____

2. I have some trouble with: _____

3. I need to learn more about: _____

الوحدة التاسعة
Family Relations and Children
الأبناء و الأسرة

Al-abnaa' wa al-osrah

Objectives:

1. Names of Arab Countries
2. Nationalities
3. Grammar: Sentence Structure (Nominal and Verbal Sentences)
4. Culture: Identifying People (sons)
5. Reading

 **Vocabulary**

Meaning	Transliteration	Plural	Transliteration	Word
Country	Dowal	دُوَل	Dawlah	دَوْلة
City	Modon	مُدُن	Madinah	مَدينة
River	Anhar	أَنْهار	Nahr	نَهْر
Mountain	Jibal	جِبال	Jabal	جَبَل
Plain	Sohool	سُهول	Sah-l	سَهْل
Desert	–	–	Sahraa	صَحْراء
Ocean	Moheetat	مُحيطاتْ	Moheet	مُحيطْ
Coast	Sawahil	سواحِلْ	Sahel	ساحِلْ
Border	Hodood	حُدودْ	Had	حَدْ
Beach	Shawati	شَواطِئ	Shati'	شاطِئ

Meaning	Transliteration	Plural	Transliteration	Word
Lie	–	–	*Waqa'/ yaqa'*	وَقَعَ /يَقَعْ
Location	*Mawaqi'*	مَواقِعْ	*Mawqi'*	مَوْقِعْ
Asia	–	–	*Aasya*	آسيا
Africa	–	–	*Afriqya*	أفْريقْيا
Europe	–	–	*Orooba*	أوروبا
Australia	–	–	*Ostoralya*	أُسْتُراليا
America	–	–	*Amreeka*	أمريكا
Continent	*Qarrat*	قارّات	*Qarrah*	قارّة
North	–	–	*Shamal*	شَمالْ
South	–	–	*Janoob*	جَنوب
East	–	–	*Sharq*	شَرْقْ
West	–	–	*Gharb*	غَرْبْ
Capital	*A'wasim*	عواصم	*A'simah*	عاصِمة
As for	–	–	*Amma*	أمّا
Consists of	–	–	*Yatakawwan*	يَتَكَوَّن
World	–	–	*Ala'alam*	العالَمْ
Region	*Aqaleem*	أقاليمْ	*Iqleem*	إقْليمْ
Sea	*Bihar*	بحار	*Bahr*	بَحْرْ
Valley	*Wedyan*	وديان	*Wadi*	وادي
Island	*Jozor*	جُزُرْ	*Jazeera*	جَزيرة
Gulf	–	–	*Khaleej*	خَليجْ

Meaning	Transliteration	Plural	Transliteration	Word
Prince	*Omaraa'*	أُمَراء	*Ameer*	أَميرْ
Sheikh (no equivalent in English) the closest is Head of or leader of	*Shiyookh*	شيُوخ	*Shaykh*	شَيْخْ
King	*Molook*	مُلوك	*Malik*	مَلِكْ
Leader of	*Ro'asaa*	رُؤساء	*Ra'ees*	رَئيسْ
Kingdom	*Mamaalik*	مَمالك	*Mamlakah*	مَمْلَكة
Emirate	*Imarat*	إمارات	*Imarah*	إمارة
Republic	*Jomhoriyat*	جُمْهوريّات	*Jomhooriyah*	جُمْهوريّة

To help you memorize your vocabulary, you may make a schedule and arrange your words into land words and water words.

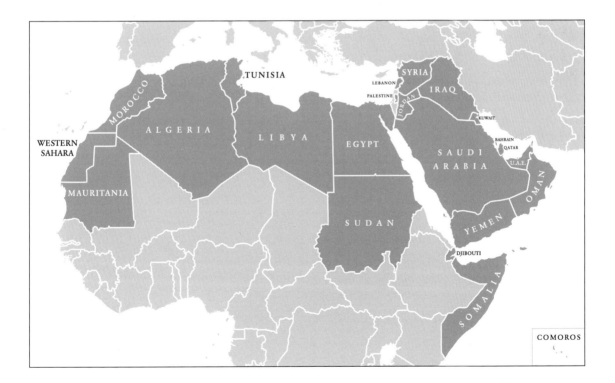

Children in Arab Societies

In the past, cultural and family pressure strongly motivated Arabs to have many children. This social pressure still exists in rural areas, but not in the entire Arab world. In the past, a strong motivation for marriage was to have children who can maintain family lineage and inherit family property, in addition to strengthening the family in numbers. A popular Arab saying is "Every baby comes with his own provision," (Fowler, Kirkham, Sawatzky & Elizabeth[1], 2012, p. 241). Similarly, a verse in the Qur'an states: "Do not abandon your children out of fear of poverty. We will provide for them and for you" (17:242). However, families are becoming smaller with fewer children born in each generation; most Arab families today have two to three children at most.

Although Arabs believe that all children are a gift from God, the birth of a baby boy is celebrated more than that of a baby girl. Males represent future security for parents, as it is the responsibility of males to take care of their parents and support them when they get old and can no longer work.

Arab parents devote their lives, time and love to their children and have great expectations of their children. Usually parents pay for their children's college education and support their children until they get married. There is almost no pressure on adult children to seek independence, as is often the case in the United States. This is to say, fulfillment of a child's economic and educational needs is the principal goal of the family.

Child discipline consists of rewards and punishment. It is common for parents to use strong verbal reprimands and even scream at or raid their children. During childhood, one's mother is the primary disciplinarian, but as children reach their teenage years, the father becomes the authority figure.

Arab children are brought up to respect and obey their parents, no matter how old they get. Obedience to parents is a lifelong commitment that supersedes all other social commitments, including marital obligations. Correspondingly, it is considered shameful in Arab culture for children to place their parents in a nursing home. Usually it is the eldest son's responsibility to provide for his parents and bring them to live with him in his own house if needed. Other male children are expected to help take care of their parents. Daughters may help with other support but are not required to contribute monetarily, usually only doing so if they can afford it. Daughters, usually help in buying clothes, cleaning their house, preparing food and all other emotional care and support. Sons provide the money as they are the ones responsible to work and they spend time with their parents in the afternoons and evenings.

---

1 *Religion, Religious Ethics and Nursing*, 2012, Edited by: Marsha D. Fowler, Sheryl Reimer Kirkham, Richard Sawatzky, Elizabeth Johnston Taylor, Springer Publishing Company, New York (p. 241).

Obedience to elders extends beyond one's parents. When an older person enters the room, for example, a child is expected to stand up and offer his seat to the older person, not raise his voice, speak politely, wait until the older person stops talking before speaking. Children must greet everyone who visits whether they know them or not. Children are taught that the family's interest comes first, and they must live according to the family's expectations (Hammad, 1989[2]). This plays a role in having strong family relation.

Arab Countries:
Arab countries lay in Asia and Africa. There are twenty-two Arab countries, as you know, and are considered as developing countries. People refer to Arab countries using the term Middle East. However, when "Middle East" is used, the first thing comes to mind is rich countries and oil. This is not very true. Yes, Saudi Arabia is the second largest in the world in producing oil, Iraq ranks the seventh, United Arab Emirate ranks the eighth and Kuwait the eleventh in the world. The economy of these countries depends on petroleum production countries. However, not all Arab countries have oil or petroleum products. Some countries are very poor while others are extremely rich. For example, Qatar is one of the highest per capita in the world while Yemen is one of the lowest.

Many of Arab countries names are the same as in English. Here is a list of the names of Arab countries:

Name in English	Transliteration	Arab Country
Kuwait	*Alkowayt*	الكويت
Qatar	*Qatar*	قطر
Sudan	*Assodan*	السودان
Oman	*Oman*	عُمان
Bahrain	*Albahrain*	البحرين
Yemen	*Alyaman*	اليمن
Syria	*Soorya*	سوريا
Lebanon	*Lobnan*	لبنان
Palestine	*Falasteen*	فلسطين

---

2 Hammad, A. 1989. *Effectiveness and Efficiency in the Management of Palestinian Health Services.* Ph.D. Thesis. University of Manchester. Jan. 1989.

Name in English	Transliteration	Arab Country
Iraq	*Aliraq*	العراق
Libya	*Leebya*	ليبيا
Mauritania	*Moretanya*	موريتانيا
Saudi Arabia	*Almamlaka alarabiyya assa'oodiya*	المملكة العربية السعودية
United Arab Emirates	*Alimarat alarabiyyah almotahidah*	الامارات العربية المتحدة
Egypt	*Jomhooriyat mesr alarabiyyah*	جمهورية مصر العربية
Tunisia	*Toonis*	تونس
Algeria	*Aljazaer*	الجزائر
Morocco	*Almaghrib*	المغرب
Somalia	*Assoomal*	الصومال
Djibouti	*Jaibooti*	جيبوتي
Comoros	*Jozor alqamar*	جزر القمر
Jordan	*Alordon*	الأردن

Note that although there might be some differences between English and Arabic names, there are many similarities and it can be easy to identify them.

Nationalities

It is very easy to learn nationalities, which is an adjective in Arabic. In most cases, you just add the suffix "*ya*" to the name of the country and remove the "*al*" (if there is an "*al*") from the beginning. The same rule applies to all countries and not only Arab countries. For example:

المغرب *almaghrib* would be مغربيّ *maghribiy*
السعودية *alsaoodiya* would be سعودي *sa'oodi*
الأردن *alordon* would be أردنيّ *ardoniy*

Many non-Arab countries have names in Arabic that are very similar to their English names: Britain بريطانيا (*Breetanya*), Russia روسيا (*Roosya*), Italy ايطاليا (*Italya*) and France فرنسا (*Faransa*).

This is also true of the words for nationalities:

Britain	بريطانيا (*Breetanya*)	British	بريطاني (*Breetani*)
Russia	روسيا (*Roosya*)	Russian	روسيّ (*Roosiy*)
Italy	ايطاليا (*Italya*)	Italy	ايطالي (*Eetali*)
France	فرنسا (*Faransa*)	French	فرنسي (*Faransey*)

This information will be reviewed in the next lesson, and more details will be provided.

9.1. **Practice** (see Answer Key)

Fill in the blanks:

Nationality	Country
عراقي	العراق
	الكويت
	اليابان
أمريكي	
سوري	
هندي	

Nationality	Country
	فلسطين
لبناني	
	الجزائر
	ليبيا
مصري	

Nominal sentences:

Sentences starting with a noun are called nominal sentences, as in:

Meaning	Transliteration	Example
The weather is hot.	*altaqs har.*	الطقس حار
The door is open.	*Albab maftooh.*	الباب مفتوح
My house is far.	*baytee ba'eed.*	بيتي بعيد

Usually the subject and the predicate have *dhamma*. The predicate agrees with the subject in gender, number and all other situations.

Note that the subject is definite while the predicate is not. You may guess the reason by reading the following sentences:

Al-bayt al-kabeer البيت الكبير means "the big house is" which indicates the sentences is not complete while: *Al-bayt kabeer* البيت كبير means "the house is big."

Verbal sentences:

Unlike English, sometimes Arabic sentences start with a verb. These are called verbal sentences. In verbal sentences the verb comes before the subject and the rest of the sentence. Some examples are:

Meaning	Transliteration	Example
Ahmad left the house.	*Kharaja ahmed men albayt.*	خرج أحمد من البيت
My father went to the office.	*Thahaba abee ila almaktab.*	ذهب أبي الى المكتب .
Mr. Ali attended the meeting.	*Hadhar assayed ali alijtimaa'.*	حضر السيد علي الاجتماع

Verbal sentences should always start with verb in the singular form even if the subject of the sentence is plural, while matching the gender. Verbs should match the subject if it comes before it but not after it.

Some examples are:

Meaning	Transliteration	Example
Students went to school.	*Thahab atalameeth ila almadrasa*	ذهب التلاميذ الى المدرسة
Students wrote the homework.	*Taktob attalibat alwajeb*	تكتب الطالبات الواجب
The family sits in the kitchen.	*Tajlis ala'ilah fee almatbakh.*	تجلس العائلة في المطبخ
My brothers live in this house.	*Yaskon ikhwatee fe hatha albayt.*	يسكن اخوتي في هذا البيت

Note that at the beginning of the sentence, the verbs match with gender but are always singular. It does not matter if the subject is singlar or plural.

9.2. Practice (see Answer Key)

Identify whether the sentence is verbal or nominal:

1.   تقع كليتي في بريطانيا.

2.   أدرس الهندسة في جامعة هارفارد.

3.   أختي تسكن بجانب المكتبة.

4.   اسم صديقي علي أحمد الأستاذ.

5.   كتابك على الطاولة.

6.   أنا أتكلم أربع لغات.

7.   هذه الدروس جميلة.

8.   يعمل أخي في البنك.

9.   سامية و أمل من لبنان.

10.   يدرس أحمد في جامعة أريزونا.

11.   تسكن مها مع أخوها بجانب الجامعة.

9.3. Practice (see Answer Key)

Change the following into nominal sentences:

1.   تدرس مها الكيمياء و الأدب. _____

2.   يتكلم والدي ثلاث لغات. _____

3.   ستسافر صديقتي يوم الأربعاء. _____

4.   يشاهد ابن عمتي الأخبار دائما. _____

5.   سنأكل الدجاج على الغداء اليوم. _____

9.4. Practice (see Answer Key)

Change the following into verbal sentences:

1.   سارة تحب القهوة مع الحليب. _____

2.   هدى و أمل تدرسان الكلمات الجديدة. _____

3.   علي يعرف هذا الرجل _____

4. _____ عائلتها تسكن في الأردن.

5. _____ صديقي يعمل في مطعم قريب.

Non-Human Plural Agreement:

All non-human nouns regardless of their gender use singular feminine adjectives, pronouns or demonstratives. This means we say:

Meaning	Transliteration	Example
These are watches	*hathihi saa'at*	هذه ساعات
These are the rooms	*hathihi heya alghoraf*	هذه هي الغرف
These are my books	*Hathihi kotobi*	هذه كُتُبي
Big cars	*Sayyarat kabeera*	سيارات كبيرة
Beautiful houses	*Beyoot jameela*	بيوت جميلة

This also means we say:

Hathihi saa'ah هذه ساعة for singular and *hathihi saa'at* for plural هذه ساعات

9.5. **Practice** (see Answer Key)

Read the following paragraph about Arab countries:

Yatakawan alalam ala'rabi men ithnatan wa eshreen dawlah. The Arab world consists of twenty-two countries.	يَتَكَوَّنُ العَالَمُ العَرَبِيُّ مِنْ اِثْنَتَانِ وَعِشْرِينَ دَوْلَةِ.
Taqa' thalath ashrat menha fee qarrat asya wa tes'dowal fee afriqya. Thirteen countries lie in Asia while the other nine are in Africa.	تَقَعُ ثلاث عَشْرَةً دَوْلَةً مِنْهَا في قَارَّةِ آسِيَا وَ تِسْعُ دُوَلٍ في قَارَّةِ أَفْرِيقَيَا
Yakhtalif attaqs feeha men balad ila akhar The weather is different from one country to another.	يَخْتَلِفُ الطَّقْسُ فِيهَا مِنْ بَلَدٍ إِلَى آخَرَ
Wa lakin yomkin taqseemoha ila khamsat aqaleem joghrafiyya hasab mawqi'oha. But we can divide into five regional parts according to its location.	وَ لَكِنَّ يُمْكِنُ تَقْسِيمها إِلَى خَمْسَةً أقاليم جُغْرَافِيَةً حَسَبَ مَوْقِعِهَا:

Conversation (continued)

1. Bilad asham wa hiya: sorya, lobnan wa alordon wa falasteen. The Asham region which consists of Syria, Lebanon, Jordan and Palestine.	١. بِلَادُ الشَّامُ وَ هِيَ: سُورِيَا وَ لُبْنَانُ وَ الأُرْدُنُّ وَ فِلَسْطِينُ.
2. Dowal alkhaleej alarabi wa hiya: alkwayt, assa'oodiya, alimarat al-Arabiya almotahida wa oman wa alyaman wa albahrain. The Gulf region: Kuwait, Saudi Arabia, United Arab Emirates, Oman, Yemen and Bahrain.	٢. دُوَلُ الخَلِيجِ العَرَبِيِّ وَ هِيَ: الكويت وَ السَّعُودِيَّةُ وَ الإِمَارَاتُ العَرَبِيَّةَ المُتَّحِدَةُ وَ عُمَانُ وَ اليَمَنُ وَ البَحْرَينِ.
3. Ma bayn annahrayn aliraq. Between the two rivers: Iraq.	٣. مَا بَيْنَ النَّهْرَيْنِ: العِرَاقُ.
4. Wadi aneel: mesr, asoodan, asoomal wa jaybooti. The Nile Valley: Egypt, Sudan, Somalia and Djibouti.	٤. وَادِي النِّيلِ: مِصْرُ وَ السُّودَانُ وَ الصُّومَالُ وَ جِيبُوتِي.
5. Shamal afriqya: toonis, wa aljaza'r wa leebya wa almaghrib wa moritanya. North Africa: Tunisia, Algeria, Libya, Morocco and Mauritania.	٥. شَمَالُ أَفْرِيقِيَا: تُونِس وَ الجَزَائِرُ وَ لِيبِيَا وَ المَغْرِبُ وَ مُورِيتَانِيَا.
Yahodo alalam alarabi men asharq iran wa bahr alarab. The Arab world is bordered from the east by Iran and the Arab Sea.	يحُدُّ العَالَمُ العَرَبِيُّ مِنَ الشَّرْقِ إِيرَانُ وَ بَحْرُ العَرَبِ
Wa men algharb almoheet alatlasi. From the west by Atlantic Ocean.	وَ مِنَ الغَرْبِ المُحِيطُ الأَطْلَسِيُّ
Wa men aljanoob almoheet alhindi wa assahra alkobra. From the south: the Indian Ocean and the great Sahara.	وَ مِنَ الجَنُوبِ المُحِيطُ الهِنْدِيُّ وَ الصَّحْرَاءُ الكُبْرَى
Wa men ashamal torkya wa albahr alahmar. From the North: Turkey and the Red Sea.	وَ مِنَ الشَّمَالِ تُرْكِيَا وَ البَحْرُ الأَحْمَرُ
Torkya wa iran homa men dowal asharq alwasat wa lakinahoma. Turkey and Iran are part of the Middle East, but they are not Arab countries.	تُرْكِيَا وَ إِيرَانُ هُمَا مِنْ دُوَلِ الشَّرْقِ الأَوْسَطِ وَ لَكِنَّهُمَا لَيْسَتَا دُوَلَ عَرَبِيَّةً

Now answer the following questions:

1. كم دولة في العالم العربي؟ _____

2. ما هي دول بلاد الشام؟ _____

3. كم دولة في اقليم الخليج العربي؟ _____

4. ما هي دول شمال أفريقيا؟ _____

5. ماذا يحد العالم العربي من الشمال ؟ من الجنوب؟ _____

9.6. Practice (see Answer Key)

To learn more about Arab countries, do some search and connect the country with its capital:

Capital – العاصمة	#	اسم الدولة	
المنامة		جزر القمر	1.
دمشق		المملكة الأردنية الهاشمية	2.
موروني		السودان	3.
عمّان		جمهورية لبنان	4.
صنعاء		الجمهورية العربية السورية	5.
بغداد		جمهورية مصر العربية	6.
القاهرة		اليمن	7.
بيروت		مملكة البحرين	8.
الخرطوم		المغرب	9.
الرباط		العراق	10.

Reflection

1. In this Lesson I learned: _____

2. I have some trouble with: _____

3. I need to learn more about: _____

Lesson 10

الوحدة العاشرة
Arabic Dress
اللباس العربي
Allibas ala'rabi

Objectives:

1. Arabic Clothes and Cultural Dress
2. Body Parts
3. Grammar: Nouns-Adjectives Agreement
4. Adjective of Place (*Nisba*)
5. Culture: Dress Code
6. Reading

🔊 Vocabulary

Meaning	Transliteration	Plural	Transliteration	Word
Buy	–	–	*Ishtara*	إشْتَرى
Sell	–	–	*Ba'*	باعَ
Job	*Mihan*	مِهَنْ	*Mihnah*	مِهْنة
Nationality	*Jinsiyat*	جِنْسِيّاتْ	*Jinseyya*	جِنْسيّة
Once / one time	*Marrat*	مَرّاتْ	*Marrah*	مَرّة
Numbers	*A'dad*	أَعْدادْ	*A'dad*	عَدَدْ
Good person	*Salihoon/ saliheen*	صالحون / صالحين	*Salih*	صالِحْ
Tooth	*Asnan*	أَسْنانْ	*Sin*	سِنْ
Hand	*Aydee*	أيْدي	*Yad*	يَدْ
Leg	*Arjol*	أرْجُلْ	*Rijl*	رِجِلْ

Meaning	Transliteration	Plural	Transliteration	Word
Face	*Wojooh*	وجوه	*Wajh*	وَجْه
Head	*Ro'oos*	رؤوس	*Raas*	رَأْسَ
Hair	*Sha'r*	شَعْرْ	*Sha'rah*	شَعْرة
Mouth	–	–	*Fam*	فَمْ
Ear	*Athan*	آذان	*Othon*	أُذُنْ
Eye	*Oyoon*	عُيونْ	*Ayn*	عَيْنْ
Mustache	*Shawareb*	شَوارب	*Sharib*	شاربْ
Ugly	–	–	*Qabeeh*	قَبيحْ
Beautiful	–	–	*Jameel*	جَميلْ
Big	–	–	*Kabeer*	كَبيرْ
Small	–	–	*Sagheer*	صَغيرْ
Broken	–	–	*Maksoor*	مَكْسورْ
Intact	–	–	*Saleem*	سَليمْ
Dress	–	–	*Fostan*	فُسْتانْ
Shirt	–	–	*Qamees*	قَميصْ
Pants	–	–	*Bantaloun*	بَنْطَلونْ
Shorts	–	–	*Short*	شورتْ
Busy	–	–	*Mash-ghool*	مَشْغولْ
Get ready	–	–	*Ista'da* (present tense) / *yasta'ed* (past tense)	استَعَد / يَسْتَعِدْ
Arrive	–	–	*Wasala* (present tense) / *yasel* (past tense)	وَصَلَ / يَصِل

Meaning	Transliteration	Plural	Transliteration	Word
Considered	–	–	*I'tabara* (present tense) / *ya'taber* (past tense)	اعْتَبَرَ / يُعْتَبَرُ
If	–	–	*Ithan*	إِذا
Shopping center	–	–	*Assoq*	السوقْ

There are some words describing outfits that have no equivalence in English. For example:

- *Abaya* عباية for women and *dishdasha* دشداشة for men: both mean long loose outfit that cover the whole body
- *Kofiyah* كوفية and *shemagh* شماغ or *ghotra* غترة for men: men's head cover, they wear it to protect them from the heat/cold, high temperature and dust
- *Hijab* حجاب: women's head cover that a woman wear to cover her hair

Dress Code

Currently, many Arabs wear Western dress, from blue jeans, t-shirts and shorts to miniskirts and three-piece suits, and they follow European and American brand names and clothing styles.

The trend began with colonialism and European dominance over Arab countries during World War I, and it has continued since then, especially among younger generations. At the same time, many Arabs young and old, continue to wear traditional attire, especially in traditional gatherings and during celebrations. Traditional Arab attire includes long, loose robes that cover the whole body. It is called *dishdasha* دشداشة for men and *Abaya* عباية for women. *Dishdasha* دشداشة and *Abaya* عباية have slight variations in styling, colors and designs from one country to the next and even from one village to another. Usually, Arab men wear a light-colored *dishdasha* دشداشة in summer or in desert environments, such as Gulf countries, Iraq or Egypt; strong breezes circulating through the *dishdasha* دشداشة provide a cooling effect in the summer. Men wear a dark-colored *dishdasha* دشداشة in winter. In countries with more rain and vegetation, such as Syria, Jordan and Lebanon, the dress is more colorful. As for *Abaya* عباية, it has assorted color according to the country. For example, in Tunisia, women wear white and green *Abaya* عباية; in Egypt the *Abaya* عباية is often solid white or blue with embroidery; in Syria and Palestine, it is often black with colorful embroidery, and in Gulf countries the *Abaya* عباية is black.

Traditional dress for men also includes a head dress **ghotra** for protection from the sun during hot summers and from the cold in winters. The color varies among countries, with men in Gulf countries using a white **ghotra** and men in Jordan and Palestine using a red-and-white checkered **ghotra**.

Noun-Adjective agreement

Adjectives come after the noun, not before it as in English. Adjectives agree with the noun it is describing in almost all its details including gender, definiteness and number. It also takes the same vowels and tanween as the noun. Some examples are:

Meaning	Transliteration	Example
A good man	*Rajol salih*	رجل صالح
Two good men	*Rajolan salihan*	رجلان صالحان
Good men	*Rijal salihoon*	رجال صالحون

The only situation that the adjectives do not follow the noun is when the noun is a non-human plural, then the adjective should be singular feminine. Some examples are:

Meaning	Transliteration	Example
Big books	*Kotob kabeerah*	كُتُب كبيرة
Small houses	*Beyoot sagheerah*	بيوت صغيرة

Additionally, if we are describing an identified noun, then we can use more than one adjective without writing the word and (و) in between for example:

Meaning	Transliteration	Example
The new small car...	*Assayarah aljadeeda assagheera...*	السيارة الجديدة الصغيرة ....
The beautiful big house ...	*albayt aljameel alkabeer...*	البيت الجميل الكبير ....

10.1. Practice (see Answer Key)

Write a check mark beside the correct noun–adjective agreement, and an X beside the wrong ones. Then correct the wrong ones:

1. _____ أحمد طالب لبنانية.

2. _____ تونس مدينة عربي.

3. _____ أريزونا ولاية أمريكية.

4. _____ أختي جميلة و قصير.

5. _____ غرفتي كبيرة.

6. _____ أتكلم اللغة العربية و الانجليزي.

7. _____ اشتريت كتب جديد.

8. _____ هذه بيت أستاذنا الأمريكية.

9. _____ الطالبان يدخلان من الباب الصغيرة.

10. _____ عندي دراجتان قديمان.

Adjectives of place (Nisba):

Adjectives of place, or nationalities, are sometimes called *nisba*. *Nisba* means "related to," so *nisba* adjectives are related adjectives because they are derived from the name of the city, region, country or family's last name. This is very easy procedure. All you have to do is add ي at the end of the word.

Words describing nationalities are considered adjectives. They are called adjectives of place as they are describing the place of origin of someone or something. Adjectives of place may be formed by adding *ya* at the end of the name of country as in:

English Name of country	Transliteration	Adjective of place (Feminine)	Transliteration	Adjective of place (Masculine)	Name of country
Qatar	*Qatariyyah*	قطريّة	*Qatari*	قطري	قطر
Egypt	*Mesriyyah*	مصرية	*Mesrey*	مصري	مصر
Lebanon	*Lebnaniyyah*	لبنانية	*lobnani*	لبناني	لبنان

Notice that when referring to females we add the *ta marbuta* after the *ya*.

If the country name ends in a *ta marbuta* or *alif*, then remove it and add the *ya* as in:

English Name of country	Transliteration	Adjective of place (Feminine)	Transliteration	Adjective of place (Masculine)	Name of country
Syria	*Sooriyyah*	سورية	*Sooriy*	سوري	سوريا
America	*Amreekiayyah*	أمريكية	*Amreeki*	أمريكي	أمريكا
Britain	*Breetaniyyah*	بريطانية	*Breetani*	بريطاني	بريطانيا

As explained earlier, if the country name starts with the definite *al*, then remove it and add the *ya* as in:

English Name of country	Transliteration	Adjective of place (Feminine)	Transliteration	Adjective of place (Masculine)	Name of country
Iraq	*Iraqiyyah*	عراقية	*Iraqi*	عراقي	العراق
Kuwait	*Kuwaytiyyah*	كويتية	*Kowaiti*	كويتي	الكويت
Sudan	*Soodaniyyah*	سودانية	*Soodani*	سوداني	السودان
Japan	*Yabaniayyah*	يابانية	*Yabani*	ياباني	اليابان

To make nationalities a plural form, we just add the ون/ين form for masculine and ات for feminine. Some examples are:

English Name of place	Transliteration	Plural-Feminine	Transliteration	Plural -Masculine	Adjective of place
Egyptian	*Misriyyat*	مصريات	*Mesriyoon/ Mesriyeen*	مصريون / مصريين	مصري
Iraqi	*Iraqiyyat*	عراقيات	*Iraqiyoon/ Iraqiyeen*	عراقيون/ عراقيين	عراقي
Qatari	*Qatariyyat*	قطريات	*Qatariyoon/ Qatariyeen*	قطريون / قطريين	قطري

English Name of place	Transliteration	Plural–Feminine	Transliteration	Plural –Masculine	Adjective of place
Algerian	*Jazairiyyat*	جزائريات	*Jaza'reyoon/ Jaza'riyeen*	جزائريون / جزائريين	جزائري
Jordanian	*Ordoniyyat*	أردنيات	*Ardoneyoon/ Ardoniyeen*	أردنيون / أردنيين	أردني

Of course, there are few exceptions for the rule as in:

English Name of place	Transliteration	Plural– Feminine	Transliteration	Plural– Masculine	Adjective of Place
English	*Ingleeziyat*	انجليزيات	*Ingleez*	إنجليز	انجليزي
Arab	*Arabiyat*	عربيات	*Arab*	عرب	عربي
Russian	*Roosiyat*	روسيات	*Roos*	روس	روسي

10.2. Practice (see Answer Key)

Fill in the blanks:

Adjective of place Feminine	Adjective of place Masculine	Country
		باكستان
		قطر
		الامارات
		لبنان
		اليمن
		تونس
		الجزائر
		ايطاليا

10.3. Practice   (see Answer Key)

Fill in the blanks:

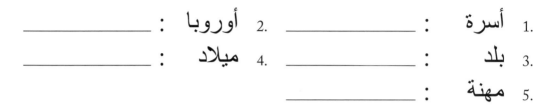

1. أسرة : _____   2. أوروبا : _____

3. بلد : _____   4. ميلاد : _____

5. مهنة : _____

10.4. Practice   (see Answer Key)

To review your understanding of verb conjugation, fill in the blanks with the conjugated verbs:

Meaning	هم	هما	هي	هو	انتِ	أنتَ	نحن	أنا	Verb in past tense
Write									كتب
Drink									شرب
Live									سكن
Read									قرأ
Go									ذهب
Love/like									أحب
Cook									طبخ
Want									أراد
Arrive									وصل
Leave									رحل

10.5. Practice   (see Answer Key)

Circle the word that does not belong:

1. أنا – أنت – هل – هم   2. هل – متى – كتاب – كم

3. دفتر – قلم – أحمد – كتاب   4. أم – أب – باب – أخ

5. قصير – طويل – أمل – سليم   6. فستان – دشداشة – أبي – قميص

7. عربي – أمريكي – كلية – انجليزي

8. قهوة – حار – بارد – ممطر

9. الأربعاء – الجمعة – يناير – السبت

10. آداب – علوم – لغات – شاي

Read the following conversation:

Almalabis altaqleediya al-Arabiya motashabiha jidan. Arab traditional clothes are very similar.	الملابس التقليدية العربية متشابهة جدا.
Wa takoon motanasiba ma'ataqs. It also fits the weather.	و تكون متناسبة مع الطقس.
Mathalan fee dowal alkhaleej wa aliraq wa alardon wa mesr takoon almalabes alwanoha fatiha mithl alabyad lita'kis ashi'at ashams fee alsayf. For example, in Gulf countries, Iraq, Jordan and Egypt people tend to wear light colors as white to reflect the sun rays.	مثلا في دول الخليج و العراق و الأردن و مصر تكون الملابس ألوانها فاتحة مثل الأبيض لتعكس أشعة الشمس في الصيف.
Wa wasi'a litasmah biharakat alhawa wa takoon masnoo'a men alqotn. And loose to allow air movement and it is made of cotton.	و واسعة لتسمح بحركة الهواء و تكون مصنوعة من القطن.
La'anna attaqs yakoon har jidan. Because the weather is very hot.	لأن الطقس يكون حار جدا.
Wa fee ashitaa yalbis alarab alalwan alghamiqa mithl aswad wa alazraq alghamiq aw alboni. In winter they wear dark colors as black, dark blue and brown.	و في الشتاء يلبس العرب الألوان الغامقة مثل الأسود و الأزرق الغامق أو البني.
Wa takoon almalabes masnoo'a men assof la'nna ataqs yakoon barid jidan. And made of wool because the weather is very cold.	و تكون الملابس مصنوعة من الصوف لأن الطقس يكون بارد جدا.

Conversation (continued)

Men almohim Aydan taghtiyat arras belkoofiya aw ashemagh aw ghita' arra's lihimayat arra's wa alwajh men ashams alharra aw arimal aw ariyah It is important too to cover the head with Kufia, or any head cover to protect the head and face from the hot sun, sands or winds	من المهم أيضا تغطية الرأس بالكوفية أو الشماغ أو غطاء الرأس لحماية الرأس و الوجة من الشمس الحارة أو الرمال أو الرياح .
Yalbis alarab allibas ataqleedi ba'dh alahyan Sometimes Arabs wear their traditional clothes	يلبس العرب اللباس التقليدي بعض الأحيان
Wa lakinnahom okhra yalbisoon albintal aw ashort ma' alqamees aw albolooza Other times they wear pants or shorts with t-shirts or blouses	و أحيانا أخرى يلبسون البنطال أو الشورت مع القميص أو البلوزة

10.6. Practice (see Answer Key)

Answer the following questions:

1. هل تتشابه الملابس العربية؟
2. لماذا يلبس العرب الملابس الفاتحة في الصيف؟
3. لماذا يلبسون الملابس المصنوعة من الصوف في الشتاء؟
4. لماذا يغطون رؤوسهم؟
5. هل يلبس الرجال الدشداشة دائماً؟

10.7. **Practice** (see Answer Key)

Rearrange the following words to form meaningful sentences:

1. المسلمون – خمس – يصلون – اليوم – في – مرات

2. سنوات – الجامعة – يدرس – الطب – طلاب – سبع – في

3. الكتاب – اسم – ما – اشتريته – الذي – أمس؟

4. تغضب ـ الواجب – أمي – لم – اذا – أعمل.

5. اللاعبون – ملابس – لكي – الفريق – يستعدوا – يلبس – للمباراة.

6. وصلوا – الى – الأردن – أصدقائي – الاثنين – يوم.

7. مدينة – كم – زرت – في – مصر؟

8. سعاد – الى – ذهبت – أمها – مع – السوق.

9. خالد – في – أن – يريد – يكون – الجامعة – دكتور.

10. أصغر – عربي – البحرين – بلد – تعتبر.

10.8. **Practice** (see Answer Key)

Connect the related words by writing the words' numbers in the parentheses:

( ) أم	2. أخ	( ) جدتي	1. أب
( ) صغير	4. الآن	( ) منذ سنة	3. جدي
( ) نشيط	6. نهار	( ) ليل	5. كسلان
		( ) أخت	7. كبير

Reflection

1. In this Lesson I learned: _____

2. I have some trouble with: _____

3. I need to learn more about: _____

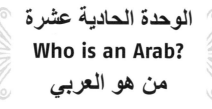

الوحدة الحادية عشرة
Who is an Arab?
من هو العربي
Man howa alarabi

Objectives:
1. Children's Value in the Arab world
2. Daily Schedule and Time Expression
3. Grammar: Ordinal and Cardinal Numbers
4. Culture: "You Know You're an Arab When…"
5. Reading

Vocabulary

Meaning	Transliteration	Plural	Transliteration	Word
Oil	*Ziyoot*	زيوت	*Zayt*	زَيْتْ
Juice	*Asa'er*	عصائر	*A'seer*	عَصيرْ
Orange	*Bortoqalat*	بُرْتَقالاتْ	*Bortoqal*	بُرْتَقالْ
Apple	*Tofah*	تُفَّاحْ	*Tofaha*	تُفَّاحة
Banana	*Mawz*	مَوْزْ	*Mooza*	مَوْزة
Egg	*Baydh*	بَيْضْ	*Baidha*	بَيْضة
Butter	–		*Zobda*	زُبْدة
Jam	–		*Moraba*	مُرَبّى
Bread	–		*Khobz*	خُبْزْ
Cheese	*Ajban*	أجبان	*Jobna*	جُبْنة
Biscuit	-	-	*Baskaweet*	بَسْكَويتْ

Meaning	Transliteration	Plural	Transliteration	Word
Salad	*Salatat*	سلطات	*Salatah*	سَلَطة
Rice	–	–	*Arz*	أرُزْ
Meat	*Lahm*	لَحْم	*Lah-ma*	لَحْمة
Chicken	*Dajaj*	دَجاج	*Dajajah*	دَجاجة
Fish	*Samak*	سَمَكْ	*Samakah*	سَمَكة
Fried	*Mashawi*	مشاوي	*Mashwi*	مَشْوي
Broiled	*Maqali*	مقالي	*Maqli*	مَقْلي
Falafel	–	–	*Falafel*	فلافِلْ
Humus	–	–	*Hommos*	حُمّصْ
Cereal	–	–	*Hoboob*	حُبوبْ
Macaroni	–	–	*Ma'karoona*	مَعْكَرونة
Cake	–	–	*Ka'k*	كَعْكْ
Food	*At'emah*	أطْعِمة	*Ta'am*	طَعامْ
Drink	*Mashroobat*	مَشْروباتْ	*Sharab*	شَرابْ
Prefer	–	–	*Faddala* (present tense)/ *yofaddel* (past)	فَضّلَ / يُفَضّلْ
Hour (o'clock)	*Saa'at*	ساعاتْ	*Saa'h*	ساعة
Minute	*Daqa'iq*	دَقائِقْ	*Daqiqa*	دَقيقة
Half	–	–	*Nisf*	نِصْفْ
Quarter	–	–	*Rob'*	رُبْعْ
Third	–	–	*Tholoth*	ثُلْثْ
Till /Except	–	–	*Illa*	إلّا
Schedule	*Jadawel*	جَداوِلْ	*Jadwal*	جَدْوَلْ

Meaning	Transliteration	Plural	Transliteration	Word
Parking lot	*Mawaqif*	مَوَاقِفْ	*Mawqif*	مَوْقِفْ
Spoon	*Mala'eq*	مَلَاعق	*Mila'qa*	مِلْعَقة
Fork	*Showak*	شُوَك	*Shawka*	شَوْكة
Knife	*Sakakeen*	سَكاكين	*Sikeen*	سِكِّينْ
Plate	*Atbaq*	أطباق	*Tabaq*	طَبَقْ
Eat	–	–	*Akala* (present tense) / *ya/kol* (past tense)	أَكَلَ/ يَأكُلْ
Cook	–	–	*Tabakha* (present tense) / *yatbokh* (past tense)	طَبَخَ/ يَطْبَخْ
Wash	–	–	*Ghasalaa* (present tense) / *yaghsel* (past tense)	غَسَلَ/ يَغْسِلْ
Reserve	–	–	*Hajaza* (present tense) / *yahjiz* (past tense)	حَجَزَ/ يَحْجِزْ
Person	*Ash-khas*	أَشْخاصْ	*Shakhs*	شَخْصْ

You know you're an Arab when:

The following list is from an email that is exchanged, as a joke, among Arabic friends. It is similar to the "Redneck" jokes told by comedian Jeff Foxworthy. The issues mentioned are part of Arabic culture, so the list below is included to add a bit of humor to the lesson. Specific cultural explanations are included below each point.

- A visa is not a credit card.
  Arabs mostly use cash in their daily monetary transactions. They do not use credit cards. In some Arabic countries, Jordan for example, you must pay an extra 7-10% if you want to use your credit card while shopping. So, it is cheaper to pay cash. In Arab countries, it is quite safe to carry large amounts of cash in your pocket and walk around.

- You refer to your dad's friends as *Amme* عمي.
  As you know, *Amme* means "uncle," which is a paternal uncle. It is very rude for people to address older people by their first names. They should use the word عمي *ammee* before mentioning his name or calling him. Females are addressed as خالتي *khaltee*, maternal aunt. As a rule of thumb and irrespective of

your age, you should always address people who are older than you in this fashion: عمي (for males) or خالتي (for females) when communicating with them.

- You have an endless supply of pistachios, dates, and pumpkin seeds.
  Arabs have a short workday. Most government offices finish their work at 2:00 P.M. They start at 7:00 A.M. and do not have lunch breaks, as lunch is considered part of the family ritual that all members of the family must attend. They go home to have their main meal (lunch) at this time and take a short nap. When they wake up, they have plenty of time to go and socialize by visiting their family and friends. During these visits, they offer juice, soda, or other cold drinks (non-alcoholic) at the beginning, and then hot tea with cakes and/or cookies, followed by pistachios and/or pumpkin seeds; finally, the coffee is served with some dates. Even without visitors, Arabs enjoy watching TV while cracking their pumpkin seeds and pistachios.

- Your parents can tell you are becoming Americanized anytime you talk back to them!
  Children are not allowed to talk back or raise their voices to their parents. Children are supposed to listen and discuss politely what they want to say. They are not supposed to look at their parents directly in the eyes or in any rude manner (rolling their eyes, making faces, etc). Therefore, when children talk back to their parents, the prevailing thought is that they must have acquired it from the TV (watching American movies, MTV, the Simpsons, etc.).

- After a family meal, the women (while visiting other families) fight to the death over who should wash the dishes while the men sit and discuss politics, waiting for their tea.
  When Arabs invite people for lunch (the main meal), they prepare many dishes. Therefore, the host is tired, and her visitors want to help her clean. The men move to a different room to get out of the way and the women start to argue who will clean the dishes, who will put the food away, and who will take care of preparing the hot tea. When women are done cleaning, either they can join the men to have tea together or they might prefer to sit in a different room and have their own chat.

- Your parents want you to become a doctor or engineer.
  Most Arabs want their children to be doctors or engineers. Perhaps they believe that doctors and engineers have excellent pay; so, they steer their children in that direction. Usually things do not turn out to this way; but parents want their children to live comfortably, so they do their best to convince them to major in either of these two fields.

- You have at least 30 cousins.
  Of course, if you know all your uncles and aunts from both sides, you would know all your cousins and have a strong relationship with them all. Brothers and sisters visit each other a lot. When visiting family members, the tradition is to take your children with you, so chil-

dren get to know all their relatives. In addition to that, it is a tradition in most families to invite all married children every weekend for lunch, for the brothers and sisters to develop close relationships. This helps to cement the strong family bond.

- You are standing next to the largest suitcases at the airport.
  When you go to visit your family, you will meet all your relatives, cousins, aunts, and uncles from both sides. All of them will come to say hello, and it will be very embarrassing if you did not give them a gift. They also will bring you a good-bye gift when you leave. Therefore, you will definitely need a big suitcase. Arabs pay attention to the way you are dressed (unless you are truly poor). Therefore, you must wear nice clean clothes at all times, and you need a variety of clothes to wear for the trip.

- Your relatives alone could populate a small city.
  Arabs believe in big families. In the past, families always aspired for more children, especially sons, to defend their tribes and villages from invaders and thugs, so the more sons (warriors) you had, the stronger you were. Despite all the changes that affected societies and cultures, the urge to have more children stayed the same. Now, if you have six uncles and each has five children as an average, this equals 30 cousins. When each of these 30 cousins has another five of their own, how many will you have? So, do the math. Remember, this is only from the father's side, and if you add your cousins from the mother's side, you would truly make up a small village.

- You still came back home to live with your parents after you graduate.
  This concept was introduced in earlier lessons. It is common to send sons and daughters to a different country to study at a university. There has been a lot of development in Arabic countries over the past 20 years. Previously, not all Arab countries had universities and if they had one, it would not have all degrees. So, a father will provide for his son(s) to go to a different country to finish his/her degree. When the sons and daughters have completed their degrees, they come back to their parents' home to reside until they find a job, establish themselves, get married, and start their own families.

Cardinal Number

Number-Noun Agreement

When talking about nouns and combining them with quantity, there are few rules to follow:

1. Numbers 1 & 2 follow the noun in gender and case. When used, they are used for emphasis. 1 & 2 come after the noun, so we would say:

Meaning	Transliteration	Example
One book	*kitab wahed*	كتاب واحد
One room	*ghorfa wahidah*	غرفة واحدة
Two rooms	*ghorfatan ithnatan*	غرفتان اثنتان

2. Numbers 3-10 come before the noun they modify, and they use the opposite word gender. For example: *sit sayyarat* ست سيارات "six cars" and *sab'at kotob* – سبعة كتب "seven books"

3. In all situations, the noun we are referring to should be **indefinite** in all situation. That is it should not have ال

4. The nouns coming after numbers 3-10 are always considered as *idafa* which means they should have *kasra*

Here is a list of the numbers in the masculine and feminine forms of 1-10:

Transliteration	Feminine form	Transliteration	Masculine form	Number
Taliba wahida	طالبة واحدة	*Talib wahid*	طالب واحد	1
Talibatan ithnatan	طالبتان اثنتان	*Talibatan ithnatan*	طالبان اثنان	2
Thalath talibat	ثلاث طالبات	*Thalathat tollab*	ثلاثة طلاب	3
Arba'talibat	أربع طالبات	*Arba'at tolab*	أربعة طلاب	4
Khams talibat	خمس طالبات	*Khamsato tollab*	خمسة طلاب	5
Sit talibat	ست طالبات	*Sitato tollab*	ستة طلاب	6
Sab'talibat	سبع طالبات	*Saba'ato tollab*	سبعة طلاب	7
Thamani talibat	ثماني طالبات	*Thamaniyato tollab*	ثمانية طلاب	8
Tes' talibat	تسع طالبات	*Tesa'to tollab*	تسعة طلاب	9
A'shr talibat	عشر طالبات	*Ashrato tollab*	عشرة طلاب	10

11.1. Practice   (see Answer Key)

1.   بيت (9) : _____   2.   حقيبة (6) : _____

3.   طاولة (4) : _____   4.   قلم (8) : _____

5.   أستاذ (3) : _____   6.   خالة (7) : _____

7.   شارع (5) : _____   8.   كلية (2) : _____

9.   كلمة (10) : _____   10.   مفتاح (1) : _____

Ordinal Numbers:

Ordinal numbers indicate things done in order. They are the same as first, second, …etc in English. The first ordinal number أول is different from the first cardinal number واحد. However, 2-10 are formed from their cardinal numbers. There are different forms for masculine and feminine forms. Yes, it is just adding *ta marbuta*. Look at the table below to learn ordinal numbers:

Meaning	Transliteration	Feminine form	Transliteration	Masculine Ordinal number	Transliteration	Number
The first	*Oola*	أولى	*Awal*	أول	*Wahid*	واحد
Second	*Thaniya*	ثانية	*Thani*	ثاني	*Ithnan*	اثنان
Third	*Thalitha*	ثالثة	*Thalith*	ثالث	*Thalathah*	ثلاثة
Fourth	*Rabi'a*	رابعة	*Rabi'*	رابع	*Arba'*	أربعة
Fifth	*Khamisah*	خامسة	*Khamis*	خامس	*Khamsa*	خمسة
Sixth	*Sadisa*	سادسة	*Sadis*	سادس	*Sitta*	ستة
Seventh	*Sabi'a*	سابعة	*Sabi'*	سابع	*Saba'h*	سبعة
Eighth	*Thamina*	ثامنة	*Thamin*	ثامن	*Thamaniyah*	ثمانية
Ninth	*Tasi'a*	تاسعة	*Tasi'*	تاسع	*Tes'ah*	تسعة
Tenth	*A'shira*	عاشرة	*A'shir*	عاشر	*Asharah*	عشرة

Ordinal numbers 11-19 are invariable which means that they do not change the case. Unlike cardinal numbers, both words in 11-19 in ordinal numbers should agree in gender with the noun. We say:

Meaning	Transliteration	Example
The twelfth lesson	*addars athani ashar*	الدرس الثاني عشر
The twelfth page	*assafhato athaniyato asharah*	الصفحة الثانية عشرة

11.2. Practice (see Answer Key)

Arrange the following sentences to form a meaningful paragraph:

سنأخذ الدجاج و نريد عصير برتقال   ـ_____

نعم – عندنا سمك مقلي و طيب جدا.   ـ_____

مرحبا بكم في مطعمنا. ما الاسم لو سمحت   ـ_____

شكرا ! ما هو طبق اليوم؟   ـ_____

مساء الخير. حجزنا طاولة لثلاثة أشخاص   ـ_____

أنا أحب السمك. هل عندكم سمك؟   ـ_____

الاسم هو محمد   ـ_____

حسنا و أنت يا سيدة ماذا تريدين؟   ـ_____

أهلا و سهلا ! طاولة رقم سبعة   ـ_____

طبق اليوم دجاج مشوي مع أرز   ـ_____

اذا طبق سمك و طبقين من الدجاج مع الأرز   ـ_____

11.3. Practice (see Answer Key)

How do you say the following using ordinal numbers?

2. البنت 4 : _____		1. الصفحة 25 : _____	
4. الطالبة 1 : _____		3. في سنة 1925 : _____	
6. البيت 19 : _____		5. الرجل 17 : _____	

Reading:

Jadwal ali alyawmi. Ali's daily schedule.	جدول علي اليومي:
Kol yawm yastayqith ali men annawm fee assa'a alkhamisa wa arrob' sabahan. Everyday, Ali wakes up at 5:15 in the morning.	كل يوم يستيقظ علي من النوم في الساعة الخامسة و الربع صباحا.
Yath-hab ila alhammam wa yonathif asnanaho wa yastahim belmaa wa assaboon. He goes to the bathroom, brush his teeth and wash himself with water and soap.	يذهب الي الحمام و ينظف أسنانه و يستحم بالماء و الصابون.
Thoma yath-hab ila almatbakh wa yohadher ta'am alfotoor. Then he goes to the kitchen and prepare breakfast.	ثم يذهب الى المطبخ و يحضر طعام الفطور.
Mo'tham alayam yaakol albaydh wa alkhobz ma' aljibn wa yashrab ashay. Most days, he eats eggs, bread and cheese and drinks tea.	معظم الأيام يأكل البيض و الخبز مع الجبن و يشرب الشاي.
Howa yohib ashay katheeran. He likes tea very much.	هو يحب الشاي كثيراً.
Fee assa'a assabi'a yath-hab ila amilihi fee albas la'anaho la yajod mawqifan lisay-yarataho. At seven o'clock, he goes to his work by bus because he cannot find a parking for his car at his work.	في الساعة السابعة يذهب علي الى عمله في الباص لأنه لا يجد موقفا لسيارته.
Fee assa'a athaniyata ashara yath-hab ila mat'am qareeb wa ya'kol ta'am alghada. At twelve O'clock, he goes to a nearby restaurant to eat lunch.	في الساعة الثانية عشرة يذهب الى مطعم قريب و يأكل طعام الغداء.
Ta'amoho almofadal alahm ma' alarz wa assalatah. His favorite food is meat with rice and salad.	طعامه المفضل اللحم مع الأرز و السلطة.

Conversation *(continued)*

Yabqa fee amalihi hata assa'a alkhamisa masaa'n. He stays at work until 5 o'clock.	يبقى في عمله حتى الساعة الخامسة مساءً.
Ahyan yahdhor endaho sadiqoho hani wa yoshahidan atilfaz wa yashraban ashay. Sometimes, his friend Hani goes to him to watch TV and drink tea.	أحيانا يحضر عنده صديقه هاني و يشاهدان التلفاز و يشربان الشاي.
Yath-hab ali ila annowm fee assa'a al'shirati masa'an. Ali goes to bed at 10:00 at night.	يذهب علي الى النوم في الساعة العاشرة مساءً.

11.4. Practice (see Answer Key)

Answer the following questions:

1. متى يستيقظ علي؟   2. ماذا يفعل كل صباح؟

3. هل يشرب علي القهوة؟   4. ما هو طعام علي المفضل؟

5. متى ينام علي؟

11.5. Practice (see Answer Key)

Connect the related words by writing the numbers in parentheses:

1. فرشاة   ( ) شراب   2. سرير   ( ) دقيقة

3. مطبخ   ( ) طعام   4. ساعة   ( ) معجون أسنان

5. عصير   ( ) ينام

11.6. Practice (see Answer Key)

Connect the related words by writing the numbers in parentheses:

1. أذهب الى المكتبة   ( ) لأتناول طعام العشاء

2. أذهب الى المطعم   ( ) لأقرا الكتاب

3. ماذا تريد أن تلعب؟   ( ) 645 شارع تمبي مدينة جلبرت

4. كان الامتحان صعب   ( ) أنا ألعب كرة القدم

5. ما عنوانك؟   ( ) و لكني نجحت في الامتحان

Reflection

1. In this Lesson I learned: _____

2. I have some trouble with: _____

3. I need to learn more about: _____

الوحدة الثانية عشرة
Relations between the Sexes
العلاقة بين الجنسين
Alilaqa bayna aljensayn

Objectives:

1. Professions and occupations vocabulary
2. Grammar
   - Negation of Nominal Sentences
   - Negation of Verbal Sentences
3. Culture: Modesty and Sex Separation
4. Reading

🔊 Vocabulary

Meaning	Transliteration	Plural	Transliteration	Word
Busy	–	–	*Mash-ghool*	مَشْغُولْ
Sleep		–	*Nama* (present tense)/ *Yanam* (past tense)	نامْ/ينام
Refuse	–	–	*Rafada* (present tense) / *yarfod* (past tense)	رفَضَ/ يَرْفُضْ
Agree	–	–	*Wafaqa* (present tense) / *yowafiq* (past tense)	وافَقَ/يُوافِقْ
Go or continue doing something	–	–	*Madha* (present tense) / *yamdhi* (past tense)	مَضَى/ يَمْضِي
Newspaper	*Jara'ed*	جَرَائد	*Jareeda*	جَريدة
Box	*Sanadeeq*	صناديق	*Sondooq*	صَنْدوقْ
Candy	–	–	*Halwa*	حَلْوى

Meaning	Transliteration	Plural	Transliteration	Word
Late	–	–	*Mota'khir*	مُتَأَخِّر
Early	–	–	*Mobakir*	مُبَكِّر
Ready	–	–	*Jahiz*	جاهِزْ
Holiday, vacation	*O'tal*	عُطَل	*Otla*	عُطْلة
End	*Nihayat*	نهايات	*Nihaya*	نِهاية
Beginning	*Bedayat*	بدايات	*Bedaya*	بِداية
About	–	–	*A'mma*	عَمّا = عَنْ ما
Employee	*Mowathafeen/ mowathafoon*	موظفين/ موظفون	*Mowathaf*	مُوَظَّفْ
Company	*Sharikat*	شَرِكات	*Sharikah*	شَرِكة
Accountant	*Mohasebeen/ mohaseboon*	محاسبين/ محاسبون	*Mohaseb*	مُحاسِبْ
Too	–	–	*Aydhan*	أَيْضاً
Then	–	–	*Thomma*	ثُمَّ
But, however	–	–	*Lakin*	لكِنْ
As for	–	–	*Amma*	أَمّا
Wake up	–	–	*Istayqatha* (present tense) / *yastayqith* (past tense)	أَسْتَيْقِظْ / يستيقظ
Take a shower, bathe	–	–	*Istahamma/ yastahim*	أَسْتَحِمْ / يستحم

Meaning	Transliteration	Plural	Transliteration	Word
Guard	*Horras*	حُرّاس	*Haris*	حارِسْ
Director, manager	*Modara'*	مُدَراء	*Modeer*	مُدِيرْ
Businessman	*Rijal a'mal*	رجال أعمال	*Rajol a'mal*	رَجُلْ أَعْمالْ
Salary	*Rawateb*	رواتب	*Ratib*	راتِبْ
Carpenter	*Najjareen/ najaroon*	نجارين/ نجارون	*Najjar*	نَجّارْ
Artist	*Fannaneen/ fannanoon*	فَنّانين/ فَنّانونْ	*Fannan*	فَنّانْ
Helper, assistant	*Mosa'deen/ mosa'doon*	مُساعِدْين/ مُساعِدْون	*Mosa'ed*	مُساعِدْ
Journalist	*Sahafiyeen/ sahafiyoon*	صَحَفِيْون/ صَحَفِيْين	*Sahafi*	صَحَفِيْ
Shoes	*Ahthiyah*	أحذية	*Hitha'*	حِذاءْ
Belt	*Ahzima*	أحزمة	*Hizam*	حِزامْ
Tie	*Rabtat onoq*	ربطات عُنُقْ	*Rabtat onoq*	رَبْطة عُنُقْ
Pajama	*Bijamat*	بيجامات	*Bijama*	بيجاما
Size	*Maqasat*	مقاسات	*Maqas*	مَقاسْ
Tight	–	–	*Dhayiq*	ضَيّقْ
Loose	–	–	*Wasi'*	واسِعْ

Modesty and Sex Separation

Generally, interaction between sexes is limited to family members. However, there is a significant difference in gender separation from one Arab country to another. Gulf countries have more restrictions than other Arab countries, whereas Levantine and North African Arab countries are more flexible.

Eye contact is not encouraged in cross-gender interactions outside the family structure. Males do not look directly at females, and females do not look directly at males when speaking together. Men and women are expected to not interact socially in public outside of their extended family. Arabs normally do not allow dating and sexual relations outside of marriage are strictly prohibited. Premarital sexual relations are considered highly shameful and divisive. An Arab girl is expected to be a virgin on her wedding night, and an unchaste bride or groom brings shame on herself or himself as well as on their family. However, the rules against sexual relations applies to females more than it does to males because a girl's pride and dignity represent the honor of her family. As explained earlier, Arabs place immense value on the family's name, reputation and honor and will protect that honor with their own lives.

When meeting an Arab woman, there are few things that are not accepted especially in front of male family members. For example, showing any interest as in staring or trying to take pictures with them; asking about female members and starting a conversation without being introduced or not respecting the woman's privacy. When meeting each other, one should ask about the family in general and not a wife, sister or daughter.

On the other hand, women do play an important role in the workforce. Separation between males and females is maintained in the workplace in Saudi Arabia only. In all other Arab countries, there is no separation between sexes. As for professional careers, females are encouraged to be teachers, nurses, doctors and caregivers, and although there are many female lawyers and engineers, depending on the country, these careers are less preferable.

Contrary to popular Western belief about Muslims, restricting women to certain jobs or professions is an Arab cultural norm rather than an Islamic tradition. There is no Islamic law that requires women to stay home or to refrain from having a job. However, when a woman chooses to work, she is entitled to equal pay, as the Qur'an states:

> "And in no wise covet those things in which Allah hath bestowed His gifts more freely on some of you than on others: To men is allotted what they earn, and to women what they earn: But ask Allah of His bounty. For Allah hath full knowledge of all things" (4:32)

Interestingly, the Prophet's Mohammed's first wife, Khadija, was a business owner and she hired him to take care of her trade before she proposed to him.

Negation of Nominal sentences

To negate nominal sentences, we just add ليس to the sentence. However, ليس should be conjugated according to the thing I am negating as it should agree with gender and number.

Here is a list of conjugations that are used according to the noun that *I* is negated:

Meaning	Transliteration	Conjugation of ليس	Pronoun
I am not	*Lasto*	لستُ	أنا
We're not	*Lasna*	لسنا	نحن
You're not (m.)	*Lasta*	لستَ	أنتَ
You're not (f.)	*Lasti*	لستِ	انتِ
You're not (dual)	*Lastoma*	لستما	أنتما
You're not (m. plural)	*Lastom*	لستم	أنتم
You're not (f. Plural)	*Lastonna*	لستن	أنتن
He's not	*Laysa*	ليس	هو
She's not	*Laysat*	ليست	هي
They're not- dual	*Laysa*	ليسا	هما
They're not (m. plural)	*Laysoo*	ليسوا	هم
They're not (f. plural)	*Lasnna*	لسن	هن

Some examples are:

Meaning	Transliteration	Example
Mohmoud is not from Syria	*Mahmood laysa men Soorya*	محمود ليس من سوريا
Your car is not white	*sayaratoka laysat baydha*	سيارتك ليست بيضاء
They (dual) are not home	*homa laysa fii albayt*	هما ليسا في البيت
They are not at the university	*hom laysoo fi aljame'a*	هم ليسوا في الجامعة

12.1 Practice   (see Answer Key)

Negate the following sentences using ليس:

1. كتابي على الطاولة. _____
2. أختي في المطعم _____
3. الطلاب قرأوا الكتاب _____
4. صورتهم على الجدار _____
5. أنا غني _____

Negating Verbal Sentences:

Negating a verbal sentence simply involves creating a negative verb according to your needs. For example, as you know, there are two types of present tense: the regular as in "he writes" and the continuous as in "he is writing." To negate these verbs in the present tense, we have two options:

1. If we are talking about the continuous present tense (which indicates an ongoing action such as "writing") we just add لا before the verb. لا has no effect on the the verb's form.
2. To negate verbs in the present tense, we add لم before the verb. For example:

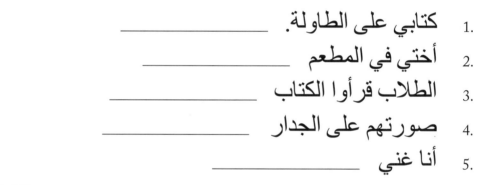

Meaning	Would be	Example
He is writing the lesson/ He is not writing the lesson.	لا يكتب الدرس *la yaktob addars*	يكتب الدرس *yaktob addars*
Do the homework/did not do the homework.	لم تعمل الواجب *lam ta'mal alwajib*	تعمل الواجب *ta'mal alwajib*

Meaning	Would be	Example
Eat breakfast/did not eat breakfast.	لم يأكل الافطار *lam ya'kol aliftar*	يأكل الافطار *ya'kol aliftar*

There is one important rule for negating present tense verbs using لم which is: after لم the verb should has *sukoon* on it, that is no vowels. The verb would be called *majzoom* مجزوم. When a verb is مجزوم and referring to the pronouns: انتِ – هما – هم we remove the ن from the verb. Look at the table below with verbs that have *sukoon* and come after لم : all of them are in negation, that is they mean "did not do."

Transliteration	Verb	Pronoun
Lam af'al	لم أفعل	أنا
Lam naf'al	لم نفعل	نحن
Lam taf'al	لم تفعل	أنتَ

Transliteration	Verb	Pronoun
Lam taf'alee	لم تفعلي	انتِ
Lam taf'ala	لم تفعلا	أنتما
Lam taf'loo	لم تفعلوا	أنتم

To negate the sentences with verbs in the past tense we just add ما before the verb. ما does not make any changes in the sentence, the same as لا. Some examples are:

Meaning	Would be	Example
Did not write the lesson	ما كتبت الدرس *ma katabto adars*	كتبت الدرس *katabto addars*
Did not study for the test	ما درست للامتحان *ma darasat lilimtihan*	درست للامتحان *darasat lilimtihan*

To negate sentences with future tense verbs, we add لن *lan* before the verb and remove the letter سـ or سوف. For example:

Meaning	Would be	Example
I will not meet	لن أقابل *lan oqabil*	سوف أقابل *sawfa oqabil*
I will not read	لن أقرأ *lan aqra'*	سأقرأ *sa'qra'*

To summarize negation:

1. To negate verbs in the continuous present tense use لا and the verb should have **dhamma** on it
2. To negate verbs in past tense use ما
3. To negate verbs in present tense use لم and the verb should have **sukoon**, that is no vowels
4. To negate verbs in future tense use لن and the verb should have **fat-ha**
5. To negate nominal sentences use ليس and conjugate it according to the subject

12.2. Practice (see Answer Key)

Negate the following sentences:

1. درست للامتحان في المكتبة أمس.
   _____
2. هم يسكنون في هذا البيت منذ شهر.
   _____
3. سيشاهد علاء المباراة غدا.
   _____
4. طبخت أختي طعاما لذيذا.
   _____
5. تحب أمي أن تشرب الشاي مع الافطار.
   _____
6. سنذهب الى السوق بعد قليل.
   _____
7. سوف يقابل علي أستاذه في الجامعة غدا.
   _____
8. انتقلت أختي الى البحرين.
   _____
9. زرنا لبنان قبل شهرين.
   _____
10. يجلسون في المقهى كل يوم.
    _____
11. هي تعرف من أنا.
    _____

12.3. Practice (see Answer Key)

Answer the following questions without using negation:

1. هل هذا أستاذك؟
   _____
2. هل درست لامتحان الكيمياء؟
   _____
3. هل ستخرج مع أصدقائك يوم الجمعة؟
   _____
4. هل تعرفين ماذا سنأكل اليوم؟
   _____
5. هل ستساعدوني في دراسة الكلمات؟
   _____
6. هل أمضيتم عطلة الأسبوع مع علي؟
   _____

12.4. Practice (see Answer Key)

How would you ask or respond to the following in Arabic?

1. Where can you get a newspaper. _____

2. Your friend said, "I'll visit you tonight!" _____

3. You want to buy a box of candy. _____

4. You are late to class. _____

5. You were busy working so you did not do your homewor.k

   _____

6. You need extra time to be ready. _____

12.5. Practice (see Answer Key)

Read the following conversation between Ali and Othman:

Masa' alkair. Good evening.	علي: مساء الخير
Masa'anoor ahlan wa sahlan. Good evening to you too. You are welcome.	عثمان: مساء النور. أهلا و سهلا
Ayna kont? Where were you ?	علي : أين كنت ؟
Konto fee almala'ab limatha? I was at the sports field, why?	عثمان: كنت في الملعب. لماذا؟
Tariq kana yabhatho ank. Tariq was looking for you.	علي : طارق كان يبحث عنك.
Limatha? Hal yoreed shaya'n? Why? Does he need anything?	عثمان: لماذا ؟ هل يريد شيئا؟
Yoreed an tadros ma'aho litosa'edaho fee maddat aloloom. He wants you to study with him to help him with his science.	علي : يريدك أن تدرس معة لتساعدة في مادة العلوم
Hasanan ayna howa al-an? Ok, where is he now?	عثمان: حسنا. أين هو الآن؟
Howa fee almaktabah. He's at the library.	علي: هو في المكتبة

Conversation *(continued)*

Sa'ath-hab ila almaktaba, hal toreed an tadros ma'ana? OK, I will go to the library. Do you want to study with us?	عثمان: سأذهب الى المكتبة. هل تريد أن تدرس معنا؟
La, oreed an ath-hab ila almat'am ana ja'e'. I want to go to the restaurant, I am hungry.	علي: لا أريد أن أذهب الى المطعم. أنا جائع
Taal ma'ee ila almatabah nadros qaleelan wa nohil alwajib thomma nath-hab ma'an ila almata'am. Come with me to the library, study for a while, do the homework then go to the restaurant.	عثمان: تعال معي الى المكتبة ندرس قليلا و نحل الواجب ثم نذهب معا الى المطعم.
Ana ja'e jidan wa oreed an aakol awalan thomma adros. I am very hungry, I want to eat first then study.	علي: أنا جائع جدا و أريد أن آكل أولا ثم أدرس
Hasanan taal linokgber tariq thomma nath-hab ila almata'm. Ok, lets go and tell Tariq then go to the restaurant.	عثمان: حسنا . تعال لنخبر طارق ثم نذهب الى المطعم
Fikrah jayyeda, haya bina. Good idea, let's go.	علي : فكرة جيدة. هيا بنا

Now answer the following questions:

1. أين كان عثمان؟ _____

2. من يبحث عن عثمان؟ _____

3. ماذا يريد طارق؟ _____

4. أين سيدرس عثمان و طارق؟ _____

5. أين يريد علي أن يذهب؟ _____

12.6. Practice (see Answer Key)

Please change into plural as in the example:

صحفيين / صحفيات	صحفي		مدرس
	محام		مهندس
	فنان		نجار
	سائق		معلم
	مساعد		مدير
	مصمم		

12.7. Practice (see Answer Key)

Connect the related words by writing the numbers in the parentheses:

شركة ( )		بداية	1.
رجل ( )		يشرب	2.
الساعة العاشرة مساء ( )		يطبخ	3.
الدجاج مع الأرز ( )		شارب	4.
عصير ليمون ( )		ينام	5.
فستان ( )		الجمعة و السبت	6.
الخامسة الا الربع ( )		قميص	7.
عطلة نهاية الأسبوع ( )		الساعة	8.
نهاية ( )		يرفض	9.
يوافق ( )		موظف	10.

Reflection

1. In this Lesson I learned: _____

2. I have some trouble with: _____

3. I need to learn more about: _____

الوحدة الثالثة عشرة
The Effect of Islam on Arabic Culture
أثر الاسلام على العادات العربية
Athar alislam ala al'adat ala'rabiyyah

Objectives:

1. Weather and Nature
2. Grammar: Past, Present and Future Tense
3. Arabs and Religious Life
4. Reading

Vocabulary

Meaning	Transliteration	Plural	Transliteration	Word
Remember	–	–	*Tathakar/ yatathakar*	تَذَكَّرَ / يَتَذَكَّرْ
Opinion	–	–	*Ra'y*	رَأْي
In your opinion	–	–	*Fee ra'yik*	في رَأْيِكْ
Building	*Imarat*	عِمارَاتْ	*Imara*	عِمارة
Floor (in a building or hotel)	*Tawabiq*	طَوابِقْ	*Tabiq*	طابِقْ
Building	*Mabani*	مَبـاني	*Mabna*	مَبْنى
Hotel	*Fanadiq*	فَنادِقْ	*Fondoq*	فُنْدُقْ
Park	*Hada'iq*	حَدائِقْ	*Hadiqa*	حَديقة
Consist	–	–	*Takkawana* (present tense) / *yatakawan* (past)	تَكوَّنَ / يَتَكَوَّنْ
Move	–	–	*Intaqala/ yantaqil*	انتَقَلَ / يَنْتَقِلْ

Meaning	Transliteration	Plural	Transliteration	Word
Transfer/Move	–	–	*Naqala/yanqil*	نَقَلَ / يَنْقِلْ
Suppose/Guess	–	–	*Thanna/yathon*	ظنّ / يَظُنْ
Graduate	–	–	*Takharraja/yatakharraj*	تخَرَّجَ / يَتَخَرَّجْ
Think	–	–	*Fakkara/yofakir*	فَكَّرَ / يُفَكِّرْ
Always	–	–	*Da'man*	دائِماً
Empty	–	–	*Farigh*	فارِغْ
Full	–	–	*Malee'*	مَليىْء
Stay	–	–	*Aqama/ yoqeem*	أقام/ يُقيمْ
Achieve	–	–	*Haqaqa/ yohaqiq*	حَقَّق/ يُحَقِّقْ
Several	–	–	*Idda*	عِدّة
Wrong	–	–	*Khati'*	خاطِىْء
Correct, true	–	–	*Sahih*	صَحيحْ
In fact, actually	–	–	*Fi alhaqiqa*	في الحَقيقة
Information	*Ma'loomat*	مَعْلومات	*Ma'looma*	مَعْلومة
As for…	–	–	*Belnisbati lee*	بِالنِسْبةِ لِـ
Horse	–	–	*Hisan*	حِصانْ
Camel	–	–	*Jamal*	جَمَلْ
Soda	–	–	*Soda*	صودا
Hobby	*Hiwayart*	هِوايات	*Hiwayah*	هِواية
Take a picture	–	–	*Sawwara/ yossawer*	صوّرْ/ يُصَوِّر

Meaning	Transliteration	Plural	Transliteration	Word
Ride	–	–	*Rakiba/yarkab*	رَكَبَ / يَرْكَبُ
Leisure	–	–	*Faragh*	فَراغْ
Authority	–	–	*assoltah*	السُّلْطة

Religious Life

As explained earlier, regional variations exist in the Arab world. Islamic philosophies and interpretations change gradually from generation to generation and from one country to another, but there are some common beliefs shared among all. For Arabs, a religious affiliation is an essential part of life. Arabs respect other religious groups and practices but do not appreciate atheists or agnostics.

Arabs tend to make their religious identity public by means of a head scarf and modest clothing for women. Additionally, almost all Arabs decorate their buildings, houses, cars and offices with ornaments and pendants inscribed with Qur'anic verses. They wear jewelry that has Qur'anic verses or with the word "Allah" engraved on it. It is common to see Arabs wearing necklaces holding miniature Qur'ans or hanging them in their cars. Businesses and residential buildings have the words "This is from Allah," "In the name of Allah" or "*Masha Allah*" written in Arabic at the entrance. Even formal letters have the words "*Bismillah ArRahman Ar-Rahim*," meaning "In the Name of Allah the Most Merciful, Most Compassionate" printed at the top of it, to symbolize that we start everything with the name of Allah. The same term is used at the beginning of speeches or when writing letters to friends and family. Additionally, the term is used at the beginning of a meal, starting a journey, going to bed or starting any task.

Another common term used by all Arabs, both Muslims and non-Muslims, is "*Inshallah*," meaning "If God wills" or "God willing." It is used to discuss future events and to respond to requests. Instead of a clear yes, an Arab might say "*Inshallah*." It is also used to indicate "Let me think about it" or to deflect additional requests. Sometimes and at home environment, parents might use "*Inshallah*," to make their children stop asking for something.

Arabs also respond first with *alhamdulillah*, meaning "thanks for Allah," when they are asked, "How are you?" The "*alhamdulillah*" precedes the rest of the response that might be news or complaints. In general, Arabs believe that humans must worship Allah and follow His orders. Yet this does not mean that all Arabs are religious. Some follow Allah's orders while others do not as the case in all religions.

Belief in Destiny

One common belief is "fate," or **qadar** in Arabic. Arabs believe that what happens in the world is controlled by Allah rather than by human beings or natural forces. They believe in the power of Allah and his authority over all things. They also believe everything that happens in the world is related to our behavior and is a consequence of our deeds; Arabs believe that our actions have a metaphysical effect on everything in the world. What we do is reflected on us. For example, natural disasters, earthquakes and volcanoes are not seen as meteorological or geological occurrences, but rather because of human behaviors. Some Westerners might view this as old-fashioned, superstitious, or even ignorant because they cannot relate to the Arab world view. Arabs think that these disasters happen because of our sins and straying from Allah's orders. At the same time, when good things happen, such as rain when we need it, it is because we humans did something good and rain is a gift for us from Allah. This perception is applied to almost all events, whether related to nature or to regular daily events. If one's car breaks down on the way to school, work or any other destination, it is because that person did something wrong. Arabs feel that Allah is watching everyone's actions, and people will be punished or rewarded for their actions here in this life as well as in the hereafter. This is not to say, Arabs do not believe in science or environmental occurrences, they believe it happened because humans are doing something wrong and at the same time, they accept its scientific factors.

Dependency on God often makes reactions to events much easier. For example, in the case of a death in the family, Arabs feel this is the will of Allah and they might not try to learn about the cause of death. Therefore, it is customary to bury the dead at the same day or the next day at the most.

As part of believing in destiny, when a woman gets pregnant, it is a gift from Allah, and every child comes with his own livelihood. Abortion after forty days of pregnancy is prohibited in Islam so it is not an option. Muslims believe that after forty days in the mother's womb the child is given a soul, so miscarriages are forbidden and are considered as killing a soul. Therefore, miscarriage is not a frequent practice in the Arab world. Hence, children are never considered a financial burden on the family.

Nevertheless, some Arabs strive for good behavior in their daily lives because they fear Allah's punishment. At the same time, others deviate completely from Islamic behavior and do whatever they please.

Death

Arabs view death as a family and community occasion requiring care and support from all family members and the larger community. When a person dies, Arab tradition encourages a quick burial with respect and dignity in a ritual called **janaza**. For Arabs, death means the person's soul is sent to the afterlife for judgement. People present at the time of death encourage the dying person to testify to their faith and recite verses from the Qur'an beside him. There is no need to call a cleric to perform these tasks. After death, a certified man for dead males and a certified woman for dead females cleans the body and wraps it in one piece of white cloth covering all the body. The white cloth represents the belief that all people are equal, coming into the world with no clothes and leaving with a simple white rag. It does not matter how rich or poor a person was in his life; all that counts are his actions and deeds.

Janaza also involves visitation of family and close friends, prayer and unfettered expression of feelings and emotion. The body is taken to a cemetery for burial as soon as possible rather than waiting for several days, as is often customary in the United States. In addition, Arabs usually refuse autopsies unless necessary, because they consider autopsies to be disrespectful to the dead, and, regardless, death is the will of Allah. Sometimes, if an Arab immigrant dies in a Western country, his family may prefer him to be buried in his country of origin. In this case, they would permit embalming to be done so they can fly the body overseas for burial; however, cosmetic preparations are not accepted.

The *janaza* prayer is announced to family, friends and community members. People are encouraged to attend a prayer and go to cemetery to attend the burial. Usually, people from the community would go and visit the closest family member for three days after the burial. Close friends would provide food for the family and their visitors and spend almost all their time with the sad family trying to comfort them. After three days, people would stop their visitation, but close friends and family members keep visiting for a while.

The death of parents with small children is taken very seriously. The oldest adult brother or closest family member of the deceased takes full responsibility for the children. No legal papers or documentations are required. If the father dies, family members ensure the well-being of the survivors. For example, my father was the oldest of seven brothers. After the death of my grandfather, my father and the second-oldest brother were responsible for their mother and other brothers. They supported them financially and paid for their housing, daily expenses and even for university educations in different countries including Lebanon, Egypt, Turkey and Jordan. If the mother dies, then the paternal grandmother takes care of the children or the father marries someone who will help him take care of the children.

Verbs in Present Tense:
In Arabic, verbs are usually sited in the past tense because it is the simplest form of verbs. Therefore, to conjugate a verb in present or future we add suffix, prefix or both to the verb in the past tense to represent the person we are talking about, as explained earlier.

Present tense verbs are verbs that describe actions that are not complete yet, but in the process. Verbs in the present tense are formed by adding a prefix, suffix or both. For example, look at the conjugation of the verb (write) كتب , I wrote the prefixed and suffixed that apply to all verbs to make it easier for you

Prefix, suffix or both	Pronoun	Verb
أ ـــــ	أنا	أكتب
ـن ـــــ	نحن	نكتب
ـت ـــــ	أنتَ	تكتب
ـت ـــــ ين	انتِ	تكتبين
ـت ـــــ ان	أنتما	تكتبان
ـت ـــــ ون	أنتم	تكتبون

Prefix, suffix or both	Pronoun	Verb
يـ ـــــ	هو	يكتب
ـت ـــــ	هي	تكتب
يـ ـــــ ان	هما (M)	يكتبان
ـت ـــــ ان	هما (F)	تكتبان
يـ ـــــ ون	هم	يكتبون

Verbs in past tense:

As you know, they are verbs describing actions that are completed or happened in the past. Unlike the present tense, only the end of the verb changes depending on who did the action. Look at the conjugation of this verb تذكر (remember)

Suffix added	Conjugation of the verb	Pronoun
تُ ـــــ	تذكرتُ	أنا
نا ـــــ	تذكرنا	نحن
تَ ـــــ	تذكرتَ	أنتَ
ت ـــــ	تذكرتِ	أنت
تما ـــــ	تذكرتما	أنتما
تم ـــــ	تذكرتم	أنتم

Suffix added	Conjugation of the verb	Pronoun
ـــــ	تذكرَ	هو
تِ ـــــ	تذكرت	هي
ا ـــــ	تذكرا	هما (M)
تا ـــــ	تذكرتا	هما (F)
وا ـــــ	تذكروا	هم

13.1. Practice (see Answer Key)

Here is a list of verbs you studied in the past tense. Conjugate them and keep them handy to use when needed:

Future Tense	Present Tense	Transliteration	Past tense	Meaning
		Shariba	شرب	Drank
		Dakhala	دخل	Entered
		Kharaja	خرج	Got out
		Tabakha	طبخ	Cooked
		Fa'ala	فعل	Did
		Rasama	رسم	Drew
		Shahada	شاهد	Watched
		Thahaba	ذهب	Went
		Akala	أكل	Ate
		Amila	عمل	Did
		A'rafa	عرف	Knew
		Qara'	قرأ	Read
		Darasa	درس	Studied
		Sakana	سكن	Inhabited
		Takkalama	تكلم	Spoke
		Samia'	سمع	Heard
		Sa'ada	ساعد	Helped
		Ista'jara	أستأجر	Rented
		ajjara	أجر	Rented someone

13.2. Practice   (see Answer Key)

How would you ask the following in Arabic?

1. Where can I rent a car? _____

2. What is the first word you learned in Arabic? _____

3. Do you like your school? Why? _____

4. What is your favorite hobby? _____

5. What was the most beautiful place you visited? _____

6. In your opinion, which is better: to buy a house or rent an apartment?

_____

13.3. Practice   (see Answer Key)

Conjugate the verb in parentheses to fit in the sentence:

1. أريد أن (غيّر) _____ ملابسي.

2. كان عندي واجبات كثيرة لذلك (تأخر) _____ عن الموعد.

3. هما لم (حقق) _____ كل ما يريدان.

4. أين (أقام) _____ ايمان؟ ماذا (عمل) _____؟

5. أمل هل (أحب) _____ أن (شاهد) _____ فيلم عربي الآن؟

6. بدأنا (شعر) _____ بالراحة بعد عمل يوم طويل.

7. هذا كتاب مهم و يجب أن (قرأ) _____ معا.

8. هم (زار) _____ أماكم كثيرة و جميلة في سوريا.

9. هما (جلس) _____ في هذا المقهى كل يوم.

10. أمي (أراد) _____ أن ترجع الى العمل.

11. هل (نام) _____ قبل الساعة التاسعة كل يوم يا أولاد؟

13.4. Practice (see Answer Key)

Underline the word that does not belong to the group:

1. راديو – كمبيوتر – أحمد – تلفزيون
2. باب – شباك – عشرة – حائط
3. أب – ايمان – عم – خال
4. معلمة – موظفة – اسم – دكتورة
5. مصر – الامارات – جامعة – قطر
6. الأربعاء – وجه – شعر – عين
7. أزرق – أبيض – أخي – أسود
8. شقة – بيت – عمارة - لوح

13.5. Practice (see Answer Key)

Reading:

هناك معلومة خاطئة عن العالم العربي و هي أن كل العالم العربي صحراء. في الحقيقة أن هناك بحار و أنهار ووديان و جبال و جزر بالاضافة الى الصحاري. مثلا هناك الخليج العربي في شرق الجزيرة العربية و تقع حوله دول الخليج العربي السبعة. و هماك خليج العقبة في جنوب الأردن و البحر الأحمر بين مصر و السعودية و البحر الأبيض المتوسط في بلاد الشام و هو متصل بالمحيط الأطلسي. و البحر العربي يقع في جنوب شرق شبه الجزيرة العربية و فيه مضيق هرمز و خليج عُمان. قناة السويس في مصر و تربط بين البحر الأحمر و البحر الأبيض المتوسط.

أما بالنسبة للأنهار فهناك نهر النيل في مصر و السودان و هو أطول نهر في العالم و نهر دجلة و الفرات في العراق و نهر الأردن في الأردن.

هناك أيضا جزر في العالم العربي مثل البحرين و جزيرة سقطرة في خليج عدن و جزيرة مصيرة في البحر العربي.

و يوجد أيضا عدة جبال مشهورة مثل جبل الشيخ في لبنان و جبل عرفات في السعودية و جبل طارق بين المحيط الأطلسي و البحر الأبيض المتوسط.

و نعم توجد صحاري في العالم العربي مثل صحراء سيناء في مصر و الصحراء الكبرى في شمال أفريقيا و صحراء النفوذ في السعودية.

Now answer the following questions:

1. ما هي المعلومة الخاطئة عن العالم العربي؟

2. هل يوجد أنهار في العالم العربي؟

3. ما هو أطول نهر في العالم؟ أين يقع؟

4. اكتب أسماء ثلاثة جزر عربية

5. كم دولة تقع على الخليج العربي؟

Reflection

1. In this Lesson I learned: _____

2. I have some trouble with: _____

3. I need to learn more about: _____

الوحدة الرابعة عشرة
Sports in the Arab World
الرياضة في العالم العربي

Alriyadda fee ala'lam ala'rabi

Objectives:

1. Animals
2. Grammar
   • Imperative Verbs
   • Negation of Imperative
3. Culture: Sports in Arab Cities
4. Reading

Vocabulary

Meaning	Transliteration	Plural	Transliteration	Word
Play	–	–	*La'iba/ yala'b*	لَعبَ / يَلْعَبْ
Watch	–	–	*Shahada/ yoshahid*	شاهَدَ / يُشاهِدْ
Game/match	*Mobarayat*	مُبارَياتْ	*Mobarah*	مُباراة
Football	–	–	*Korat alqadam*	كُرةُ القَدَم
Basketball	–	–	*Korat assallah*	كُرةُ السَلّة
Volleyball	–	–	*Korat atta'rah*	كُرةُ الطائِرة
Hand ball	–	–	*Korat alyad*	كُرةُ اليَدْ
Tennis	–	–	*Korat attawelah*	كُرةُ الطاوِلة
Team	–	–	*Fareeq*	فَريقْ
Win	–	–	*Rabiha/ yarbah*	رَبِح / يَرْبَحْ

Meaning	Transliteration	Plural	Transliteration	Word
Lose	–	–	*Khasira/yakhsar*	خَسَرَ / يَخْسَرْ
Train	–	–	*Taddaraba/ yatadarrab*	تَدَرَّب / يَتَدَرَّب
Trainer	–	–	*Moddarib*	مُدَرِّبْ
Ball	*Korat*	كُراتْ	*Korah*	كُرة
Bat	*Madharib*	مَضارِبْ	*Madhrab*	مَضْرَبْ
Dance	–	–	*Raqasa/yarqos*	رَقْصْ / يرقُص
Dancing	–	–	*Arraqs*	الرَقْصْ
Swim	–	–	*Sabiha/yasbah*	سَبَحَ / يَسْبَحْ
Swimming	–	–	*assibaha*	السِباحة
Boxer	–	–	*Molakim*	مُلاكِمْ
Boxing	–	–	*Molakamah*	مُلاكَمة
Decide	–	–	*Qarrara/yoqarrir*	قَرَّرْ / يُقَرِر
Spent	–	–	*Qadha/yaqdhi*	قَضى / يَقضي
Important	–	–	*Mohim*	مُهْمْ
Airplane	*Ta'rat*	طَائِراتْ	*Ta'rah*	طائِرة
Ship	*Sofon*	سُفُنْ	*Safeenah*	سَفِينة
Cheap	–	–	*Rakhees*	رَخِيصْ
Expensive	–	–	*Ghali*	غالِي
Show	–	–	*Isti'radh*	إِسْتِعْراضْ
Walk	–	–	*Sara/yaseer*	سارَ/ يَسِير

Meaning	Transliteration	Plural	Transliteration	Word
Respect	–	–	*Ihtarama/yahtarim*	احْتَرَمَ / يَحْتَرِمْ
Close	–	–	*Aghlaqa/yoghliq*	أَغْلِقْ / يُغْلِق
Draw	–	–	*Rasama/yarsom*	رَسْمْ / يَرْسُمْ
Sent	–	–	*Arsala/yorsel*	أَرْسَلْ / يَرْسُلْ

Sports in the Arab World

Sports in the Arab world, as in all parts of the world, are an important aspect of society as they represent a source of entertainment, encouraging teamwork and discipline while, and at the same time, providing a good source of income for the players. In almost all Arab countries, international games are watched via satellite broadcast while people wear their team's or favorite player's jerseys.

Sports have gained a lot of attention in the Arab world. Looking back in history you will find many stories and legends regaridng sports. In the past, popular sports included hunting, falconry, camel and horse racing, archery and sailing. In one of the Prophet Mohammed's sayings, he encouraged his followers to teach their children "swimming, archery and horse-riding." Additionally, Islamic scholars encouraged people to exercise due to its benefits for the mind and body. One example is Abu Hamid Al-Ghazali (1058-1111) who was a prominent Islamic theologian, jurist, and mystical thinker (*Fates*, 1994:26). Some examples of these traditional sports that are still practiced are:

> Fantasia, a combination of horse riding and shooting, still practiced in the *Maghreb*; Falcon hunting, traditional sailing, and camel racing, still popular in the Arabian Peninsula; Bullfighting in Oman and the UAE; traditional wrestling, known as *Gourrara* in Morocco, and *Taabaz* or *Debli* in Algeria; *Kharbaga, kharbga* (in the *Maghreb*), games of strategy that use a square checkerboard, known also as "*Seega*" or "*siga*" in Egypt.[1]

The first Formula One World Championship racing event was held in Bahrain in 2004 and sponsored by Gulf Air.

As for current sports, Egypt was the first Arab country to participate in international competitions. In 1934, Egypt participated in the FIFA World Cup, the first African country to do so. Al-Ahly and Zamalek are popular soccer teams in Egypt which are very well known throughout the Arab world. The Moroccan team won the African Cup of Nations in 1976 and also qualified four times, in 1970, 1986, 1994 and 1998, for the FIFA World Cup.

---

1 Festivals for the promotion of traditional games are organized in Morocco: http://www.mjs.gov.ma/fr/Page-32/sauvegarde--des-jeux--sportifs-traditionnels

As for other Arab countries in North Africa, such as Tunisia, Morocco and Algeria, their participation in international sports started almost immediately after they gained independence from France. For example, Tunisia was liberated in 1956 and became a member of International Olympic Committee in 1957, Morocco joined in 1959 while Algeria became a member in 1964. Additionally, in 2010, the third Euro-Mediterranean Heritage Games was held in Tunisia.

Although, the most popular game in Arab countries is soccer, there are other sports that are thriving as well. No one can ignore the inspiring performance of Moroccan athletes in Track and Field such as Nawel Moutawakel, who was the first Muslim women to win a gold medal at the Olympics, Saïd Aouita, Nezha Bidouane, Kalid and Brahim Boulami, Khalid Skah, Hasna Benhassi and Hicham Al-Guerrouj.

In the Gulf region, many sports are held. For example, in 2006, the Asian Games competition was held in Doha, Qatar. Additionally, Qatar won the bid to host the FIFA World Cup in 2022 which is considered a historical win, not only for Qatar but the entire Gulf countries.

In United Arab Emirates there are several popular sport centers as in: Dubai Sport City and Zayed Sports City in Abu Dhabi. Despite the heat and humidity in UAE, it became a member of the International Ice Hockey Federation in 2001 and they were the first to participate in the International Ice Hockey Federation (IIHF) World Championship in Europe in 2009. As for Saudi Arabia, some members of the royal family are professional football players in Saudi Arabia team.

Imperatives:

As in other languages, there are four forms of Arabic verbs: past, present, future and imperative. As you know imperative is used for commanding or asking someone to do something. It is used with the second person as you should be talking to someone in front of you to ask him/her to do something. You can simply use the stem of the present tense verb, remove its prefix (ﺗـ or ﺑـ) and add ﺍ instead. There are five forms of imperatives depending on the person/persons you are addressing. Usually imperatives start with an *alif* ﺍ.

Look at the conjugation of the verbs "write" and "go" below

أنتن	أنتم	أنتما	أنتِ	أنتَ
اكتبن	اكتبوا	اكتبا	اكتبي	اكتب
Oktobna	oktoboo	Okyoba	Oktobee	Oktob
اذهبن	اذهبوا	اذهبا	اذهبي	اذهب
Ith-habna	Ith-habo	Ith-haba	Ith-habee	Ith-hab

14.1. Practice   (see Answer Key)

Ask the following groups of people to do the following:

1. Two people to sit down: _____

2. A man to write: _____

3. Two girls to study: _____

4. Mixed group of people to leave: _____

5. Group of girls to play: _____

Negating Imperatives

Negating imperatives is done by just using لا before the imperative verb, and in this situation it would mean "do not." When using لا the verb should be in present tense. For example, we say: لا تذهب *la that-hab* – لا تجلس *la tajlis*.

Verbs after لا should have *sukoon* on them, that is they are not vowelled.

14.2. Practice   (see Answer Key)

How do you say this in Arabic?

1. Ask a woman not to forget her purse: _____

2. Tell your female friend not to give your phone number to Ali: _____

3. Tell students there is no class today: _____

4. Tell a boy not to throw his shoes: _____

5. Ask your female friends not to run and slow down: _____

14.3. Practice   (see Answer Key)

Conjugate the verb in parentheses into the imperative form:

1. _____ بتحضير العشاء بعد مشاهدة الفيلم. (بدأ)

2. عندك عمل كثير غدا لذلك _____ مبكرا. (نام)

3. لا _____ الى السوق الآن يا امل. (ذهب)

4. أنت و صديقك _____ سيارة جديدة من هذا المحل! (اشترى)

5. _____ الشاي مع قليل من السكر يا أولاد. (شرب)

14.4. Practice   (see Answer Key)

Conjugate the verb in parentheses using negation into the imperative form:

1. _____ الى المطعم لأنكم مشغولين. (ذهب)

2. _____ الى شقة أكبر يا أحمد و علي. (انتقل)

3. _____ السلطة يا سعاد! (أكل)

4. _____ الصودا قبل طعام الغداء يا أبنائي. (شرب)

5. _____ في النهر يا بنات لأن الماء بارد جدا الآن. (سبح)

14.5. Practice   (see Answer Key)

Choose the correct word in parentheses:

1. (يوم – أيام – يوما) الجمعة و السبت هما عطلة نهاية الأسبوع في العالم العربي.

2. هل (تريد – تريدين – أرادت) أن تشربي القهوة الآن يا أمل.

3. عيونه (أخضر – خضراء) مثل أبيه.

4. أمل و هدى (قررا – قررتا – قرروا) أن يسكنان في شقة واحدة معا.

5. جميعهم (عاد – عادا – عادوا) الى البيت مبكرين أمس.

14.6. Practice (see Answer Key)

Negate using ليس

1. هذا الكتاب _____ مهما.

2. السيارة _____ أسرع من الطائرة.

3. الفستان و الحقيبة _____ رخيصان و لكنها تريدهما.

4. جامعتنا _____ أقدم جامعة و لكنها أفضل جامعة.

5. الجبال _____ عالية و لكنها جميلة.

14.7. Practice (see Answer Key)

Conjugate the verbs in parentheses to fit the sentences:

1. وقف الاعبين في الملعب و (بدأ) _____ التمرينات الرياضية.

2. في كرة القدم (ربح) _____ فريق جامعتنا على كل الجامعات.

3. بدأت المباراة باستعراض الاعبين الذين (سار) _____ بملابسهم الرياضية.

4. بعد أن دخل المدرب جميع الاعبين (وقف) _____ احتراما له.

5. (يصبح) مدرسا بعد أن يتخرج من الجامعة.

6. طلب أحمد و علي من الأستاذ أن (ساعد) في عمل الواجب.

7. هل (أغلق) _____ الباب بعد أن خرجت من البيت.

8. (استمع) _____ الى كلامي يا أولادي.

9. الطالبان (يريد) _____ وقتا أطول للدراسة.

10. الصديقتان (شاهد) _____ الكثير من الأماكن الجميلة في المدينة.

14.8. Practice (see Answer Key)

Connect the related phrases by adding numbers in the parentheses:

1. اقرأوا   ( ) عن الأسئلة

2. استمع الى   ( ) صورة لشاطئ البحر

3. أجب   ( ) الكتاب صفحة 50-70

4.	ارسم	( ) رسالة في البريد
5.	ارسل	( ) التلفون داخل الفصل
6.	لا تستعمل	( ) كلاما الأستاذ

Reading:

14.9. Practice (see Answer Key)

Read the following conversation between friends:

جلس الأصدقاء في النادي و طلبوا الشاي الساخن و بدأوا يتحدثون عن عطلة نهاية الأسبوع.

قال أحمد: كان عندي تدريب لمباراة كرة القدم فقضيت يوم الجمعة كلة في النادي نتدرب

قال محمد: أنا شاهدت فيلما مع أسرتي في السينما ثم ذهبنا الى العشاء في مطعم صيني. كان الفيلم جميلا و الطعام لذيذا جدا.

قال علي: في كل يوم جمعة نذهب الى بيت جدي حيث تجتمع العائلة. هناك نجلس مع أعمامي و أخوالي و أبناؤهم و نتحدث عما حدث معنا خلال الأسبوع ثم نجلس أنا و أبناء عمتي نلعب على الكمبيوتر

قال جمال: أنا لعبت مع أولاد الجيران كرة القدم و قد فاز فريقنا على الفريق الآخر لذلك فقد دعونا الى مطعم قريب و أكلنا طعام الغداء و تعرفنا على أفراد الفريق الآخر و اتفقنا أن نلتقي و نتدرب مرة أخرى .

Answer the following:

2.	أين قضى أحمد يوم الجمعة؟	1.	أين جلس الأصدقاء؟
4.	ماذا فعل جمال؟	3.	أين أكل محمد طعام العشاء؟

14.10. Practice   (see Answer Key)

The teacher entered the class and gave the following instructions to students. Translate these in-structions into Arabic using the imperative form:

1. Come to class on time. _____

2. Put your phone in your bag. _____

3. Don't talk to students beside you. _____

4. Work on your assignment alone. _____

5. Don't forget to write the date on your paper. _____

Reflection

1. In this Lesson I learned: _____

2. I have some trouble with: _____

3. I need to learn more about: _____

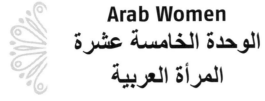

Arab Women
الوحدة الخامسة عشرة
المرأة العربية
Almar'a al'arabiyyah

Objectives:
1. Shopping in Arab World
2. Grammar: Nouns Used as Adjectives (*idafa* and *modaf ileeh*)
3. Culture: Status of Arab Woman
4. Reading

🔊 Vocabulary

Meaning	Transliteration	Plural	Transliteration	Word
Meet	–	–	*Qabala/yoqabil*	قَابَلْ/يُقابل
Driver	–	–	*Sa-iq*	سائِقْ
A sleep	–	–	*Nawm*	نَوْمْ
Neighbor	*Jeeran*	جيران	*Jar/jarrah*	جارْ/جارة
Still	–	–	*Ma zala*	ما زال
Video	–	–	*Vidyoo*	فيدْيو
Cinema	–	–	*Sinema*	سينما
Trip	*Rihlat*	رحلات	*Rihla*	رِحْلة
Leave	–	–	*Ghadara/ yoghader*	غَادَرْ/يُغادر
Walking	–	–	*Mashitan*	ماشِياً

Meaning	Transliteration	Plural	Transliteration	Word
Passenger	*Rokkab*	رُكّاب	*Rakeb*	راكب
Touristic	–	–	*Siyahi*	سِياحيْ
Monument / historical structures	*Athar*	آثارْ	*Athar*	أَثَر
Lose	–	–	*Faqada/yafqid*	فَقَدْ/ يفقد
Find	–	–	*Wajada/yajid*	وَجَدْ/يَجد
Call	–	–	*Itasala/yatasil*	إتَّصَلْ/ يتصل
Send	–	–	*Arsala/yorsel*	أَرسَلَ/ يُرْسِلْ
Receive	–	–	*Istalama/ yastalim*	استَلَمَ/يَسْتَلِمْ
Letter	–	–	*Risalah*	رِسالة
Police	–	–	*Ashortah*	الشُرْطة
Center	*Marakiz*	مراكز	*Markaz*	مَرْكَزْ
Post office	*Makatib albareed*	مكاتب البريد	*Maktab albareed*	مَكْتَبُ البَريدْ
Gas station	*Mahataat albanzeen*	محطات البنزين	*Mahatat albanzeen*	مَحَطّةُ البِنْزين
Train station	*Mahataat alqitar*	محطات القطار	*Mahatat alqitar*	مَحَطّةُ القِطارْ
Ticket	*Tathaker*	تَذاكِرْ	*Tathkirah*	تَذْكِرة

Meaning	Transliteration	Plural	Transliteration	Word
Travel agency	*Makateb/ safariyyat*	مكاتب سفريات	*Maktab safariyyat*	مَكْتَبْ سَفَرِيّاتْ
Project	*Masharee'*	مشاريع	*Mashroo'*	مَشْروعْ
Continue	–	–	*Istamara/ yastamer*	إِسْتَمَرَّ/ يَسْتَمِرْ
Period	–	–	*Moddah*	مُدَّة
Type	*Anwa'*	أَنْواعْ	*Naw'*	نَوْعْ
Pain	*Aalaam*	آلام	*Alam*	أَلَمْ
Practice	–	–	*Marasa/ yomares*	مارَسَ/ يُمارِسْ
Fat	*Dohoon*	دُهونْ	*Dihn*	دِهْنْ
To increase	–	–	*Kath-thara/ yokther*	كَثَّرَ/ يُكْثِرْ

Arab Women and Veiling

Arabs use the word *hijab* to refer to the veil that many Muslim women wear. The exact meaning of the word *hijab* is a garment or curtain that separates things. The *hijab* is a scarf covering the hair, neck and sometimes the shoulders, leaving the face uncovered, depending on how large a scarf the woman chooses or the style she prefers. This modest apparel covers the hair, trunk and limbs, but not necessarily the face.

Most Muslim scholars understand Islamic veiling as covering the entire body except for the face and hands (*Stowasser*, 1993, p. 17[1]). There is also the *niqab*, which is a small piece of cloth that women may use in addition to the *hijab* to cover their faces, leaving an opening for the eyes.

Yet head coverings are not exclusive to Islamic tradition. Throughout history, women have covered their hair for several reasons, including religious beliefs, a mark of social status, cultural traditions or fashion statements. The first records of veiling go back to the thirteenth century

---

1 Stowasser, B., 1993, "Women's issue in Modern Islamic Thought," in Arab Women: Old Boundaries, New Frontiers, ed. Judith E. Tucker, Indiana University Press: Bloomington and Indianapolis, 1993, p. 17

BC in Assyria. To differentiate themselves from women of a lower social status, noblewomen began to cover their hair (*Cross-Cultural Head Coverings*, p. 1[2]). Veiling was practiced in Mesopotamia, Greece, ancient Persia, and pre-Islamic Arabia (*Scarce*, 1975, p. 5-6). In medieval times, to wear a veil meant "to become a nun" or "to enter a convent" (*Oxford English Dictionary* 2, 1971, p. 3599). In Islam, Judaism and Christianity, covering women's hair was associated with modesty and respectability. This is clear in Judaism and Christianity, in that all representations of Mary, the mother of Jesus, show her wearing a head covering and a long, loose dress. Christian women used to cover their hair in public (*Yohannan*, 2011[3]), and it is still quite common to see elderly non-Muslim women in Europe wearing headscarves, especially in Russia.

Today, head or hair coverings for religious reasons are most frequently associated with Muslim women, Catholic nuns, and Amish and Mennonite women. In addition, some Jewish sects require married women to wear scarves as a sign of modesty. These scarves are known as **tichels** or snoods (*Elisabet*, 1997[4]). Currently, married women in some Near East countries wear a veil as an announcement that their beauty and magnetism are only for their husbands and they will not expose themselves to other men, which is precisely why Muslim women wear veils.

In the Qur'an, Allah told the Prophet: "O Prophet, tell your wives, your daughters, and the womenfolk of the believers to draw their **hijab** close about them. That is most appropriate so that they be recognized and not be molested. God is forgiving and merciful" (33:59). Some might say that this order is for the Prophet's wives only, but that is not the case. For Muslims, all orders and practices of the Prophet apply to all Muslims to imitate and follow. In another chapter of the Qur'an, Allah says: "Tell the female believers that they should lower their gaze, guard their chastity, to reveal of their adornments only that which is apparent, and to cast their veils over their bosoms" (24:31). This is a clear admonishment for Muslim women to practice modesty. Muslim or not, however, because of the Islamic influence in Arab countries, many but not all Arab women wear modest clothing, whether European or traditional, when going out in public.

Of course, not all Arab women cover their hair, but veiling is widespread in all Arab countries. The difference lies in the degree of how much of her body a woman should cover. In all Arab countries, one can see women wearing the **abaya** with their heads and faces covered, walking side-by-side with women wearing tight, colored dresses or pants. Some restrictions exist in Saudi Arabia and in rural areas, but there is a vast array of veils with assorted colors and styles in use by women.

---

2 Cross-Cultural Head Coverings, Created by the Center for South Asian & Middle Eastern Studies, University of Illinois at Urbana-Champaign Retrieved from: http://www.csames.illinois.edu/documents/outreach/Cross-Culture_Head_Coverings.pdf

3 Yohannan, K., 2011, Head Coverings, What the Bible Teaches about Head Coverings for Women, Believers Church Publications

4 Elisabet, 1997, On Account of the Angels: Why I Cover My Head, Orthodox Christian Information Center, From the Spring 1997 issue of The Handmaiden, Conciliar Press, retrieved from: http://orthodoxinfo.com/praxis/head-coverings.aspx

Throughout the second half of the nineteenth century, the process of forsaking the veil in the Arab world started first with Christian and Jewish Arab women due to a strong European influence. In Beirut in 1890, Christian women had abandoned the veil (*Baer*, 1964, p. 42[5]); however, the abandonment of the hijab by Muslim women started much later. The earliest occurrences of Muslim women abandoning the *hijab* took place in Turkey, which is not an Arab country. In the nineteenth century, upper-class women started to wear European-inspired clothing as a sign of modernization. Initially they wore European styles indoors while keeping the face covering when outdoors. Later, they started to wear thin, transparent face veils exposing their features (*Micklewright*, 1986, p. 217[6]). The second step in abandoning the *hijab* took place in the early twentieth century, with some Turkish women wearing "European-style face veils that were attached to large European-style women's hats" (*Norton*, 1997, p. 155[7]). Following that, Egyptian women were the first Arab women to forsake the *hijab*. In the middle of the twentieth century, many Muslim women stopped wearing the *hijab*, which invited Oxford historian Albert Hourani to publish an article in the UNESCO *Courier* titled "The Vanishing Veil a Challenge to the Old Order" in 1956. In his article, he described the disappearing *hijab* in many Arab countries (*Hourani*, 1956, p. 35-37[8]). However, there is another phenomenon taking place, which is the return of hijab or veiling in its different forms.

As an interesting side note, most of the time Western media describe the *hijab* using words *niqab* or *burqa*. Both *niqab* and *burqa* refer to an extra piece of cloth worn to cover the nose and mouth but keep the eyes uncovered. However, *burqa* is an Afghani word for a cloth that covers the whole body. Although it is a Muslim country, Afghanistan is not an Arab country, and the Afghani *burqa* is not an accurate term to describe the head covering used by Arab women.

Nouns Used as Adjectives—Idafa-modaf ileeh:

Idafa is a fundamental structure in Arabic. *Idafa* is the same as "annexation" in English. It is the ownership or possession. Simple *idafa* is when two nouns following each other while the second noun is identifying the first or explaining what it is. Usually the second noun is definite or proper noun. The first noun is called مضاف meaning "added" and the second is called مضاف اليه meaning "added to it."

5 Baer, G., 1964, Population and Society in the Arab East (Routledge and Kegan Paul: London, 1964), p. 42.
6 Micklewright, N., "Women's Dress in Nineteenth-Century Istanbul: Mirror of a Changing Society" (Ph. D. diss., University of Pennsylvania, 1986), p. 217.
7 Norton, J., 1997, "Faith and Fashion in Turkey," in Languages of Dress in the Middle East, ed. Nancy Lindisfarne-Tapper and Bruce Ingham, London, Curzon Press, 1997, pp. 155-157
8 Hourani, A., 1956, "The Vanishing Veil a Challenge to the Old Order." UUNISCO Courier, January 1956, 35-37.

Some examples are:

Meaning	Transliteration	Example
The niece	*Bint al-akh*	بنت الأخ
My niece	*Bint akhee*	بنت أخي
Students of the class	*Tollab assaf*	طلاب الصف
Students of my class	*Tollab saffee*	طلاب صفي
The book of my teacher	*Kitab mo'alimee*	كتاب معلمي

When the *idafa* is dual or plural then it loses the *na* in it as in: سيارتا الطالبين or غرفتا المعلمين

You may realize that the construction of **Idafa** exists in English language too. Some examples are: cat food, post office, mail man, school bus or fire truck.

Simple *idafa* is when we have two nouns connected while complex *idafa* is when we have more than two nouns as in: *ibn a'm walidee* .... ابن عم والدي

Please note that the *ta marbuta* ة – ـة should be pronounced all the time when it appears in all the nouns in *idafa* except on the final noun of *idafa* as in: مدينة دمشق *Madinat Dimashq* – جامعة ولاية أريزونا *jame'at Wilayat arizona*

15.1. Practice (see Answer Key)

Translate the following using idafa. Please note that *idafa* defines the first noun:

1. The classroom windows are big. _____

2. The college of Science is close to my house. _____

3. He lost his car keys. _____

4. Ahmad's bicycle is in the parking lot. _____

5. The newspaper is on the teacher's desk. _____

15.2. Practice (see Answer Key)

Put a check mark beside the correct sentences and correct the wrong ones. Keep in mind the *idafa* and noun-adjectives agreement:

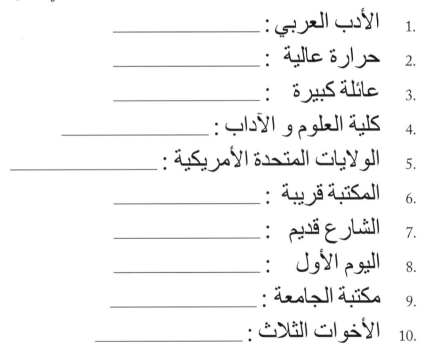

1. _____ الحاسوب القديم على الطاولة.

2. _____ الأستاذة عربية في المكتب.

3. _____ مكتب الجديد واسع.

4. _____ عند أخي سيارة القديمة.

5. _____ على الجدار صورة قديمة.

6. _____ المفاتيح صغيرة في الحقيبة

15.3. Practice (see Answer Key)

Write whether the following is *idafa* or noun and adjective:

1. الأدب العربي : _____

2. حرارة عالية : _____

3. عائلة كبيرة : _____

4. كلية العلوم و الآداب : _____

5. الولايات المتحدة الأمريكية : _____

6. المكتبة قريبة : _____

7. الشارع قديم : _____

8. اليوم الأول : _____

9. مكتبة الجامعة : _____

10. الأخوات الثلاث : _____

15.4. Practice (see Answer Key)

Write whether the following is *idafa* or noun and adjective:

1. هناك سيارات (كثيرة – قصيرة – أحمر) في الشارع.

2. هم (يحبون – يحب – أحب) الشوكولاتة كثيرا.

3. هي لا (تعرف – تعرفين – تعرفون) أين أجد المتحف.

4. (انا – أنت – نحن) نلعب الورق كل مساء.

5. سينتهي (الدرس – المباراة – الشتاء) الساعة الثالثة بعد الظهر.

6. سنتحدث معا الساعة الخامسة (بعد – قبل – الا) ربعا.

7. علي لا يحب الاستماع الى (الرياضة – الموسيقى – الدفتر).

8. أمي (تشرب – تشربين – شربت) القهوة مع جارتها كل يوم.

9. (حملت – حمل – تحماين) الطالبة حقيبتها و خرجت من الغرفة.

10. هم (يقرأ – يقرآن – يقرأون) الكتاب في المكتبة.

15.5. Practice (see Answer Key)

Here are some places in the Arab world. Identify the *idafa* ones and circle them:

2. جبل الشيخ		1. البحر الأحمر	
4. وادي النيل		3. نهر دجلة	
6. المحيط الأطلسي		5. الخليج العربي	
8. خليج العقبة		7. قارة أفريقيا	
10. العالم العربي		9. الصحراء الكبرى	

15.6. Practice (see Answer Key)

Using the new vocabulary in this lesson fill in the blanks:

مكتب البريد ـ محطة البنزين – الشرطة مركز – مكتب السفريات –
السوق ـ مكتب البريد

1. نشتري تذاكر السفر من _____

2. نملا السيارة بالبنزين من _____

3. نشتري الملابس من _____

4. نرسل الرسائل في _____

5. فقدت سيارتي و اتصلت في _____

15.7. Practice (see Answer Key)

Reading:

عمي أحمد عمره 65 سنة. يسكن هو و زوجته في بيت واسع من طابقين. في الطابق الأول يجد غرفة نوم واحدة ة غرفة الجلوس و غرفة السفرة و مطبخ كبير و حمام. و في الطابق الثاني يوجد ثلاث غرف نوم و حمامين و غرفة مكتب. تخرج أولاده و بناته من الجامعة و تزوجوا لذلك خرجوا من البيت.

تقول زوجة عمي أن البيت كبير و فارغ و تريد أن تنتقل الى بيت أصغر. لكن عمي لا يريد أن ينتقل و يقول سنؤجر غرفة أو غرفتين الى طلبة الجامعة. هم ما زالوا يفكرون في هذا الموضوع.

عمي و زوجته يحبون أن يطبخوا طعام العشاء معا و يجلسون و يتحدثون عن أبنائهم دائما. هم أيضا يحبون السفر و تصوير كل المناطق الجميلة التي يزورونها. عندهم مكتبة مليئة بالفيديوات التي فيها رحلاتهم.

Answer the following:

2. كم طابق في بيته؟   1. كم عمر عمي أحمد؟

4. لماذا خرج أولادة من البيت؟   3. كم غرفة في الطابق الثاني؟

5. ماذا يحب أن يفعل عمي و زوجته؟

15.8. Practice (see Answer Key)

Rearrange the following words to form meaningful sentences:

1. المشروع – سنة – سيبدأ – 2020

2. الفيلم – ساعتين – استمر – لمدة

3. عشرة – أيام – سيقضون – لبنان – في

4. الدواء – هذا – استعملي – و اشربي – كثيراً – ماءً

5. ألم - رأسي - عندي – في

6. الرياضة – هم – بجميع – يحبون – أنواعها

7. مدير – هو – شركة – يعمل – الكترونية

8. الخضار – و الفواكه – كلي – و لا – الدهون – تكثري – من

Reflection

1. In this Lesson I learned: _____

2. I have some trouble with: _____

3. I need to learn more about: _____

الوحدة السادسة عشر
Marriage in the Arab World
الزواج عند العرب
Azzawaj enda al'arab

Objectives:

1. Health Symptoms and General Medical Conditions
2. Grammar: *kana wa akhawatoha*
3. Culture: Marriage in the Arab World
4. Reading

Vocabulary

Meaning	Transliteration	Plural	Transliteration	Word
People	–	–	*Nas*	ناسْ
Yesterday	–	–	*Ams*	أَمْسْ
Tomorrow	–	–	*Ghadan*	غَداً
Day	*Ayam*	أيام	*Yawm*	يَوْمْ
Coming	–	–	*Qadim*	قادِمْ
Past	–	–	*Madhi*	ماضي
Present	–	–	*Hadher*	حاضر
Future	–	–	*Mostaqbal*	مستقبل
Airport	*Matarat*	مَطارات	*Matar*	مَطارْ
Sit	–	–	*Jalasa/ yajlis*	جَلَسَ/يَجْلِسْ
Arrive	–	–	*Wasala/ yasil*	وَصَلَ/يَصِلْ

Meaning	Transliteration	Plural	Transliteration	Word
Accident	*Hawadith*	حوادث	*Hadith*	حادِثْ
Cup	*Akwab*	أكواب	*Koob*	كوبْ
Pharmacy	–	–	*Saydaliyah*	صَيدَليّة
Medicine	–	–	*Dawa'*	دَواءْ
Sunstroke	–	–	*Dharbat shams*	ضَربةُ شَمْس
Cold	–	–	*Bard*	بَرْدْ
Flu	–	–	*Inflowanza*	إنْفِلْوَنْزا
Fever	–	–	*Homma*	حُمى
Blood pressure	–	–	*Dhaght addam*	ضَغطْ الدم
Diabetic	–	–	*Sokkari*	سُكّري
Allergy	–	–	*Hasasiyyah*	حَساسيّة
Headache	–	–	*Soda'*	صُداعْ
Sick	*Mardha*	مَرضى	*Mareedh*	مَريضْ
Disease	*Amradh*	أمراض	*Maradh*	مَرَضْ
Smoking	–	–	*Tad-kheen*	تَدْخينْ
Weight	–	–	*Wazn*	وَزْنْ
Pill	–	–	*Habbat dawa'*	حَبّةُ دَواءْ
Decrease	–	–	*Inkhifad*	إنْخِفاضْ
Suffering	–	–	*Mosab*	مُصابْ
Necessary	–	–	*Men allazim*	مِنْ اللازِمْ
Probably	–	–	*Men almohtamal*	مِنْ المحتمل

Meaning	Transliteration	Plural	Transliteration	Word
Stomach	–	–	*Batn*	بَطْن
Foot	–	–	*Qadam*	قَدَم
Fracture	–	–	*Kasr*	كَسْر
Transport	–	–	*Naql*	نَقْل

Marriage

One of the primary foundations of Arab society is marriage. From an early age, whenever a child does something good, it is customary to praise him with a wish for a happy married life and wish that parents live long enough to see their children's weddings and enjoy their grandchildren.

The age of marriage differs from one region to another. In the past, girls and boys married in their teenage years. However, now most parents encourage their children to finish their studies with a university degree and have well-established careers before getting married. According to a United Nations World Fertility Report in 2003, in the 1970s about forty percent of women in Kuwait and Libya were married by the age of fifteen to nineteen. However, by 1990 this percentage had dropped to five percent. Women now tend to marry in their late twenties or early thirties. Although less common overall today, early marriages are still prevalent in Yemen, Oman, rural areas in Egypt and Palestine in Gaza (Rashad, H., Osman, M. & Roudi-Fahimi, F., 2005). Additionally, women now tend to have jobs, which has changed the role of women and marriage trends.

One common Western perception is that first-cousin marriages are the norm in the Arab world. Looking through history reveals that marriage between close biological relatives is not an Arab tradition, and the practice predates Islam. First cousin marriage goes back to the Greeks and Romans. Even in more recent history, members of royal families in Europe often married cousins because traditionally they were not allowed to marry non-royals, because they are from a lower status. Recently, members of royal families have permission to marry for love and not just for status (*Sennels*, 2010[1]), thereby allowing them to marry non-royals and reducing first-cousin marriages.

First-cousin marriages are still popular in some areas of the Middle East, Africa, the United

1 Sennels, N., 2010, Muslim Inbreeding: Impacts On Intelligence, Sanity, Health and Society. Islam under Scrutiny, Australian Islamist Monitor. Retrieved from: http://islammonitor.org/index.php?option=com_con-

Kingdom and Australia. However, parts of Europe, China, and the United States prohibit these marriages (*Bittles*, 1994[2]). Permission and prohibitions also vary from one religion to the next. First-cousin marriage is permitted in Islam and Buddhism but forbidden by "Christian Orthodox churches and require special permission for members of the Roman Catholic Church" (Shareen Joshi, Sriya Iyer & Quy Toan Do, p. 1). Marriage rates between close relatives range "from 30-50% in Middle Eastern countries, 20-40% in North Africa, and 10-20% in South Asia" (*Kapadia*, 1958: 117-137; *Naderi*, 1979; *Maian and Mushtaq*, 1994; *Bittles*, 1998; *Bittles*, 2001; *Bittles*, 2008).

First-cousin marriage was encouraged in the past because daughters get a percent of the inheritance, so and to keep the property in the family it was the norm. Researchers explain that marriage between cousins was encouraged to mainly preserve cultural values, secure a family's wealth, strengthen family relationships and develop closer bonds between a wife and her in-laws (*Conniff*, 2003[3]). Bittles and Hussain confirm these reasons and add that first-cousin marriages would reduce the possibilities for conflict and sometimes reduce dowry payments (*Bittles*, 1994; *Hussain*, 1999). The larger the family or clan, the more control they would have over land and wealth, and consequently the more powerful they would be, especially in rural societies as almost all Arab countries were in the past. The percentage of first-cousin marriage reaches ninety percent among Bedouins of Saudi Arabia and Kuwait, compared with forty percent in all other Arab countries (*Teebi*, 1997[4]) and ten percent worldwide (*Kershaw, Sarah*, 2009[5]). Marriage between relatives of the same family, not only first cousin, is high in Saudi Arabia, Libya and Sudan. Marriage of a relative does not mean arranged marriages, it might be because the couple see each other a lot in family occasion and fell in love.

Islam neither encourages nor prohibits first-cousin marriages. Although the Prophet Mohammed did not forbid Muslims from practicing it, he advised against it, as children of first-cousin marriages might have genetic disorders. Scientists have shown that children of first-cousin marriages do indeed have double the risk (six percent) of genetic diseases, as opposed to three percent for children whose parents are genetically not related (*Paul DB, Spencer HG*, 2008[6]). First-cousin marriage was a cultural norm but with decreased tribal influence in modern Arab culture, this practice is disappearing. Young people today usually refuse first-cousin marriages because they consider their cousins to be like sisters or brothers rather than future spouses.

In Islam, marriage is the only accepted way to produce children and replenish the earth, as family is considered the basic unit of society. The Prophet Mohammed said, "Marriage is

tent&view=article&id=3910:muslim-inbreeding-impacts-on-intelligence-sanity-health-and-society&-catid=294:social-practices-interactions&Itemid=61

2 Bittles, AH (1994), "The Role and Significance of Consanguinity as a Demographic Variable," Population and Development Review, 561-584.

3 Conniff, R. (2003), Go Ahead Kiss Your Cousin, Heck, marry her if you want to, August issue, Discover science for the curious from: http://discovermagazine.com/2003/aug/featkiss

4 Teebi, A.S., Farag, T.I., eds. 1997, Genetic Disorders Among Arab Populations, New York: Oxford University Press.

5 Kershaw, S., 2009, "Shaking Off the Shame." The New York Times, Nov. 26, P. D1

6 Paul DB, Spencer HG (2008) "It's Ok, We're Not Cousins by Blood": The Cousin Marriage Controversy in Historical Perspective. PLoS Biol 6(12): e320. doi:10.1371/journal.pbio.0060320

my Sunnah (divinely guided way of life). Whoever is displeased with my Sunnah is not from among us" (*Al-Bukhari*, Vol. 7, pp. 1-2, # 1). This is to say that marriage is designed to protect people against immortality, and it is highly appreciated and encouraged in Islam. In many hadith, he asked men to be gentle and kind to their wives. One such **hadith** is: "The most perfect believer in faith is the best of them in character and the best of you in character is he who is best to his family" (*At-Tirmithi*, Vol. 1, pp. 340, # 928). Another **hadith** is: "Fear Allah in dealing with your women because you have taken them in your trust by Allah's permission..." (*Muslim*, Vol. 2, pp. 615-6, # 2083). Two verses from the Qur'an are: "And women have right corresponding to the obligations on them, according to what is equitable..." (2:228) and "... Live with them (women) in equity...." (4:19).

Traditionally, the groom, with the support of his family, is responsible for marriage expenses as: ceremonies, bridal gifts, housing and paying a dowry for the bride. The festive culture surrounding the marriage, makes it costly and in some cases as an economic burden on the groom. One popular culture in wedding is to invite all relatives, neighbors and friends to the wedding. The attendees would be in hundreds of numbers and dinner should be served for all. To conclude this section, in the Arab world, marriage is the norm as pre-marital relations are not allowed and considered shameful.

Grammar: Kana wa akhawatoha كان و أخواتها
The verb كان in Arabic is almost the same as the verb "to be" in English. It is used to state actions in the past. كان is conjugated like other verbs, according to the subject it is describing. It means was and it is used to mean that the whole sentence happened in the past. If we want to describe things in the future we may use سيكون . It is conjugated as all other verbs as it has its forms in present, past and future tense. An example is:

Future	Past	Present
سأكون في مكتبي	كنت في مكتبي	أكون في مكتبي
Sa'koono fee maktabi	*Konto fee maktabi*	*Akoon fee maktabi*

Here is the conjugation of the verb كان :

Transliteration	Future	Transliteration	Present	Transliteration	Past	Pronoun
Sa'koon	سأكون	Akoon	أكون	Konto	كنت	أنا
Sanakoon	سنكون	Nakoon	نكون	Konna	كنا	نحن
Satakoon	ستكون	Takoon	تكون	Konta	كنتَ	أنتَ
Satakooneen	ستكونين	Takooneen	تكونين	Konti	كنتِ	انتِ
Satakoonan	ستكونان	Takoonan	تكونان	Kontoma	كنتما	أنتما
Satakoonoon	ستكونون	Takoonoon	تكونون	Kontom	كنتم	أنتم
Sayakoon	سيكون	Yakoon	يكون	Kana	كان	هو
Satakoon	ستكون	Takoon	تكون	Kanat	كانت	هي
Sayakoonan	سيكونان	Yakoonan	يكونان	Kana	كانا	هما
Sayakoonoon	سيكونون	Yakoonoon	يكونون	Kanoo	كانوا	هم

Note the conjugation is almost the same as other verbs.

An example (the room is big)

كانت الغرفةُ كبيرةً *alghorfato kabeeraton* would be *kanat alghorfato kabeeratan* الغرفةُ كبيرةٌ

كان has sisters. They are called sisters because they have the same effect on the nominal sentence when they precede it. The subject of the nominal sentences is called اسْمُ كَانَ and it keeps its nominative case, that is مَرْفُوعٌ while the predicate or الْخَبَرُ in Arabic takes the accusative case and it is called خَبَرُ كَانَ *khabar kana*.

The sisters of كَانَ are:

Example	Meaning	Transliteration	
كان الطقسُ غائما *Kana attaqso gha'man.* The weather was cloudy.	Was	*Kana*	كَانَ
مازال الطالبُ سعيداً *Ma zala attalibo sa'eedan.* The student is still happy.	Still is	*Ma zala*	مازال
أصبح العالمُ قريةً واحدة *Asbaha ala'lam qaryatan wahida.* The world becomes one village.	Became, something happened in the morning	*Asbaha*	أصبح
ظلّت المدرسةُ مفتوحةً *Thallat alghorfato maftohatan.* The school is still open.	Continue	*Thalla*	ظلّ
صارت الغرفةُ فارغةً *Sarat alghorfato farigha.* The room became empty.	Became, something changed	*Sara*	صار
أمسى الطقسُ جميلاً *Amsa attaqso jameelan.* The weather became beautiful in the evening.	Became, something happened in the evening	*Amsa*	أمسى

In short, there are several features of كان and its sisters, when added to nominal sentences:

a) It provides a time frame
b) It affects the predicate of the nominal sentence. It should be accusative (have **fat-ha**) all the times
c) The subject of the nominal sentence will keep its **dhamma** all the time
d) The same rules of كَانَ conjugation are applied to all the sisters.

16.1. Practice (see Answer Key)

Fill in the blanks with the correct form of كان:

1. أحمد في دبي غداً. ـ_____

2. صديقتي أمل و أختها _____ في المدرسة أمس.

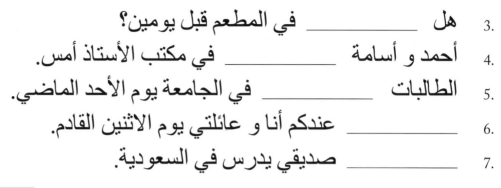

3. هل _____ في المطعم قبل يومين؟

4. أحمد و أسامة _____ في مكتب الأستاذ أمس.

5. الطالبات _____ في الجامعة يوم الأحد الماضي.

6. _____ عندكم أنا و عائلتي يوم الاثنين القادم.

7. _____ صديقي يدرس في السعودية.

16.2. Practice   (see Answer Key)

1. أين (كان + انتم) _____ يوم الأحد؟

2. هل (أصبح + هم) _____ يدرسون الأدب معك؟

3. (أمسى + نحن) _____ نستمع الى الموسيقى.

4. (ظلّ + هي) _____ أمي تعمل في المطعم.

5. (صار + أنا) _____ أسكن هنا في السنة الماضية.

6. هل (كان + أنتَ) _____ تأكل في السيارة أمس؟

7. أين (كان + أنت) _____ في الأسبوع الماضي؟

8. هل (ما زال + هي) _____ تدرس معك؟

9. (أصبح + نحن) _____ نشرب القهوة العربية كل يوم.

10. (ظلّ + هم) _____ في الفندق أربعة أيام.

16.3. Practice   (see Answer Key)

Rearrange the words to form meaningful sentences:

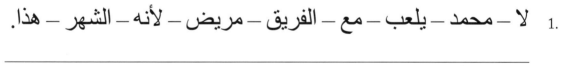

1. لا – محمد – يلعب – مع – الفريق – مريض – لأنه – الشهر – هذا.

_____

2. الطيور – ساعات – عبدالله – في – كان – يقضي – طويلة – صيد.

_____

3. جدتي – العلاج – الطبيعي – تفضل.

_____

4. الحادث۔ ناجحة – عملية – اُجريت – في – له – المستشفى۔ بعد.

_____

5. الطب – تدرس – هي – في ۔ أمريكا.

_____

16.4. Practice (see Answer Key)

Fill in the blanks with words from the list:

أريد – جلست – الذي – التي ۔ أخذت – يدرسون – ستذهبين –
اشتريت

1. _____ أمل على الكرسي بجانب الباب.

2. _____ الكتاب من علي.

3. أنا _____ كوبا من الشاي الساخن.

4. _____ سيارة جديدة سوداء قبل اسبوعين.

5. هم _____ في كلية العلوم بجانب العمارة القديمة.

6. متى _____ الى المدرسة يا سارة.

7. أكل الضيوف من الطعام _____ كان على الطاولة.

8. استمعنا الى الأستاذة _____ تدرس اللغة العربية.

16.5. Practice (see Answer Key)

Write the following using the correct form of كان :

1. You used to love scientific films. _____

2. They were reading the novel. _____

3. We were watching the horror movie. _____

4. They (2 people) have left before we came. _____

5. I used to enjoy reading poetry. _____

6. Tea was cold so I did not drink it. _____

7. I was afraid. _____

8. Our room was very big and cold. _____

9. The winds were very strong. _____

10. She had a flu, so she went to the doctor. _____

16.6. Practice   (see Answer Key)

To review your comparatives, conjugate the adjectives between brackets:

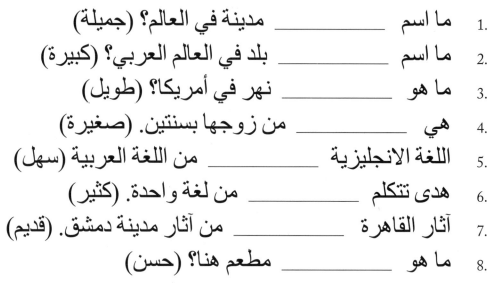

١.   ما اسم _____ مدينة في العالم؟ (جميلة)

٢.   ما اسم _____ بلد في العالم العربي؟ (كبيرة)

٣.   ما هو _____ نهر في أمريكا؟ (طويل)

٤.   هي _____ من زوجها بسنتين. (صغيرة)

٥.   اللغة الانجليزية _____ من اللغة العربية (سهل)

٦.   هدى تتكلم _____ من لغة واحدة. (كثير)

٧.   آثار القاهرة _____ من آثار مدينة دمشق. (قديم)

٨.   ما هو _____ مطعم هنا؟ (حسن)

16.7. Practice   (see Answer Key)

Change the following into singular:

١.   أيام   : _____   ٢.   أسماء   : _____

٣.   أخوات: _____   ٤.   أعداد   : _____

٥.   أوراق : _____   ٦.   أسابيع : _____

٧.   أسئلة   : _____   ٨.   فناجين : _____

٩.   أبناء   : _____   ١٠. أمراء : _____

16.8. Practice   (see Answer Key)

Reading:

في معظم الدول العربية تكون أيام العمل الرسمية تبدأ يوم الأحد و حتى يوم الخميس. و بذلك فان يومي الجمعة و السبت هما يوما عطلة نهاية الأسبوع. عادة يبدأ الدوام في الشركات من الساعة السابعة و النصف

صباحا حتى الساعة الثانية عشرة ظهرا و ثم من الساعة الثالثة و النصف عصرا حتى الساعة السادسة و النصف مساء طوال أيام العمل الأسبوعية. أما بالنسبة للمؤسسات الحكومية و المدارس فتكون ساعات العمل فيها من الساعة السابعة و النصف صباحا حتى الساعة الثانية ظهرا.

Now answer the following questions from what you read:

1. ما هي أيام العمل في الدول العربية؟

2. ما هي أيام عطلة نهاية الأسبوع؟

3. متى يبدأ الدوام في الشركات؟

4. متى ينتهي الدوام في المؤسسات الحكومية؟

5. قارن بين ساعات العمل في بلدك و بين ساعات العمل في الدول العربية!

16.9. Practice (see Answer Key)

Underline the suitable word in parentheses:

1. أنا (أدرس – تدرس – يدرس) التجارة في جامعة الكويت.

2. (على – من – في) مكتبي مجلات و كتب كثيرة.

3. أحب أن أشرب القهوة مع أصدقائي في (المتحف – الشارع – المقهى).

4. في عطلة نهاية (اليوم – الأسبوع – الشهر) أصحو من النوم متأخرا.

5. أمل و عائلتها (تذهب – ذهبوا – ذهبا) الى المطعم اليوم.

6. أحمد و محمد (يقضيان – يقضون – يقضي) وقتهم في اللعب و مشاهدة التلفاز.

7. لا (تنسى – نسيَ – تنسون) أن تعمل الواجب يا خالد.

8. (ماذا – من – متى) تفعل مع العائلة كل أسبوع؟

9. (هي – هما – هم) يعملان في محطة البريد.

10. (صغير – صغيرة ـ أصغر) دولة عربية هي البحرين.

Reflection

1. In this Lesson I learned: _____

2. I have some trouble with: _____

3. I need to learn more about: _____

الوحدة السابعة عشر
Arabic Proverbs
أمثال عربية

Amthal Arrabiyyah

Objectives:

1. Grammar: *ina w a akhawatuha*
2. Culture: Most Popular Idioms

3. Reading

 **Vocabulary**

Meaning	Transliteration	Plural	Transliteration	Word
Belongings	*Aghradh*	أَغْراضْ	*Gharad*	غَرَضْ
Father	–	–	*Walid*	والِدْ
Mother	–	–	*Walida*	والِدة
Magazine	*Majjalat*	مَجَلّاتْ	*Majjallah*	مَجَلَّة
Story	*Qissas*	قِصَصْ	*Qissa*	قِصّة
Stay	–	–	*Baqiya/yabqa*	بقى/تَبْقى
Author	*Mo'lifoon/ mo'lifeen*	مُؤَلِّفونْ/مُؤَلِّفينْ	*Mo'alif*	مُؤَلَّفْ
Producer	*Mokhrijoon/ mokhrijeen*	مُخْرِجونْ/ مُخْرِجينْ	*Mokhrij*	مُخْرِجْ
Actor	*Momathiloon/ momathileen*	مُمَثِّلونْ/مُمَثِّلين	*Momathil*	مُمَثِّلْ

Meaning	Transliteration	Plural	Transliteration	Word
Actress	Momathilat	مُمَثِّلات	Momathilah	مُمَثِّلة
A play	Masrahiyyat	مَسْرَحيّات	Masrahiyyah	مَسْرَحيّة
Film	Aflam	أَفْلام	Film	فيلْم
Story	Qissas	قِصَص	Qissa	قِصّة
Novel	Riwayat	رِوايات	Riwaya	رواية
Horror	–	–	Ro'b	رُعْب
Romantic	–	–	A'tifi	عاطِفيْ
Science	-	-	Elmi	عِلْميْ
Imagination	Khayalat	خيالات	Khayal	خَيالْ
Science fiction	–	–	Khayal elmi	خَيالْ عِلْميْ
Poem	Asha'ar	أَشْعارْ	Sh'er	شِعْرْ
Poet	Sho'ra'	شُعَراءْ	Sha'ar	شاعِرْ
Song	Aghani	أَغاني	Oghniyyah	أُغنية
Effect	–	–	Ta'theer	تَأْثيرْ
Affecting	–	–	Mo'ather	مُؤَثِّرْ
Criticism	–	–	Naqada	نَقْدْ
Absence	–	–	Ghiyab	غِيابْ
Unanimous	Maj-hooleen	مَجْهولْين	Majhool	مَجْهولْ
Written by	–	–	Men ta'leef	مِنْ تأليفْ
Cupboard	Khaza'en	خَزائِن	Khezana	خَزانة
Mirror	Maraya	مرايا	Mera'ah	مِرآة

Meaning	Transliteration	Plural	Transliteration	Word
Washer	*Ghassalat*	غسّالات	*Ghassalah*	غَسّالة
Stove	*Afran*	أفران	*Forn*	فِرْن
Refrigerator	*Thallajat*	ثلاجات	*Thallaja*	ثَلّاجة
Village	*Qora*	قُرَى	*Qaryah*	قَرْية
Morning	–		–	*Sabah*	صَباح
Evening	–		–	*Massa'*	مَساء
Fruit	*Fawakih*	فواكه	*Fakihah*	فاكِهة

Most popular idioms and Proverbs

As in all world languages, Arabic has its own idiomatic expressions أمثال *amthal* / تَعْبِيرَات
أو اِصْطِلاحِيَّة or *ta'beerat istilahiyah*. Idiomatic expressions أمثال refer to idioms that cannot
be understood literally but they have a story behind them and are used in certain situations.
These expressions might be difficult to comprehend for non-native speakers. Here are few
examples of idioms:

"Returned back with pair of Hunain's shoes" (رجع بخفّي حُنَين *raja' bekhofay honain*).

The meaning of this idiom is "to come back empty-handed." The origin of the idiom goes back
to the following story: A man came by Hunanin, a shoemaker, to buy pair of shoes. He kept
on bargaining with Hunanin hoping he'd sell him the shoes for lowest price. Not reaching a
figure he'd be satisfied with, he decided to leave Hunain without buying the shoes. Hunain
became dismayed that the buyer wasted his time haggling with him and not appreciating
the quality of his craftsmanship. He then decided to teach him a lesson. Predicting travel
route the man would take, Hunain took the pair of shoes he wanted and threw the shoes on
the road at a distant from each other's and hid at the side of the road
where he could watch the buyer's route and could not be seen. The man
eventually came riding on his camel and saw the first piece of the pair
in the middle of road and said to himself: This looks like the shoes I
wanted to buy from Hunain but kept on riding. After few yards, he
saw the other piece of the pair. This time he descended from his camel
and walked back to where he saw the first pair to pick it up. Hunain
immediately came out of his hiding place, stole the camel with its all
goods and ran away. When the man came back there was nothings. He
looked and looked but could not find his belongings, so he went back

to his town on foot. People in the town asked him about his trip and the goods he brought back with him, he answered with disappointment: "I returned with Humanin's shoes." Later on, when anyone goes to do something and cannot achieve what he wants, people would use the expression "Returned back with pair of Hunain's shoes" meaning: رجع بخفّي حنين

The second example is: *jawe' kalbak yatba'ak* «جوِع كلبك يتبعك» meaning: "Starve your dog so it follows you."

The proverb is attributed to one of Himyarite's tyrant kings. It is common fact throughout history that dictators and tyrants use all kinds of cruelties and inhumane practices, including starving the people to subjugate and force them to surrender to their demands. Witnessing the dire situation of the starving citizens and fearing grave consequences, the king's advisors as well as his wife expressed their deep concerns of the continuous worsening conditions and recommended to the king to ease their distress. With utter contempt and disregard to their advice he replied: "starve your dog and it will follow you." The idiom is continued to be used when someone wants to be in control and make his people follow his orders without discussion, so he will control their benefits.

Other few idioms that have English equivalents are:

- لا يُلدَغ المؤمن من جحر مرتين *la yoldagh almo/men men johr maratayn*: the exact meaning is that a believer will not be bitten twice from the same hole. It is the same as "Fool me once, shame on you. Fool me twice, shame on me."

- التكرار يعلّم الحمار *attikrar yo'alim alhimar* means repetition teaches the donkey. It is the same as "Practice makes perfect."

- الطيور على اشكالها تقع *attoyyor ala ashkaliha taqa'* is the same as "Birds of feather flock together."

- هاك الشبل من ذاك الأسد *hatha ashiblo men hathat alasad* means this cub is from that lion. It is the same as "Like mother, like daughter."

انّ و أخواتها: *ina w a akhawatuha*
انّ و أخواتها are used to identify or highlight the topic of the sentence. As in the case of كان و أخواتها they highlight the noun following it as the topic of the sentence. Both introduce the nominal sentences.

The difference between كان و أخواتها and انّ و أخواتها is that: كان و أخواتها are verbs while انّ و أخواتها are particles. Additionally:
1. The subject of the sentences is called اسْمُ انّ and the predicate is called خَبَرُ انّ
2. The subject or اسْمُ انّ takes the accusative case, that is منصوب while the predicate or خَبَرُ انّ keeps its nominative case, that is مَرْفُوعٌ

The sisters of انّ are:

Meaning / Transliteration	Example	Meaning / Transliteration	انّ و أخواتها
The test is close. *Inna alimtihan qareeb.*	انّ الامتحانَ قريبٌ.	It gives confirmation *Inna*	انّ
It looks like her house is ready. *Ka'anna baytaha asbaha jahizan alaan.*	كأن بيتها أصبح جاهزا الآن.	Used for comparison, as if *Ka'anna*	كأن
He wants to come but he is busy. *Howa yoreed an yahdor lakinnaho mash-ghool.*	هو يريد أن يحضر لكنه مشغول.	But or however *Lakinna*	لكن
He might be sleeping. *La'llaho na'im.*	لعلة نائم.	Gives the impression of expectation *La'alla*	لعلّ
He knows how to swim because he learned at the club. *Howa ya'rif assibaha linnaho ta'lama fii annadi.*	هو يعرف السباحة لأنه تعلم في النادي.	Because *Lia'nna*	لأن

When اسمُ انّ *ism inna* is a pronoun, then it should be attached to اسمُ انّ. Look at the table for a detailed conjugation:

Transliteration لأنّ /	Transliteration لعلّ /	Transliteration لكن /	Transliteration كأن /	Transliteration انّ /	Pronoun
Lia'nnani لأنني	*La'allani* لعلني	*Lakinnani* لكنني	*Ka'annani* كأنني	*Innani* انّني	أنا
Lia'nnana لأنا	*La'allana* لعلنا	*Lakinnana* لكننا	*Ka'annana* كأننا	*Innana* اننا	نحن
Lia'nnaka لأنكَ	*La'allaka* لعلكَ	*Lakinnaka* لكنكَ	*Ka'annaka* كأنكَ	*Innaka* انكَ	أنتَ

Transliteration لأنَّ /	Transliteration لعلّ /	Transliteration لكن /	Transliteration كأنّ /	Transliteration أنّ /	Pronoun
Lia'nnaki لأنَّكِ	*La'allaki* لعلكِ	*Lakinnaki* لكنَّكِ	*Ka'annaki* كأنَّكِ	*Innaki* انكِ	انتِ
Lia'nnakoma لأنكما	*La'allakoma* لعلكما	*Lakinnakoma* لكنكما	*Ka'annakoma* كأنكماا	*Innakoma* انكما	أنتما
Lia'nnakom لأنَّكم	*La'allakom* لعلكم	*Lakinnakom* لكنكم	*Ka'annakom* كأنكم	*Innakom* انكم	أنتم
Lia'nnaho لأنه	*La'allaho* لعلّه	*Lakinnaho* لكنّه	*Ka'annaho* كأنه	*Innaho* انه	هو
Lia'nnaha لأنهاَ	*La'allaha* لعلّها	*Lakinnaha* لكنّها	*Ka'annaho* كأنها	*Innaha* انها	هي
Lia'nnahoma لأنهماَ	*La'allahoma* لعلّهما	*Lakinnahoma* لكنهما	*Ka'annahoma* كأنهما	*Innahoma* انهما	هما
Lia'nnahom لأنهمَ	*La'allahom* لعلّهم	*Lakinnahom* لكنهم	*Ka'annahom* كأنهم	*Innahom* انهم	هم

Some examples are:

Meaning	Transliteration	Sentence
She prefers walking more than riding a car.	*Innaha tofaedl almashi akthar men rokoob assayarah*	انها تفضل المشي أكثر من ركوب السيارة
It looks like its going to rain today.	*La'la attaqs momter alyawm*	لعلّ الطقس ممطر اليوم
I know her but I am not sure of her name.	*Ana a'refoha lakinnani ghair mota'kida men ismoha*	أنا أعرفها و لكني غير متأكدة من اسمها

Meaning	Transliteration	Sentence
She's late because she slept late yesterday.	*Hiya ta'kharat li'naha namat mota'khira ams.*	هي تأخرت لأنها نامت متأخرة أمس.

17.1. **Practice** (see Answer Key)

Underline (اسْمُ انّ *ism inna*) and circle خَبَرُ انّ (*khabar inna*) and add the case endings on them in the following sentences:

1. انهما يكتبان كتابا جديدا

2. كأنه تعبان اليوم.

3. قلت لهم أن يحضروا لكنهم اعتذروا

4. لم تحضر الى الحفل لأنها مريضة

5. اسألهم لعل أفكارهم جديدة

6. ان أبوهم رجل ناجح جدا

7. لا يوجد أحد هنا لعلهم ذهبوا الى مكان آخر.

17.2. **Practice** (see Answer Key)

Reading:

يذهب علاء مع أبيه الى السوق كل يوم جمعة بعد صلاة الظهر ليساعده في شراء ما يحتاجونه من أغراض للبيت. يأخذ أبو علاء حقيبة كبيرة معة ليضع فيها الأغراض و يحمل علاء حقيبة أخرى ليساعد والده في حمل بعض ما يشترونه. في البداية يذهبا الى المكتبة لشراء مجلة "العربي" لأنهما يحبانها كثيرا. أحيانا يشتري علاء قصة ليقرأ فيها قبل أن ينام.

بعد ذلك يذهبا الى سوق اللحم و يشتريا اللحم و الدجاج ليكفيهم خلال الأسبوع. ثم يذهبا الى محل الفاكهة و يشتريان الموز و التفاح و البرتقال و العنب الأخضر. أبو علاء يحب الموز و البرتقال و أم علاء تحب العنب الأخضر أما علاء فيحب التفاح.

وضع علاء و أبيه الأغراض في السيارة و لكن قبل أن يعودا الى البيت تذكر أبو علاء أنهم يحتاجون القهوة فذهبا الى محل القهوة بجانب بيتهم و اشتريا القهوة. ثم عادوا الى البيت و هم يحملون كل ما اشتروه من السوق.

كانت أم علاء قد أعدت طعام الغداء فجلسوا جميعا يأكلون و يتحدثون عما حدث معهم و عما سيفعلون خلال الأسبوع القادم.

Now answer the following questions:

1. أين يذهب علاء مع أبيه؟
2. متى يذهب مع ابيه؟
3. لماذا يذهب علاء و أبوه الى المكتبة؟
4. ماذا يحب أبو علاء من الفاكهة؟
5. ماذا تذكر أبو علاء قبل أن يذهب الى البيت؟

17.3. Practice (see Answer Key)

Underline the most suitable word between brackets:

1. يصل (أحمد – منى) الى شيكاغو الساعة السادسة صباحا.
2. كم (عندك – يوما – متى) ستبقى في لبنان؟
3. أين (تدرس – أدرس ـ تدرسين) يا ايمان؟
4. خالد (يسافرون – سيسافر – ستسافر) مع عائلته غدا الى السعودية.
5. هل (تريد – تريدان – تريدون) الذهاب الى المقهى يا أصدقائي.
6. هذا الرجل (طويل – طويلة – قصيرة) جدا.
7. بيتنا (صغير – عطشان – تعبان).
8. سأذهب الى المباراة (مع – في – فوق) أصدقائي.
9. هل (هذه – هذا ـ هؤلاء) خالتك منى؟
10. هم لا (يحب – يحبون – تحبين) الأكل في المطعم.

17.4. Practice (see Answer Key)

Change into plural:

1. الكرسي مريح. ـــــــــــــــــــــ

2. البنت طويلة. ـــــــــــــــــــــ

3. غرفة النوم كبيرة و فارغة. ـــــــــــــــــــــ

4. يوجد حديقة جميلة. ـــــــــــــــــــــ

5. هذه شقة صغيرة في عمارة كبيرة. ـــــــــــــــــــــ

17.5. Practice (see Answer Key)

Fill in the blanks with the suitable word from the list:

مؤثرة – الأغاني – رسالة – الجريدة – الأخبار

1. أحب أن أقرأ ـــــــــــــــــــــ كل صباح.

2. يكتب علاء ـــــــــــــــــــــ لأبيه كل يوم جمعة.

3. هل تحب أن تستمع الى ـــــــــــــــــــــ ؟

4. هو مؤلف مشهور و كتبه ـــــــــــــــــــــ جدا.

5. أصدقائي يقرأون ـــــــــــــــــــــ على الانترنت.

17.6. Practice (see Answer Key)

Rearrange the words to form meaningful sentences:

1. أحمد – سيارة – أمريكية ـ اشترى.

_____

2. البحر – الناس – يذهب – في – الى – الصيف.

_____

3. مفتاح – هذا – الأستاذ – مكتب.

_____

4. سافرت – تركيا – من – الى – بالطائرة – امريكا.

_____

5. الى – في – نوفمبر – الأردن – وصلت – شهر.

_____

17.7. `Practice` (see Answer Key)

To review question words, form questions from the following statements:

2. هذه حقيبة أحمد. 1. أذهب الى المكتبة لأقرأ.

4. لوني المفضل هو الأحمر. 3. في منزلي عشرين نافذة.

6. اسم صديقتي هو سعاد. 5. عندي أربع قطط و كلب واحد.

17.8. `Practice` (see Answer Key)

To review your attached pronouns, attach the suitable pronoun for the following nouns:

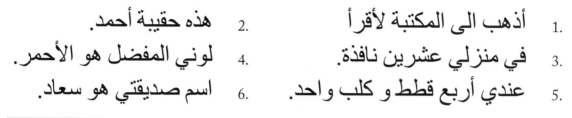

2. سائق + هم = _____ 1. طائرة + هي = _____

4. قصة + هي = _____ 3. والدة + هما = _____

6. نظارة + انا = _____ 5. مدرسة + نحن = _____

8. ساعة + انت = _____ 7. دراجة + هما = _____

10. مفتاح + أنتَ = _____ 9. مخبز + نحن = _____

Reflection

1. In this Lesson I learned: _____

2. I have some trouble with: _____

3. I need to learn more about: _____

الوحدة الثامنة عشر
The Term "Middle East"
الشرق الأوسط
Asharq alawsat

Objectives:

1. Vocabulary: The Environment
2. Grammar: Relative Nouns: الذي – التي – الذين

3. Culture: The Term "Middle East"
4. Reading

 Vocabulary

Meaning	Transliteration	Plural	Transliteration	Word
Bank	*Bonook*	بُنُوكْ	*Bank*	بَنْكْ
Win	–	–	*Faza/ yafooz*	فازْ/ يفوز
Believe	–	–	*Saddaqa/ yossadiq*	صدّقْ/يُصَدِّقْ
Lie	–	–	*Kathaba/ yokkathib*	كذّبْ/يُكَذِّبْ
Game	*Ala'ab*	ألعابْ	*Lo'ba*	لُعْبة
Electronics	–	–	*Ilktrooni/ ilktrooniya*	الكْترونيْ/ الكترونية
Screen	–	–	*Shasha*	شاشة
Subject	*Mawad*	مَوادْ	*Maddah*	مادّة
All	–	–	*Kol*	كُلْ
Almost	–	–	*Mo'tham*	مُعْظَمْ
Media	–	–	*I'lam*	إعْلامْ

Meaning	Transliteration	Plural	Transliteration	Word
Revolution	*Thawrat*	ثَوْرَاتْ	*Thawra*	ثَوْرَة
Animal	*Haywanat*	حَيْوَانَاتْ	*Hayawan*	حَيْوَان
Dig	–	–	*Hafara/yahfor*	حَفَرَ/يَحْفُرْ
Possibly	–	–	*Men almomkin*	مِنْ المُمْكِنْ
Stone	*Ahjar*	أَحْجَارْ	*Hajar*	حَجَرْ
Print	–	–	*Taba'a/ytba'*	طَبَعْ/يطبع
Printing or publishing	–	–	*Tiba'a*	طِباعة
Storage	–	–	*Takhzeen*	تَخْزِينْ
Show	*Oroodh*	عروض	*Ard*	عَرْضْ
Move	–	–	*Naqala/yanqol*	نَقْلْ/ينقل
Society	*Mojtama'at*	مجتمعات	*Mojtama'*	مُجْتَمَعْ
Technology	–	–	*Teknolojia*	تِكْنُولوجْيا
Climate, weather	–	–	*Manakh*	مَناخْ
Raise, height	–	–	*Irtifa'*	إِرْتِفاعْ
Reduction, drop	–	–	*Inkhifad*	إِنْخِفاضْ
Temperature	*Darajat alhararah*	دَرَجاتُ الحَرارة	*Darajat alhararah*	دَرَجةُ الحَرارة
Rule	*Qawaneen*	قَوانينْ	*Qanoon*	قانونْ
Storm	*Awasef*	عَواصِفْ	*A'sifa*	عاصِفة
Traffic	–	–	*Moroor*	مُرورْ

Meaning	Transliteration	Plural	Transliteration	Word
Local	–	–	*Mahalli*	مَحَلّي
National	–	–	*Dowali*	دُوَلي
Immigration	*Hijrat*	هجرات	*Hijrah*	هِجْرة
Directly	–	–	*Mobasher*	مُباشِرْ
Industrial	–	–	*Sina'I*	صِناعِيْ

The Term "Middle East"

Throughout history, the Middle East has been home for different peoples with different languages and religions, although Arabs represent the main group living there today. Several terms are used to refer to these Arab countries, including the *Middle East, the Near East, the Fertile Crescent,* and *the Levant.* The term Middle East is undoubtedly the most popular, but it was not a term people living in the area used for themselves. Rather, it was created by the Europeans stemming from the colonial description of the area between Europe and distant parts of Asia. Dividing the world into east and west goes back to the time of the Roman Empire. The word east refers to east of Britain. Sometimes, use of *Middle East* is a problematic as it does not describe the precise geographical area for people in Africa, Canada, or Europe. Different opinions exist on the most accurate geographical area that in reality represents the Arab world. However, the term is the most popular, and it refers to all Arab countries.

The term *Middle East,* as it is used now, refers to all Arab countries in Asia as well as Africa. Some scholars wrote that the term was originated in the 1850s in Britain (*Beaumont, Blake, and Wagstaff,* 1988, pp. 16[1]), but its use was limited until the American naval strategist Alfred Thayer Mahan used the term in 1902 to refer to the area between India and Arabia (*Koppes,* 1976, pp. 95–98[2]). Mahan realized the strategic significance of the region, especially with the Persian Gulf at its center. He explained, "After the Suez Canal, it was the most important passage for Britain to control in order to keep the Russians from advancing towards British India" (*Laciner,* 2006, para. 2[3]). Mahan first used the term in one of his articles, titled "The Persian Gulf and International Relations," which was published in the British journal *The National Review* in September 1902 (*Adelson,* 1995, pp. 22).

Before World War II, the areas centered on the Mediterranean and its eastern shores were

1 Beaumont, P., Blake, G. H., & Wagstaff, J. M. (1988). The Middle East: A geographical study. Oxford, UK: David Fulton.

2 Koppes, C. R. (1976). Captain Mahan, General Gordon and the origin of the term "Middle East." Middle East Studies 12, 95–98.

3 Laciner, S. (2006). Is there a place called "the Middle East"? The Journal of Turkish Weekly. Retrieved from http://www.turkishweekly.net/2006/06/02/comment/is-there-a-place-called-the-middle-east

referred to as *the Near East*, while *the Far East* referred to China. In the1930s, however, the British established a center for their military forces based in Cairo called the *Middle East Command Center*. Later, the term *Middle East* became more common in Europe and the United States, especially after the foundation of the Middle East Institute in Washington, DC, in 1946 (*Held*, 2000, p. 7[4]). The colonial application of the term *Middle East* became so common that the Arabs themselves use the term to refer to their region.

The southern section of the Middle East includes Jordan, Syria, Lebanon, and Palestine, an area well known in history as the *Fertile Crescent*. The western area of the Middle East includes Egypt, Sudan, Djibouti, Ethiopia, Mauritania, Somalia, and the Comoros Islands. The Arab countries in northern Africa are Algeria, Morocco, Libya, and Tunisia; the Gulf States are Qatar, Saudi Arabia, Kuwait, Bahrain, the United Arab Emirates (UAE), Oman, Yemen, and Iraq. In all, there are 22 Arab countries, so called because Arabic is their official language.

Relative Pronouns

Relative pronouns are used to modify the noun phrase. It agrees with the noun in gender and number. They are the same as who or which in English and there is no difference in use with human or non-human words. Look at the table

Meaning	Transliteration	Plural	Transliteration	dual	Transliteration	singular
Who/which – masculine	*Allatheena*	الذين	*Allatahn*	اللذان	*Allathi*	الذي
Who/which – Feminine	*allawati*	اللواتي	*Allatan*	اللتان	*allati*	التي

With non-human plural, the same rule applies of using the singular feminine. For example, we say:

Meaning	Transliteration	Plural
The books that I read are in the library.	*Alkotob allati qara'toha fee almaktaba*	الكُتُب التي قرأتها في المكتبة .
The friends who I know are not here	*Alasdiqa allatheen a'rifohom layso hona*	الأصدقاء الذين أعرفهم ليسوا هنا

---

4 Held, C. C. (2000). Middle East patterns: Places, peoples, and politics. Boulder, CO: Westview Press.

Meaning	Transliteration	Plural
These are the streets that I know	*Hathihi hiya ashawari' allati a'rifoha*	هذه هي الشوارع التي أعرفها.
Who/which - Feminine	*Attalibat allawati fee almaktaba fee saffi*	الطالبات اللواتي في المكتبة في صفي
The countries which I visited are few	*Albilad allati zortoha qalilah*	البلاد التي زرتها قليلة

18.1. Practice (see Answer Key)

Use the suitable relative pronoun الذي, التي or الذين and its conjugations to fill in the blanks:

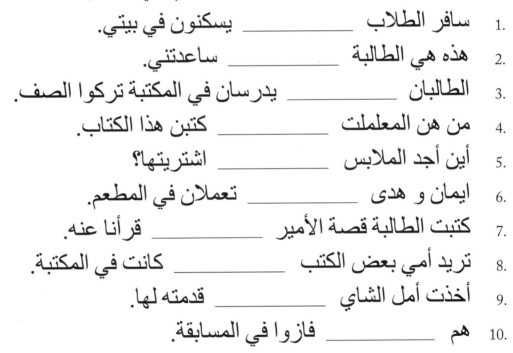

1. سافر الطلاب _____ يسكنون في بيتي.

2. هذه هي الطالبة _____ ساعدتني.

3. الطالبان _____ يدرسان في المكتبة تركوا الصف.

4. من هن المعلمات _____ كتبن هذا الكتاب.

5. أين أجد الملابس _____ اشتريتها؟

6. ايمان و هدى _____ تعملان في المطعم.

7. كتبت الطالبة قصة الأمير _____ قرأنا عنه.

8. تريد أمي بعض الكتب _____ كانت في المكتبة.

9. أخذت أمل الشاي _____ قدمته لها.

10. هم _____ فازوا في المسابقة.

18.2. Practice (see Answer Key)

What is it:

ما هو؟

1. نشربه مع القهوة. _____

2. نكتب به على الدفتر. _____

3. مكان يصلي الناس فيه. _____

4. يلبسها كبار السن عند القراءة. _____

5. نضع فيها الكتب و الأقلام. _____

6. نشرب فيه العصير أو الماء. _____

7. نشتري منه الملابس. _____

8. نضع فيه الأموال. _____

9. أكبر دولة عربية. _____

10. أصغر دولة عربية. _____

18.3. Practice   (see Answer Key)

Rearrange the words to form a meaningful sentence:

1. الأم – تحضر – الغداء – طعام: _____

2. الحائط – على – الصور – هناك : _____

3. الملابس – الحقيبة – في – أمل – تضع : _____

4. المطبخ – في – القهوة – يعمل – أحمد : _____

5. الطلاب ـ الى – رجع – الكلية – شهر – أغسطس – في : _____

6. الطابق – بيتي – هذه – في – العمارة – في – الرابع : _____

18.4. Practice   (see Answer Key)

Fill in the blanks with the suitable word from the list:

معتدل- تنخفض – بارد – درجة الحرارة –المرور – شهري – الهجرة

1. المناخ في لبنان _____ في الشتاء و

_____ في الصيف.

2. في الصحراء _____ عالية جدا في الصيف.

3. في بلدي _____ درجة الحرارة في الليل.

4. سيكون لنا لقاء _____ في أول يوم ثلاثاء من كل شهر.

5. ستراجع الدولة قانون _____ الأسبوع القادم.

6. أدرس قانون _____ قبل أن تتعلم قيادة السيارة.

18.5. Practice (see Answer Key)

Rearrange the following sentences to form a meaningful paragraph:

– ركبنا سيارة الأجرة من بيتنا الى المطار

– اشترينا تذاكر من مكتب السفريات

– قررنا أنا و أصدقائي أن نذهب الى الأردن

– ركبنا في الطيارة لمدة ست ساعات

– استمتعنا بالرحلة كثيرا

– رجعنا و معنا الكثير من الهدايا لعائلاتنا

– ذهبنا الى الأردن و زرنا الكثير من الأماكن السياحية و الآثار

– أعددنا حقائبنا للسفر

18.6. Practice (see Answer Key)

Translate the following to plan a conversation with an Arabic friend:

1. Do you have some time to meet on Friday?
2. Shall we play football, or do you prefer video games?
3. Can you help me with my Arabic homework?
4. Today it will be much colder than yesterday.
5. I just finished printing my first book.
6. Do you know immigration law?
7. This is the storm that I was talking about.
8. Where is the community center that you told me about?
9. What is your favorite animal? Do you have one at home?
10. What is the temperature outside? Do I have to wear a jacket?

18.7. Practice (see Answer Key)

Reading:

عَبْد الله: السَّلَامُ عَلَيْكُمْ.

حسن: وَ عَلَيْكُمُ السَّلَامْ! أَهْلًا, عَبْدالله

عَبْد الله: بِمَاذَا تُفَكِّرُ؟ تَبْدُو مَشْغُوْلًا.

حسن: الطَّقْسُ أَصْبَحَ بَارِدًا وَ اِحْتَاجَ إِلَى جَاكِيتٍ وَ حِذَاءٍ.

عَبْد الله: هَلْ تُرِيدُ الذَّهَابَ إِلَى السُّوقِ؟

حسن: نَعَمْ وَ لَكِنَّ سَيَّارَتَيْ لَا تَعْمَلُ.

عَبْد الله: حَسَنًا. أَنَا سَآخُذُكَ إِلَى السُّوقِ.

حسن: هَلْ أَنْتَ مُتَأَكِّدٌ؟

عَبْد الله: نَعَمْ. اِسْتَعِدَّ وَ لِنَذْهَبْ مَعًا.

حسن: أَنَا جَاهِزٌ.

عَبْد الله: هَيَّا بِنَا.

حسن: هَلْ تُرِيدُ شَيْئًا مِنْ السُّوقِ؟

عَبْد الله: نَعَمْ. أُرِيدُ أَنْ أَشْتَرِيَ بَنْطَالًا جَدِيدًا.

حسن: حَسَنًا. هَيَّا بِنَا.

Now answer the following questions:

1. بماذا يفكر حسن؟
2. لماذا لا يستطيع أن يذهب الى السوق؟
3. هل أاطقس حار عند حسن؟
4. ماذا يريد عبدالله من السوق؟

18.8. **Practice** (see Answer Key)

Specify the people or places by using الذي – التي – الذين then use in a sentence:

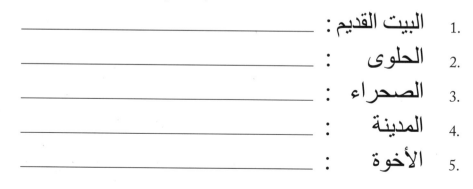

1. البيت القديم : _____
2. الحلوى : _____
3. الصحراء : _____
4. المدينة : _____
5. الأخوة : _____

6. العالم : _____

7. الساعة : _____

8. المدينة : _____

9. الرياضة : _____

18.9. Practice (see Answer Key)

Underline all words that belong to or found in a given place:

1. شارع : حاسوب – سيارة – بيت – عمارة – شباك

2. جامعة : مكتب – مكتبة – مدرسة – كلية – مادة

3. ملابس : فستان – ثلج – بنطال – شورت – طقس

4. مطبخ : ملعب – كوب – طبق – حليب – كرة

5. شقة : غرفة نوم – مخبز – حمام – غرفة سفرة – مكتب بريد

6. صيدلية : قهوة – دكتور – دواء – صيدلي – شركة

7. عائلة : زوجة – أب – ابن عم – صباح – خالة

8. دولة : نهر – جبل – صحراء – محيط – أوروبا

9. طعام : دجاج – لحم – تفاح – ساعة – سمك

10. رياضة : سباحة – كرة قدم – فندق – ملعب – صندوق

Reflection

1. In this Lesson I learned: _____

2. I have some trouble with: _____

3. I need to learn more about: _____

الوحدة التاسعة عشر
Holidays and Celebrations
أعياد و احتفالات
A'yad wa ihtifalat

Objectives:

1. Holidays
2. Grammar: Active and Passive verbs
3. Culture: Celebrations and Islamic Holidays
4. Reading
5. Holidays (from Islam as Identity *ch*)

 Vocabulary

Meaning	Transliteration	Plural	Transliteration	Word
Now	–	–	*Al-aan*	الآن
All	–	–	*Kol*	كُلْ
Party, celebration	*Haflat*	حَفْلاتْ	*Half*	حَفْلْ
Receive	–	–	*Yatassalam*	يتسّلّم/ تَسَلّم
Prize	*Jawa'iz*	جَوائِزْ	*Ja'zah*	جائِزة
Company	*Sharikat*	شَرِكاتْ	*Sharikah*	شَرِكة
Pass by	–	–	*Marra/Yamor*	مرّ/ يَمُرْ
Considered	–	–	*Ya'tabir*	يُعْتَبَرْ
Historical	–	–	*Tareekhi*	تاريخيْ
Too	–	–	*Aydhan*	أَيْضاً
Pharoah	*Fara'ina*	فَراعِنة	*Fer'awn*	فِرْعَوْنْ

Meaning	Transliteration	Plural	Transliteration	Word
Come	–		*Atta/Ya'tee*	أتي/يأتى
Funny	–		*Mod-hik*	مُضْحِكْ
Sad	–		*Hazeen*	حَزينْ
Wise	–		*Hakeem*	حَكيمْ
Stupid	–		*Ghabi*	غَبيْ
Popular	–		*Mahboob*	مَحْبوبْ
Famous	–		*Mash-hoor*	مَشْهورْ
Bedouin	*Bado*	بدو	*Badawi*	بَدَويْ
Citizen (from the city)	–		*Madani*	مَدَنيْ
Simple	–		*Baseet*	بَسيطْ
Quiet	–		*Hadi'*	هادِئْ
Prohibited	–		*Mamnoo'*	مَمْنوعْ
Traditional	–		*Taqleedi*	تَقْليدي
Use	–		*Istakhdama/yastakhdim*	استَخْدِم/يَسْتَخْدِم
Meeting	*Ijtima'at*	اجتماعات	*Ijtimaa'*	إجْتِماعْ
Center	*Marakiz*	مَراكِزْ	*Markaz*	مَرْكَزْ
Festival	*A'yad*	أعياد	*Eid*	عيد
Eid Al-Fitr	–		*Eid alfitr*	عيد الفطر
Eif Al-Adha	–		*Eid alad-ha*	عيد الأضحى

Islamic Holidays

All Arab and Islamic countries use a lunar calendar to determine religious dates such as fasting during the month of Ramadan, performing the Hajj, taking the pilgrimage to Mecca, and celebrating Islamic holidays. Lunar calendars, like the Gregorian calendar, have twelve months. Each month has twenty-nine to thirty days depending on the lunar cycle.

The Islamic calendar is also called the Hijri calendar. Umar ibn Al-Khattab, companion of the Prophet Mohammad, introduced it after the Prophet's death to resolve dating conflictions. He consulted his advisors at that time, and all agreed to use the Hijra, migration of the Prophet, as the beginning of the Hijri dating system. Some may refer to the Islamic calendar as a lunar calendar as it follows the orbit of the moon. It was started in 622 AD and the current Islamic year is 1437.

The first month of the Islamic calendar is called Muharram and therefore, the first day of Muharram is equivalent to January 1 or New Year's Day. This day is celebrated by closing schools, stores, government agencies. There are no fireworks or counting down to the beginning of the New Year. Arabs celebrate the day by visiting each other and having a fun day with family and friends.

Some Arab and Islamic countries celebrate the Prophet Muhammad's birthday, Mawlid al Nabi, which is on the twelfth day in the third month of the Islamic calendar. Others believe Muslims should not celebrate birthdays since the Prophet did not celebrate his own, or any other, birthday. Therefore, in general, Arabs and Muslims do not pay much attention to birthdays.

There are two major holidays in all Arab and Islamic countries, *Eid al-Fitr* and *Eid al-Adha*. The word Eid means celebration. Eid al-Fitr refers to the conclusion of Ramadan, the month of fasting, and celebrates the first day of breaking the fast. Muslims celebrate three days for Eid al-Fitr.

Eid al-Adha is celebrated at the conclusion of the Hajj, the fifth pillar of Islam. All Muslims celebrate it whether they are performing Hajj or not. The story behind Eid al-Adha goes back to

the time of the Prophet Ibrahim. Unlike in the Jewish and Christian traditions which believe Ibrahim (Abraham) was commanded by God to sacrifice his son Isaac, most Muslims believe that the Prophet Ibrahim was told in a dream to slaughter his son Ismail. Prophets' dreams are believed to be orders from Allah and are to be fulfilled.

Therefore, the Prophet Ibrahim, told his son about the dream, and Ismael's response was acceptance of Allah's order. When the Prophet Ibrahim held the knife and put it close to his son's throat, Allah sent down a lamb from Heaven to be sacrificed in his place. This is the reason that Muslims celebrate Eid al-Adha by slaughtering a lamb, cow or camel depending on availability and affordability. Sacrificing an animal is not an obligation but it is recommended. When sacrificing an animal, Muslims must divide their sacrifice into three parts: one third is to be given to friends and family, the second for the needy and they keep the third part for themselves. Muslims celebrate Eid Al-Adha for four days.

For Muslims, Friday is a holy day, the same as Saturday for Jews and Sunday for Christians. Males have to attend a lecture or ceremony introduced by the imam, a religious scholar, followed by the noon prayer. Women can attend the Friday ceremony if they wish, but it is not mandatory. I think this is because mothers need to tend to their babies and take care of them when the father is not available, so it was meant to make it easier for family.

Active and Passive verbs: المبني للمجهول

Arabic verbs, as in English, may be transitive or passive. To change a transitive verb into passive, there are few changes you are going to make to the verb:

1. Verbs in the past tense, you just put *dhamma* on the first letter and *kasra* on the second letter as in: كتب would be كُتِبَ and فَتَحَ would be فُتِحَ
   In weak verbs, that is verbs with *alif* ا , *waw* و or *ya* ي in the middle of the verb, we just change the long vowel into *ya* as in: قال would be قيل and جاء would be جِيئَ
   When the last letter is a long vowel, we change it into *ya* as in: سمّى would be سُمِّيَ and مشى would be مُشِيَ

2. Verbs in Present tense: we put *dhamma* on the present tense prefix (ن , ي , تـ , أ), and *fat-ha* on the middle consonant of the verb for example: يقرأ would be يُقرأ and يفتح would be يُفتَح
   As for weak verbs in the Present tense, we put *dhamma* on the first letter that is the prefix and replace the weak letter with *alif* as in: يقول would be يُقال and يصول would be يُصال
   When the last letter is a long vowel, then we change it into *alif maqsoura* as in: يُسمي would be يُسمى and يمشي would be يُمشى

19.1. Practice (see Answer Key)

Change the following sentences into the passive tense and remember to remove the doer of the action:

1. قال علي أن لبنان بلد جميل.
   _____

2. تشرب أمي القهوة بعد الافطار.
   _____

3. يحتفل المسلمون بعيد الفطر بعد رمضان.
   _____

4. اشترى أبي حلويات كثيرة.
   _____

5. يصلى المسلمون خمس مرات في اليوم.
   _____

19.2. Practice (see Answer Key)

Indicate whether the sentence has a passive or active tense:

1. اجتمع المدير مع الموظفين أمس.

2. شُربَ الدواء.

3. يُباع الرز بثلاثة دولارات.

4. أُعطيَ الفقير مالا.

5. أُكلت البرتُقالة.

6. لبستُ فستانا جميلا.

7. نام الطفل في غرفته.

8. قيل أن أفكارك ذكية.

19.3. Practice (see Answer Key)

Rearrange the words to form meaningful sentences:

1. أخوك – يدرس – ماذا – الجامعة – في؟

2. والدتي – مدينة – في – تسكن – دبي.

3. أخت – الآن – عندي – تعمل – واشنطن – في

4. لعرب – الجبن – و – الخبز – في – يأكل – معظم – الصباح.

5. موعد – في – السادسة – مساء – الطائرة – كان – وصول – و النصف.

6. العشاء – الأم – و جلسوا – أحضرت – حول – جميعا – الطاولة.

7. أزور – أن – أريد – البلاد – جميع – العربية

8. يعملون – الصباح – هم – من – الى – المساء.

9. الضيفان – هذان – الذان – أمس – زارانا.

10. يوم – سأراك – الثامنة – الأربعاء – الساعة – و النصف – صباحا.

19.4. Practice (see Answer Key)

Translate the following sentences into Arabic:

1. There is a café on the second street _____

2. January is the first month of the year _____

3. It is 8:30 now, I have to leave at 9:00 o'clock _____

4. Bilal is 75 years old, he is my maternal uncle _____

5. This is my Syrian friend Elham _____

6. I am Jordanian and he is a Kuwaiti _____

7. My paternal aunt is at home with her husband and daughter

_____

8. I am hungry. I want to eat falafel and humus _____

9. What is the name of the closest hotel to the airport? _____

10. What day comes after Sunday? _____

19.5. Practice (see Answer Key)

Change the following sentences into plural form:

1. وصل الطالب الى الحفلة ليتسلم جائزته.

2. المسافر وصل الى المطار ليركب الطائرة.

3. جاء الاعب الى النادي ليسبح.

4. المهندس يذهب الى الشركة كل يوم الساعة السابعة صباحا.

5. المدرسة كتبت الأسئلة على اللوح.

6. صديقتي تحب أن تشرب الشاي في المقهى.

7. الولد يأكل الفلافل و الحمص مع أخته.

8. هل عملت الواجب يا أخي؟

9. من أين اشتريت ساعتك؟

10. اشتريت تذكرة لاشاهد مباراة كرة القدم.

19.6. Practice   (see Answer Key)

Underline the most suitable word in parentheses:

1. عندي طائر (حمراء – أحمر – زرقاء).

2. هذا فستان (أحمر – حمراء – بنية).

3. (هذا – هذان - هؤلاء) الرجلان طويلان.

4. أنت (لست – ليسا – ليسوا) سعيد اليوم.

5. (هل متى – كم) هذه خالتك هدى؟

6. الساعة الآن (الخامسة عشرة – الثانية عشرة – الثالثة عشرة) مساء.

7. اليوم هو (الثالث – ثالث – الثالثة) من شهر يناير.

8. يوم الخميس يأتي (بعد – قبل – من) يوم الأربعاء.

9. سيارتي ليست جديدة هي (طويل – قديم – قديمة).

10. هم يريدون أن (يساعد – يساعدان – يساعدوا) في عمل الواجب.

19.7. Practice   (see Answer Key)

Connect the related words by writing the number in parentheses:

حزين	( ) دخل	2.		يتذكر	( ) صباح	1.
يوم	( ) أبيض	4.		مساء	( ) ينسى	3.
طالب	( ) سعيد	6.		الخميس	( ) أسود	5.
شتاء	( ) قهوة	8.		مدرس	( ) خرج	7.
مقهى	( ) سؤال	10.		ثلج	( ) جواب	9.

19.8. Practice   (see Answer Key)

Reading:

تعتبر جمهورية مصر العربية أكبر دولة عربية في عدد سكانها. و هي أيضا أكبر دولة في أفريقيا. يمر فيها نهر النيل و هو أطول نهر في العالم. عاصمة مصر هي القاهرة و هي تقع في شمال شرق جمهورية مصر العربية. عدد سكانها الآن تقريبا 17 مليون نسمة و هي مزدحمة جدا. يُقال أن في القاهرة يوجد أربع ملايين و خمسمائة ألف سيارة و دائما الشوارع مزدحمة جدا فيها. هناك محطة للقطار فيها و تنقل يوميا حوالي أربعة ملايين راكب يوميا.

تم بناء مدينة القاهرة في سنة 969 قبل الميلاد و كان يحكمها الفراعنة ثم الدولة الرومانية و الأتراك و فرنسا ثم بريطانيا.

من أشهر الأماكن الموجودة في مصر هي الأهرامات و تمثال أبو الهول في منطقة الجيزة و التي بناها الفراعنة في سنة 2500 قبل الميلاد و هي تمتد لمسافة 53 الف كيلو متر مربع و ترتفع 140 متر فوق سطح الأرض.

في القاهرة أيضا يوجد المتحف المصري و الذي يحتوي على أكثر من 130 الف معروض فيها.

و هناك أيضا أقدم جامعة في العالم و هي جامعة الأزهر و قد كانت مسجدا و تسمى مدينة الألف مئذنة بسبب الهندسة المعمارية الموجودة فيها.

هناك أيضا خان الخليلي و هو واحد من أكبر الأسواق في القاهرة.و يعود تاريخه إلى القرن الرابع عشر. وينقسم إلى أقسام مختلفة تبيع السجاد والتوابل والأشغال المعدنية والعديد من العناصر الأخرى

هناك أيضا مساجد كثيرة مشهورة فيها مثل جامع السيدة زينب و جامع عمرو بن العاص و مسجد الحسين. الكثير من الناس يذهبون كل سنة

الى جمهورية مصر العربية لزيارة الآثار التاريخية الجميلة الموجودة فيها

Now answer the following questions:

1. متى بُنيت القاهرة؟ 2. ما هي أكبر دولة في أفريقيا؟

3. ما هي أقدم جامعة في العالم؟ 4. ما هي أشهر الأماكن في القاهرة؟

5. ما هي أشهر المساجد فيها؟

19.9. Practice (see Answer Key)

Connect each two sentences using the relative pronouns (الذي – التي – الذين):

1. أين البنطال البني؟ غسلت البنطال أمس.

2. هل أكل الأولاد؟ الأولاد كانوا في المطعم.

3. اشترت هدى فستان. الفستان كان في الخزانة.

4. اجتمع المدير مع الموظفين. الموظفون طلبوا اجتماعا.

5. زرت الأهرامات. الأهرامات في مصر.

19.10. Practice (see Answer Key)

Change the following words into plurals then use them to fill in the blanks:

مكان – مهندس – كوب – ابن – محطة – حمام – مركز – الهدية –

1. عندي سبعة ـــــــــــــــ : ثلاث بنات و أربعة أولاد

2. أستأجرنا بيتا كبيرا فيه أربع غرف نوم و ثلاثة ـــــــــــــــ

3. تطبخ أمي أربعة ـــــــــــــــ من الرز للغداء.

4. رأينا ـــــــــــــــ بنزين كثيرة في رحلتنا

5. أصدقائي يعملون ـــــــــــــــ في الحكومة.

6. في عطلة نهاية الأسبوع ذهبنا الى الكثير من ـــــــــــــــ التسوق في المدينة.

7. استمتعنا بزيارة ـــــــــــــــ السياحية.

8.   اشترينا الكثير من ـــــــــــــــ لعائلتي.

19.11. Practice   (see Answer Key)

Write questions that correspond to the given answers:

1.   في بيتي غرفة نوم واحدة.

2.   نعم عندي سؤال.

3.   نسيت هاتفي في البيت.

4.   لا أنا أسكن مع أختي في أمريكا.

5.   أقمنا في الفندق ثلاثة أيام.

6.   أنا أعمل في البنك الوطني.

7.   أدرس الرياضيات في كلية جلبرت.

8.   سنذهب الى المقهى في الساعة السابعة مساء.

9.   لا عندي خال واحد.

10.   أمي لا تعمل . هي في البيت.

Reflection

1.   In this Lesson I learned: _____

2.   I have some trouble with: _____

3.   I need to learn more about: _____

Lesson 20

الوحدة العشرون
Review
مراجعة

Moraja'a

Objectives:

1. Describing things in the Past, Present and Future
2. Grammar: كـ- مثل – كأن – كما
3. Culture: Body Language
4. Review
5. Reading

Vocabulary

Meaning	Transliteration	Plural	Transliteration	Word
Child	*Atfal*	أَطْفال	*Tifl*	طِفْلْ
Behave	–	–	*Tasarrafa/ yatasaraaf*	تصرَّف/يَتَصرَّفْ
Luxurious	–	–	*Fakhma*	فَخْمة
Winner	–	–	*Fa'iz/Fa'iza*	فائِزْ/فائِزة
Grade	*Darajat*	دَرَجاتْ	*Darajah*	دَرَجة
Contest	*Mosabaqat*	مُسابَقاتْ	*Mosabaqa*	مُسابَقة
Test/Exam	*Imtihanat*	إِمْتِحاناتْ	*imtihan*	إِمْتِحانْ
Final	–	–	*Niha'ee*	نَهائيْ
Veiled	*Mohajabbat*	مُحَجَّبات	*mohajabbah*	مُحَجَّبة
Imagine	–	–	*Takhayyala/ yatakhayyal*	تَخَيَّلْ/يتخيّل

Meaning	Transliteration	Plural	Transliteration	Word
Clean	–	–	*Natheed*	نَظِيفْ
Dirty	–	–	*Qathir*	قَذِرْ
Suddenly	–	–	*Faj'a*	فَجْأة
Laugh	–	–	*Dhahika/ yadh-hak*	ضَحِكَ/يَضْحَكْ
Cry	–	–	*Baka/yabki*	بَكى/يَبْكي
Taxi	*Sayyarat Ojra*	سيارات أجرة	*Sayyarat Ojra*	سيّارة أُجرة
Bus	*Basat*	باصات	*Bas*	باصْ
First	–	–	*Awalan*	أوّلاً
Last	–	–	*Akheeran*	أخيراً
Dawn	–	–	*Alfajr*	الفَجْرْ
Noon	–	–	*Adhohr*	الظُّهْرْ
Afternoon	–	–	*Ala'sr*	العَصْرْ
Sunset	–	–	*Almaghrib*	المَغْرِبْ
Evening	–	–	*Alisha*	العِشاءْ
After that	–	–	*Ba'da thalik*	بَعْدَ ذلِكْ
Clear/pure	–	–	*Saffi*	صافي
Cloudy	–	–	*Gha'm*	غائِمْ
Crowded	–	–	*Mozdahim*	مُزْدَحِمْ
Empty	–	–	*Farigh*	فارِغْ
Invent	–	–	*Ightara'/ yakhtari'*	اخترَع/يَخْتَرِعْ

Meaning	Transliteration	Plural	Transliteration	Word
Information	*Ma'loomat*	مَعْلومات	*Ma'looma*	مَعْلومة
Procedure	*Ijra'at*	اجْراءْات	*Ijra'*	إِجْراءْ
Expect	–	–	*Tawaqa'/ yatawaqa'*	توقع/يتوقع

Gestures and Body Language

We will conclude this book culture part with examples of some common Arab gestures and displays of body language which may have different meanings in the West. Below are some examples.

- Usually, when using the hand for eating, drinking or shaking hands, the right hand is used.
- Nodding the head down is a sign of agreement and it means yes.
- Raising the eyebrows, moving the head from right to left, moving an open palm from right to left, using the tongue to make a clicking sound or tilting the head up are all different ways of saying "no."
- To open the left-hand palm and hit it with the right fist means condescension or offensiveness.
- Making a circle using the thumb and index fingers indicates a threat or "I am coming to get you."
- Holding the fingers together while pointing the tips up and moving the hand up and down is a sign to slow down, be careful or wait.
- Touching the forehead with the fingertips and bowing the head shows respect and appreciation.
- A man stroking his mustache reflects seriousness and honesty.

- To point at someone with the index finger and move it up and down indicates condescension toward that person or threatening him to stop what he is doing.
- To open the right-hand palm and move it right to left means no, in contrast to its meaning as "hello" for Westerners.
- To put the right-hand forefinger in the mouth and pretend to bite it means "I am angry with you" or "I am coming to get you."
- To touch the tip of the nose or the lower eyelid with the right hand or its forefinger means a promise to do something or an obligation.
- To grasp the chin with the right-hand thumb indicates wisdom or "I am thinking."

As the cradle of Judaism, Christianity and Islam and a crossroads of international commerce, the Arab world shows elements of a unified culture as well as a great deal of cultural variation. Despite differences in clothing, music, food and dialects from one Arab country to another, common fundamental values of Arab culture and customs merit exploration and explanation to foster greater understanding.

Grammar

ك _ مثل – كأن – كما , are used to show similarities. They mean "the same as." However, they are used differently.

مثل: *mithla* means "like" and is treated as the first noun in *idafa*. It can be suffixed according to the subject.

For example here is the conjugation of مثل *mithla*:

Transliteration	It would be:	Pronoun	
Mithlee	مثلي	أنا	مثل
Mithlona	مثلنا	نحن	مثل
Mithloka	مثلك	أنتَ	مثل
Mithloki	مثلكِ	أنتِ	مثل
Mithlokoma	مثلكما	أنتما	مثل
Mithlokom	مثلكم	أنتم	مثل
Mithloho	مثله	هو	مثل
Mithloha	مثلها	هي	مثل
Mithlohoma	مثلهما	هما	مثل
Mithlohom	مثلهم	هم	مثل
Mithlohonna	مثلهنّ	هن	مثل

Some examples are:

Meaning	Transliteration	Example
He is as short as I am.	*Howa qaseer mithlee.*	هو قصير مثلي
She is as smart as you.	*Hiya thakiyyah mithlokom.*	هي ذكية مثلكم

كـ: means "like" comes at the beginning of the nouns only and is connected to it. It does not come by itself and it does not make any changes. Some examples:

Meaning	Transliteration	Example
My house is as small and beautiful as his house.	*Bayti kabaytoho sagheer wa jameel.*	بيتي كبيته صغير و جميل
I want a car like yours.	*Oreed sayyarah kasayyaratok.*	أريد سيارة كسيارتك

كأن : means "as if." It should be followed by a nominal sentence. It gives the idea that whatever it is describing might not be true. Some examples:

Meaning	Transliteration	Example
The year passed as if it's a month.	*Marrat assanah ka'naha shahr.*	مرّت السنة كأنها شهر
He behaves like a child.	*Yatasarraf ka'nnaho tifl sagheer.*	يتصرف كأنه طفل صغير

كأن can be used by itself or attached to a pronoun, when it is attached it would be like this:

Transliteration	It would be:	Pronoun	
Ka'nanee	كأنني	أنا	كأن
Ka'nana	كأننا	نحن	كأن
Ka'naka	كأنك	أنتَ	كأن
Ka'naki	كأنكِ	أنتِ	كأن
Ka'nakoma	كأنكما	أنتما	كأن

Transliteration	It would be:	Pronoun	
Ka'nakom	كأنكم	أنتم	كأن
Ka'naho	كأنه	هو	كأن
Ka'naha	كأنها	هي	كأن
Ka'nahoma	كأنهما	هما	كأن
Ka'nahom	كأنهم	هم	كأن
Ka'nahonna	كأنهن	هن	كأن

Kama كما: means "as" and must be followed by a verb. It does not make any changes to the verb. Some examples are:

Meaning	Transliteration	Example
As you know	*Kama ta'lam*	كما تعلم
As I want	*Kama oreed*	كما أريد

20.1. **Practice** (see Answer Key)

Fill in the blanks using one of the following: كـ _ مثل – كأن – كما

1. هي لا تهتم بشيئ و تتصرف _____ تريد.

2. أريد أن أشتري فستانا جميلا _____ فستانك.

3. لم يفهموا شيئا من الدرس _____ الأستاذ كان يتكلم لوحده.

4. هي لا تريد أن تكون _____ صديقتها أمل.

5. _____ تعرفون أنا لا أحب النوم متأخرة.

6. القهوة العربية ليست _____ القهوة الأمريكية.

7. علاقتة بوالده جيدة جدا _____ يريد أنت تكون.

8. هل أنت _____ أمك؟

9. هو يأكل _____ ما يريد.

10. بيت الطلاب يبدو _____ عمارة فخمة.

20.2. Practice (see Answer Key)

Read. Then pretend you are the student and answer the questions to review your information on the Arab World:

دخل الأستاذ الصف و قال لطلابه أنه سيعمل لهم مسابقة. و الفائز في هذه المسابقة سيحصل على خمسة درجات سيضيفها الى درجة الامتحان النهائي. فرح الطلاب و أعدوا الورقة و القلم ليبدأوا في حل الأسئلة. كتب الأستاذ على اللوح:

1. ما هو أصغر بلد عربي؟
2. ما هو أكبر بلد عربي؟
3. ما اسم أطول نهر في العالم؟
4. ما هي أقدم جامعة في العالم ؟ أين توجد؟
5. ماذا يفعل المسلمون في شهر رمضان؟
6. ما هو الشهر السابع في السنة؟
7. ما الفرق بين السنة الميلادية و السنة الهجرية؟
8. أي بلد تحب أن تزور من العالم العربي ؟ لماذا؟
9. ما هو أول يوم في الأسبوع في العالم العربي؟
10. هل جميع النساء العربيات محجبات؟

تخيل أنك في هذا الصف و حاول الاجابة على هذه الأسئلة

20.3. Practice (see Answer Key)

Write the opposite of the following sentences:

1. شقته واسعة و ايجارها رخيص.
2. المطبخ ضيق و فيه شباك صغير.
3. غرفة النوم صغيرة و السرير قديم.
4. الطاولة و الكراسي جديدة.
5. الحمام نظيف.

6. المكتبة فارغة و ليس فيها كتب.

7. غرفة الجلوس بعيدة عن المطبخ.

8. الطقس حار و السماء صافية.

9. جاء أحمد الى أمريكا.

10. عند أمل سيارة تويوتا.

20.4. Practice   (see Answer Key)

Replace the numbers with words:

1. كل يوم أعمل واجبي في 3 _____ ساعات.

2. في مدرستي كنت أدرس 7 _____ مواد.

3. سعر الفستان 56 _____ دولارا.

4. في السنة 12 _____ شهرا.

5. كل سنة يكون عندي 2 أسبوع _____ اجازة.

6. قضينا 10 _____ أسابيع في السودان.

7. وصلنا الى المطار الساعة 6 _____ صباحا.

8. اليوم هو الخميس 2019/8/15 _____

9. قرأت 25 _____ كتابا في السنة الماضية.

10. أحتاج 1260 _____ دولارا في الشهر.

20.5. Practice   (see Answer Key)

Circle the word that does not belong:

1. شجرة – زهرة – أخضر – أستاذ

2. بارد – حار – معتدل – أسبوع

3. شاطئ – نهر – درجة – بحر

4. ربيع – جامعة – خريف – شتاء

5. اللغة العربية – الرياضيات – العلوم – المقهى

6. شاي – ماء – سيارة – قهوة

7. المطبخ ـ غرفة الجلوس – الأم – الصالة

8. تفاح – يشرب – يأكل – يطبخ

9. دقيقة – حديقة – ساعة – يوم

10. الافطار – الأمير – الغداء – العشاء

20.6. Practice (see Answer Key)

Circle the word that does not belong:

2. شاي   : _____   1. الطعام : _____

4. كتاب   : _____   3. السوق : _____

6. طائرة : _____   5. قلم   : _____

8. شقة   : _____   7. ملابس: _____

10. كرسي : _____   9. سيارة : _____

12.. التلفاز : _____   11. راديو : _____

20.7. Practice (see Answer Key)

Underline the most suitable word in parentheses:

1. (ماذا – هل – كيف) ستفعل الليلة؟

2. (ماذا – أين – كيف) الطقس اليوم؟

3. (كم – ماذا – من أين) تعملين يا هدى؟

4. (كيف – أ – لا) مستعد للسفر؟

5. الطلاب لا (يحب – يحبون – يحبان) الزي المدرسي.

6. (سأتناول – أتناول – يتناولان) الطعام بعد أن أنهي واجبي.

7. أريد أن أسرع لكن الشارع (قصير – فارغ – مزدحم).

8. هي (تشترين – تشتري – يشتري) الملابس الغالية دائما.

9. لا (يستطيع – يستطيعون – يستطيعان) المسافرون زيارة كل الأماكن في يوم واحد.

10. (بدأت – ستبدأ – يبدأ) عطلة الصيف يعد شهر واحد.

20.8. Practice (see Answer Key)

Read the sentence then form into questions:

1. أنا من مدينة القاهرة.

2. نعم أحب الفلافل كثيرا.

3. هو يعمل في الجامعة الأمريكية.

4. هم يدرسون التجارة في جامعة نيويورك.

5. أمل تسكن مع صديقتها هدى في سكن الطالبات.

6. ذهبت الى الأردن لأدرس اللغة العربية.

7. الرياض هي عاصمة السعودية.

8. تسقط أوراق الشجر في فصل الخريف.

9. بومباي هي أكبر ميناء في الهند.

10. لا لم أعمل الواجب حتى الآن.

20.9. Practice (see Answer Key)

Reading:

هل فكرت يوما أن بامكان دكتور من بريطانيا المساعدة باجراء عملية جراحية لمريض في الأردن؟

من يصدق أن الأولاد و البنات بامكانهم التسوق في كل المحلات الالكترونية بدون سيارة و يشترون كل ما يريدون و هم في بيوتهم دون الذهاب الى السوق؟

هل تصدق أن بامكانك اختيار كل ما تريده من الكتب و المجلات و تذاكر دروسك مع أصدقائك و أنت في بيتك؟ بامكانك أيضا أن تلعب

ما تشاء من الألعاب الألكترونية مع أصدقائك عبر الشاشة الألكترونية دون أن تذهب الى بيوتهم. و أخيرا من الممكن أن تدرس كل ما تريد من المواد الدراسية و تحصل على شهادة دون أن تذهب الى المدرسة أو الجامعة و أن تدرس و أنت جالس على شاطئ البحر أو في أي مكان تريد. هذه هي الثورة الاعلامية

في البداية و قبل آلاف السنين اخترعوا الكتابة و كانوا يكتبون على جلود الحيوانات و أوراق الشجر و أحيانا يحفرون على الحجر. ثم اخترعوا الطباعة و مع تقدم الوقت انتشرت الكتب في كل مكان و الآن تكنولوجيا المعلومات تمكنك من تخزين كل ما تريد من معلومات و عرضها و نقلها من مكان لاخر في أقل من دقيقة على تلفونك الخاص.

ترى: ماذا سيخترعون بعد ذلك ؟ كيف سيكون العالم بعد خمسين سنة؟

Answer the following questions from the reading:

1. ما رأيك في التكنولوجيا الحديثة؟
2. من أين تشتري كتبك؟
3. هل تذهب الى السوق لتشتري ملابسك؟
4. كم مادة درست على الكمبيوتر دون أن تذهب الى الجامعة؟
5. كيف تتوقع أن يصبح العالم بعد خمسين سنة؟

Reflection

1. In this Lesson I learned: _____

2. I have some trouble with: _____

3. I need to learn more about: _____

Answer Key

Lesson 1

1.2. Practice

11. قطر	9. طازج	7. شيطان	6. طرابلس	4. طائر	2. طماطم

1.9. Practice:

5. مسجد	4. تبذير	3. بركان	2. جلال	1. صبور
10. كلاب	9. تصدير	8. حروب	7. طالبة	6. مسلمون

Lesson 2

2.5. Practice

5. سكون	4. ضحك	3. دجاج	2. شكر	1. كشف
10. اثبات	9. ورود	8. تأثير	7. بارد	6. يبحث

2.7. Practice:

1. بــ___ور = **بدور**   2. با___د = **بارد**   3. تأ___ير = **تأثير**
4. ___رز = أرز   5. ___زواج = أزواج   6. ___ديد = **حديد**
7. و___حد = **واحد**   8. شبا___ = **شباك**   9. و___ير = **وزير**
10. أخ___ات = أخوات

2.8. Practice:

5. المدينة	4. طاولةً	3. الشارع	2. قلما	1. **الأستاذ**

2.9. Practice

(5) الى اللقاء   (2) الحمدلله أنا بخير

(3) و عليكم السلام   (1) أهلا

(4) تشرفنا . اسمي أحمد

Lesson 3

3.1. Practice:

3. زُجَاجَةٌ	2. دَجَاجَةٌ - جَرِيدَةٌ.	1. خَيْمَةٌ – بِنْتُ
6. مَجَلَّةٌ	5. سَعِيدَةٌ	4. طَاوِلَةٌ – زَوْجَةٌ
9. كُلِّيَّةٌ - جَامِعَةٌ.	8. كَاتِبَةٌ	7. بَطَّةٌ - غُرْفَةٌ
		10. جَامِعَةٌ

3.2. Practice:

15 (6)	13 (5)
17 (2)	10 (1)
9 (3)	10 (4)

3.3. Practice:

5. ٦٧	4. ٧٥	3. ٨	2. ٧١	1. ٥٣
10. ٩٦	9. ١١١	8. ٠٢	7. ٥١	6. ٤٢

3.4. Practice:

2. أربعة عشر قلما

1. أحد عشر كتابا

4. ست و سبعين بنتا

3. خمسة و ستين كرسيا

6. خمسين طاولة

5. مئتان و تسعة و ثمانين بيتا

8. ثلاث مائة و أربع و ثمانين محاية

7. اثنان و عشرين مفتاحا

10. خمس مائة و ثلاث و ستين ورقة

9. مائة و أربع غرف

3.5. Practice:

3. ض ر ب = **ضرب**

2. ك س ب = **كسب**

1. ن س ك = **نسك**

6. ع د ل = **عدل**

5. ك ش ف = **كشف**

4. ص ر خ = **صرخ**

9. ع م ل = **عمل**

8. ع ل م = **علم**

7. ك ت ب = **كتب**

12. غ ر ق = **غرق**

11. ق ر أ = **قرأ**

10. غ س ق = **غسق**

13. ق م ر = **قمر**

3.6. Practice:

Read and respond to the following:

هدى : <u>**الحمدلله أنا بخير**</u>

أمل : مرحبا !

أمل : من أين أنت؟

هدى : <u>أهلا</u>

هدى : **أنا من سوريا**_____ من أين أنت؟

أمل : ما اسمك ؟

هدى : **أنا من الكويت**

هدى : اسمي <u>هدى</u>

أمل : الى اللقاء

هدى : و انت؟ ما اسمك؟

هدى : **مع السلامة**

أمل : اسمي <u>أمل</u>

أمل: كيف حالك؟

3.8. Practice:

2. ك : مكتب – سكن – سبيكة

1. **هـ** : وردة – هدى - يهدي

4. ن :– نلعب – منال

3. م :– اسمي – مثال – سمر

6. ٦. ت :– تعليم

5. ي : جنسية – جديد – ادريس – يبحث

8. ش شارك – مشرك

7. ج : جنوب

10. ف : زفاف – فاز

9. غ غروب

Lesson 4

4.1. Practice:

النهاية

الصف

الشارع

4.2. Practice:

الولد   شمساً

كتابٍ   الساعة

مكتبةً   مسجدا

4.3. Practice:

2. غُرْفَةٌ.   1. وَاحِدٌ.

4. بَابٌ.   3. مَدِينَة

5. أَنَا

4.4. Practice:

1. مِنْ أَيْنَ أَحْمَدُ؟

أحمد من تمبي

2. أَيْنَ دِمَشْقُ؟

دمشق في سوريا

3. مَاذَا تَعَلَّمَ أَحْمَدُ اليَوْمَ؟

تَعَلَّمَ أَسْمَاءُ الأَشْيَاءَ المَوْجُودَةَ فِي الغُرْفَة

4. مَا هِيَ الأَشْيَاءُ المَوْجُودَةَ فِي الغُرْفَةِ؟

طَاوِلَةٌ وَ كُرْسِيٌّ وَ شُبَّاك .

5. أَكْتُبُ ثَلَاثَةَ أَشْيَاءٍ مَوْجُودَةٍ فِي غُرْفَتِكَ

مكتب – قلم - باب

4.5. Practice:

1. الحَقِيبَةُ   2. الطَّاوِلَةُ   3. بِجَانِبِ   4. سَأَفِرُّ   5. أَيْنَ   6. أُرِيدُ

4.7. Practice:

1. نظارة   2. بعيد   3. أمال   4. يكتب   5. ارتفاع

6. حصانة   7. نهضات   8. سفينة   9. جريدتي   10. فنادق

Lesson 5

5.1. Practice:

1. بَعْدُ   2. قَبْلَ   3. أَيَّامٌ   4. أَسَابِيعُ

5. لُغَتَيْنِ   6. الجَامِعَةُ   7. عنظَّارَاتٌ   8. مَادَّةٌ

5.2. Practice:

1. يجلس الطلاب أمام الأستاذ في الفصل.

2. كل طالب يجلس على الكرسي و معه دفتر و قلم على الدرج.

3. هناك أستاذين في هذا الصف.

4. يقف الأستاذ أمام ثلاثة و عشرين طالبا في الصف.

5. كم مادة تدرس؟

5.3. Practice:

1. تسكن الطالبات في غرف صغيرة   2. ذهب الطلاب الى الكلية   3. أدرس لغات

4. هناك معلمون في المكتبة   5. كتب الطلاب على الألواح

5.4. Practice:

1. أوراق   2. كلمات   3. لغات   4. سوريين   5. كويتيون

5.5. Practice:

3. كفي السنة أربعة فصول	2. في السنة اثنا عشر شهرا	1. في الأسبوع سبعة أيام
6. عمري .... سنة	5. عندي .... اخوة	4. في صفي عشرين طالبا؟
9. الأربعاء بعد يوم الثلاثاء	8. في اليوم أربع و عشرين ساعة	7. عيد ميلادي في شهر ....

10. آخِرُ شَهْرٍ فِي السَّنَةِ هو ديسمبر

5.6. Practice:

(6) قرأ عادل الكتاب.

(5) أخذ كتاب مادة التاريخ.

(3) لم يجد عادل الكتاب في البيت.

(4) ذهب عادل الى المكتبة.

(2) كتب معلم التاريخ الأسئلة على اللوح.

(7) أجاب على كل الأسئلة.

(1) في الصباح ذهب عادل الى فصل التاريخ .

5.7. Practice

2. أين فؤاد ؟ هُوَ فِي المَكْتَبَةِ

1. من هو محمد ؟ مُحَمَّدٌ صَدِيقُ فُؤَاد

4. في أي صف أيمن ؟ أيمن فِي الصَّفِّ التَّاسِعُ

3. كم عمر أيمن؟ عُمرُأيمن ثلاث عشرة سنة

5. أين سيذهب محمد ؟ سيذهب محمد الى المكتبة

5.8. Practice:

5. سيدة	4. بنت	3. أميرة	2. طالبة	1. معلمة
10. حضرت	9. قطة	8. كثيرة	7. هي	6. تعبانة

5.9. Practice:

5. سيارة	4. يلعب	3. كتاب	2. مكتبة	1. أنا

Lesson 6
6.1. Practice:

هم	هما	هما	نحن	هي	هو	أنتِ	أنتَ	أنا	Verb	Meaning
يحددون	تحددان	يحددان	نحدد	تحدد	يحدد	تحددين	تحدد	أحدد	حدّد	Assign
يحفظون	تحفظان	يحفظان	نحفظ	تحفظ	يحفظ	تحفظين	تحفظ	أحفظ	حفظ	Keep
يدرسون	تدرسان	يدرسان	ندرس	تدرس	يدرس	تدرسين	تدرس	أدرس	درس	Study
يرسمون	ترسمان	يرسمان	نرسم	ترسم	يرسم	ترسمين	ترسم	أرسم	رسم	Draw
يشاهدون	تشاهدان	يشاهدان	نشاهد	تشاهد	يشاهد	تشاهدين	تشاهد	أشاهد	شاهد	Watch
يأكلون	تأكلان	يأكلان	نأكل	تأكل	يأكل	تأكلين	تأكل	آكل	أكل	Eat
يسمعون	تسمعان	يسمعان	نسمع	تسمع	يسمع	تسمعين	تسمع	أسمع	سمع	Hear
يخرجون	تخرجان	يخرجان	نخرج	تخرج	يخرج	تخرجين	تخرج	أخرج	خرج	Go out
يفتحون	تفتحان	يفتحان	نفتح	تفتح	يفتح	تفتحين	تفتح	أفتح	فتح	Open

6.2. Practice:

4. يتكلم	3. يذهبان	2. يسكنون	1. ترسمين
8. يتكلمون	7. تكتب	6. يشاهدان	5. أدرس
		10. نسمع	9. أحب

6.3. Practice:

2. الاثنين هو أول أيام الأسبوع .   1. أنا أدرس الكيمياء و الأدب

4. أين حقيبتك ؟   3. تبدو متعبا هل أنت بخير ؟

5. أنا أحب الفن و لكن أكرة العلوم

6.4. Practice:

5. تعرف	4. يعرفون	3. تعرفين	2. نعرف	1. أعرف

6.5. Practice:

3. أختها أمريكية   2. هو استاذ   1. هي طالبة

6. هما طويلتان   5. هما انجليزيان   4. أبوه مهندس

6.6. Practice:

6. ماذا	5. أين	4. متى	3. كم	2. هل 1. أين

6.7. Practice

Form questions to ask your friend in Arabic:

2. كم غرفة في بيتك؟   1. أين المكتبة؟

4. ما اسم استاذ اللغة العربية؟   3. ما رقم تلفونك؟

6. هل تذهب الى الكلية بالباص أم بالسيارة؟   5. هل عندك سيارة؟

8. من أين أتيت؟   7. ما معنى كلمة ..... بالعربي؟

10. كيف أتيت الى المدرسة؟   9. كم أخ و أخت عندك؟

6.8. Practice:

5. لأنهم	4. لأنها	3. لأنها	2. لأنه	1. لأننا

6.9. Practice:

2. ماذا يدرس أحمد ؟   1. متى سنذهب الى المكتبة ؟

4. كم أخ عندك ؟   3. ما هو أول يوم في الأسبوع ؟

5. هل عائلتك كبيرة ؟

6.10. Practice:

2. أَجْمَلُ الفُصُولِ هُوَ فَصْلُ الرَّبِيعِ   1. في السنة أربعة فصول.

4. يَكُونُ الطَّقْسُ حَارٌّ في الصيف   3. يُنَزِّلُ المطر والثلج في فصل الشتاء

5. أحب فصل ....

6.11. Practice:

(1) أخضر   (5) أزهار   (4) حار   (3) مطر و ثلج   (2) رياح

Lesson 7

7.1. Practice:

1. السماء زرقاء.   2. سيارتي بنية.   3. أنا أحب اللون الأحمر.

4. الأشجار تكون خضراء في فصل الربيع.   5. لون الباب أسود.

7.2. Practice:

1. هما   2. هو   3. أنتِ   4. أنت   5. سيارتهما

7.3. Practice:

1. أنت   2. أنتم- نحن   3. هو   4. هما   5. أنتم

7.4. Practice:

أنتن	أنتم	نحن	أنتما	أنتِ	أنتَ	الكلمة
دفتركن	دفتركم	دفترنا	دفتركما	دفترك	دفترك	دفتر
فستانكن	فستانكم	فستاننا	فستانكما	فستانك	فستاني	فستان
مكتبكن	مكتبكم	مكتبنا	مكتبكما	مكتبك	مكتبي	مكتب
جامعتكن	جامعتكم	جامعتنا	جامعتكما	جامعتك	جامعتي	جامعة
اسمكن	اسمكم	اسمنا	اسمكما	اسمك	اسمي	اسم
أمكن	أمكم	أمنا	أمكما	أمك	أمي	أم
ولدكن	ولدكم	ولدنا	ولدكما	ولدك	ولدي	ولد
أختكن	أختكم	أختنا	أختكما	أختك	أختي	أخت
بيتكن	بيتكم	بيتنا	بيتكما	بيتك	بيتي	بيت
سيارتكن	سيارتكم	سيارتنا	سيارتكما	سيارتك	سيارتي	سيارة
غرفتكن	غرفتكم	غرفتنا	غرفتكما	غرفتك	غرفتي	غرفة

7.5. Practice:

Preposition would be	preposition	pronoun
عليها	على	هي
فوقنا	فوق	نحن
تحتك	تحت	أنتَ
يمينك	يمين	انتِ
يسارنا	يسار	أنتم

Preposition would be	preposition	pronoun
عليه	على	هو
أمامها	أمام	هي
بجانبهما	بجانب	هما
بينهم	بين	هم

7.6. Practice:

1.	اسمي	2.	والدتها	3.	بيتنا	4.	عنوانكم
5.	خالته- بيتي.	6.	جامعتهم	7.	عمها	8.	عمها

7.7. Practice

1.	هذا	2.	هذه	3.	هذه	4.	هذا	5.	هذه

7.8. Practice

1. هذا مكتبه
2. هؤلاء أصدقائي.
3. هذه جدتها.
4. هذان الدفتران لك.
5. هذا كلبه.
6. هذه كلية الآداب.
7. هؤلاء البنات في صفي.
8. هذا اسم عربي.
9. هذه بيوت جديدة .
10. هاتان البنتان صديقاتي.

7.9. Practice:

1.	هي	2.	الكلمات	3.	هذه	4.	لونها	5.	كليتها

7.10. Practice:

1. يوجد في الصف سبع طالبات.
2. المكتبة في الطابق الرابع.
3. آكل طعام الغداء في المطعم.
4. هل تذهب معي الى المخبز؟
5. يلعب الأصدقاء كرة السلة في الملعب.
6. أخو عادل يعمل في السوق.
7. في بيتي أربع غرف و ثلاثة حمامات.

7.11. Practice:

1. أين أمل ؟ أمل في المطبخ
2. ماذا يريد أحمد ؟ أحمد يريد فِنْجَانًا مِنْ القَهْوَة
3. كيف يشرب أحمد قهوته ؟ أحمد يشرب قهوته مع سكر
4. ماذا ستأكل أمل مع قهوتها ؟ أمل ستأكل الشُّوكُولَاتَةِ

Lesson 8

8.1. Practice:

Comparisons	Adjective	Romanization
أقدم	قديم	Qadeem
أكثر	كثير	Katheer
أكبر	كبير	Kabeer
أشدّ	شديد	Shaded
أهم	هام	Ham
أفقر	فقير	Faqeer

Comparisons	Adjective	Romanization
أغنى	غني	Ghaniy
أرخص	رخيص	Rakhees
أغلى	غالي	Ghalee
أحسن	حسن	Hasan
أرحم	رحيم	Raheem

8.2. Practice:

5. أطول   4. أجدد   3. ألذّ   2. أرخص   1. أصغر

10. أجمل   9. أنشط   8. أسرع   7. أنظف   6. أكثر

8.3. Practice:

(2) فتحت الأم العلبة   (1) اشترى الأب علبة شوكولاتة   (5) فرح الأولاد بها كثيرا

(3) أعطت الأم كل واحد أربع قطع   (4) في العلبة اثنتا عشرة قطعة

8.4. Practice:

5. رمادي   4. بيضاء   3. أسود   2. زرقاء   1. أصفر/ ذهبي

8.5. Practice:

3. كم عم و خالة عندك؟   2. ماذا تعمل خالتك؟   1. هل عندك أخوة؟

5. ما اسم ابن عمك؟   4. هل خالتك مصرية؟

Lesson 9

9.1. Practice:

Fill in the spaces:

Nationality الجنسية	Country البلد	Nationality الجنسية	Country البلد
عراقي	العراق	**فلسطيني**	فلسطين
كويتي	الكويت	لبناني	**لبنان**
ياباني	اليابان	**جزائري**	الجزائر
أمريكي	**أمريكا**	**ليبي**	ليبيا
سوري	**سوريا**	مصري	**مصر**
هندي	**الهند**		

9.2. Practice:

1. verbal   تقع كليتي في بريطانيا.

2. verbal   أدرس الهندسة في جامعة هارفارد.

3. nominal   أختي تسكن بجانب المكتبة.

4. nominal   اسم صديقي علي أحمد.

5. nominal   كتابك على الطاولة.

6. nominal   أنا أتكلم أربع لغات.

7. nominal   هذه الدروس جميلة.

8. verbal   يعمل أخي في البنك.

9. nominal   سامية و أمل من لبنان.

10. verbal   يدرس أحمد في جامعة أريزونا.

11. verbal   تسكن مها مع أخوها بجانب الجامعة.

9.3. Practice:

1. مها تدرس الكيمياء و الأدب.

2. والدي يتكلم ثلاث لغات.

3. صديقتي ستسافر يوم الأربعاء.

4. ابن عمتي يشاهد الأخبار دائما.

5. نحن سنأكل الدجاج على الغداء اليوم.

9.4. Practice:

1. تحب سارة القهوة مع الحليب.

2. تدرس هدى و أمل الكلمات الجديدة.

3. يعرف علي هذا الرجل.

4. تسكن عائلتها في الأردن.

5. يعمل صديقي في مطعم قريب.

9.5. Practice:

1. يَتَكَوَّنُ العَالَمُ العَرَبِيُّ مِنْ اثْنَتَانِ وَعِشْرِينَ دَوْلَةٍ.

2. بِلَادُ الشَّامُ وَ هِيَ: سُورِيَا وَ لُبْنَانُ وَ الأُرْدُنُّ وَ فِلَسْطِينُ.

3. هناك سبع دول في الخليج العربي

4. دول شمال أفريقيا هي تُونس و الجَزَائِرُ و لِيبيَا و المَغْرِبُ و مُورِيتَانِيَا.

5. يحد العالم العربي من الشمال تُرْكِيَا وَ البَحْرُ الأَحْمَرُ من الجنوب المُحِيطُ الهِنْدِيُّ وَ الصَّحْرَاءُ الكُبْرَى

9.11. Practice:

اسم الدولة		#	العاصمة - Capital
جزر القمر	.1	8	المنامة
المملكة الأردنية الهاشمية	.2	5	دمشق
السودان	.3	1	موروني
جمهورية لبنان	.4	2	عمّان
الجمهورية العربية السورية	.5	7	صنعاء
جمهورية مصر العربية	.6	10	بغداد
اليمن	.7	6	القاهرة
مملكة البحرين	.8	4	بيروت
المغرب	.9	3	الخرطوم
العراق	.10	9	الرباط

Lesson 10

10.1. Practice:

1. X   أحمد طالب لبناني.

2. X   تونس مدينة عربية.

3. correct   أريزونا ولاية أمريكية.

4. X   أختي جميلة و قصيرة.

5. X   غرفتي كبيرة.

6. X   أتكلم اللغة العربية و الانجليزية.

7. X   اشتريت كتب جديدة.

8. X   هذا بيت أستاذنا الأمريكية.

9. X   الطالبان يدخلان من الباب الصغير.

10. X   عندي دراجتان قديمتان.

10.2. Practice:

Adjective of place F	Adjective of place M	Country	
باكستانية	باكستاني	باكستان	Bakistan
قطرية	قطري	قطر	Qata
اماراتية	اماراتي	الامارات	Alimarat
لبنانية	لبناني	لبنان	Lebnan
يمنية	يمني	اليمن	Alyaman
تونسية	تونسي	تونس	Toonis
جزائرية	جزائري	الجزائر	Aljaza'er
ايطالية	ايطالي	ايطاليا	Italya

10.3. Practice:

١. أُسري   ٢. أوروبي   ٣. بلدي   ٤. ميلادي   ٥. مهني

10.4. Practice:

Meaning	هم	هما	هي	هو	اَنتِ	أنتَ	نحن	أنا	Verb in past tense
Write	يكتبون	كتبا	تكتب	يكتب	تكتبين	تكتب	نكتب	أكتب	كتب
Drink	يشربون	يكتبان	تشرب	يشرب	تشربين	تشرب	نشرب	أشرب	شرب
Live	يسكنون	يشربان	تسكن	يسكن	تسكنين	تسكن	نسكن	أسكن	سكن
Read	يقرأون	يسكنان	تقرأ	يقرأ	تقرأين	تقرأ	نقرأ	أقرأ	قرأ
Go	يذهبون	يقرآن	تذهب	يذهب	تذهبين	تذهب	نذهب	أذهب	ذهب
Love/like	يحبون	يذهبان	تحب	يحب	تحبين	تحب	نحب	أحب	أحب
Cook	يطبخون	يحبان	تطبخ	يطبخ	تطبخين	تطبخ	نطبخ	أطبخ	طبخ
Want	يريدون	يطبخان	تريد	يريد	تريدين	تريد	نريد	أريد	أراد
Arrive	يصلون	يريدان	تصل	يصل	تصلين	تصل	نصل	أصل	وصل
Leave	يرحلون	يصلان	ترحل	يرحل	ترحلين	ترحل	نرحل	أرحل	رحل

10.5. Practice:

١. هل   ٢. كتاب   ٣. أحمد   ٤. باب   ٥. أمل

٦. أبي   ٧. كلية   ٨. قهوة   ٩. يناير   ١٠. آشاي

10.6. Practice:

١. الملابس التقليدية العربية متشابهة جدا

٢. لأن الطقس يكون حار جدا.

٣. يلبسون الملابس المصنوعة من الصوف في الشتاء لأن الطقس يكون بارد جدا.

٤. لحماية الرأس و الوجة من الشمس الحارة أو الرمال أو الرياح.

٥. يلبس العرب الدشداشة بعض الأحيان.

10.7. Practice:

1. المسلمون يصلون خمس مرات في اليوم
2. يدرس طلاب الطب سبع سنوات في الجامعة
3. ما اسم الكتاب الذي اشتريته أمس؟
4. تغضب أمي اذا لم أعمل الواجب.
5. يلبس اللاعبون ملابس الفريق لكي يستعدوا للمباراة.
6. أصدقائي وصلوا الى الأردن يوم الاثنين.
7. كم مدينة زرت في مصر؟
8. ذهبت سعاد مع أمها الى السوق.
9. يريد خالد أن يكون دكتور في الجامعة
10. تعتبر البحرين أصغر بلد عربي.

10.8. Practice:

(4) منذ سنة	(1) أم	(3) جدتي
(5) نشيط	(6) ليل	(7) صغير
		(2) أخت

Lesson 11

11.1. Practice:

1. تسعة بيوت
2. ست حقائب
3. أربع طاولات
4. ثمانية أقلام
5. ثلاثة أساتذة
6. سبع خالات
7. خمسة شوارع
8. كليتان
9. عشر كلمات
10. مفتاح واحد

11.2. Practice:

10 سنأخذ الدجاج و نريد عصير برتقال	3 الاسم هو محمد
8 نعم – عندنا سمك مقلي و طيب جدا.	9 حسنا و أنت يا سيدة ماذا تريدين؟
2 مرحبا بكم في مطعمنا . ما الاسم لو سمحت	4 أهلا و سهلا ! طاولة رقم سبعة
5 شكرا ! ما هو طبق اليوم؟	6 طبق اليوم دجاج مشوي مع أرز
1 مساء الخير . حجزنا طاولة لثلاثة أشخاص	11 اذا طبق سمك و طبقين من الدجاج مع الأرز
7 أنا أحب السمك . هل عندكم سمك؟	

11.3. Practice:

1. الخامسة و العشرين
2. الرابعة
3. ألف و تسعمائة و خمس و عشرين
4. الأولى
5. السابع عشر
6. التاسع عشر

11.4. Practice:

1. يستيقظ علي من النوم في الساعة الخامسة و الربع صباحا
2. يذهب الي الحمام و ينظف أسنانه و يستحم بالماء و الصابون
3. لا هو يحب الشاي
4. طعامه المفضل اللحم مع الأرز و السلطة
5. بذهب علي الى النوم في الساعة العاشرة مساءً.

11.5. Practice:

1. (5) شراب   فرشاة
2. (4) دقيقة   سرير   3. (3) طعام   ساعة
4. (1) معجون أسنان   ساعة
5. (2) ينام   عصير

11.6. Practice:

(2) لأتناول طعام العشاء

(1) لأقرا الكتاب

(5) 645 شارع تمبي مدينة جلبرت

(3) أنا ألعب كرة القدم

(4) و لكني نجحت في الامتحان

Lesson 12

12.1. Practice:

1. كتابي ليس على الطاولة.
2. أختي ليست في المطعم   3. الطلاب لم يقرأوا الكتاب
4. صورتهم ليست على الجدار   5. أنا لست غني

12.2. Practice:

1. ما درست للامتحان في المكتبة أمس.
2. هم لا يسكنون في هذا البيت منذ شهر.
3. لن يشاهد علاء المباراة غدا.
4. ما طبخت أختي طعاما لذيذا.
5. لا تحب أمي أن تشرب الشاي مع الافطار.
6. لن نذهب الى السوق بعد قليل.
7. لن يقابل علي أستاذه في الجامعة غدا.
8. ما انتقلت أختي الى البحرين.
9. ما زرنا لبنان قبل شهرين.
10. لم يجلسوا في المقهى كل يوم.
11. هي لا تعرف من أنا.

12.3. Practice:

1. لا هذا ليس استاذي
2. لا لم أدرس لامتحان الكيمياء
3. لا لن أتخرج مع أصدقائي يوم الجمعة
4. لا أعرف ماذا سنأكل اليوم
5. لا لن نساعدك في دراسة الكلمات
6. لا لم نمض عطلة الأسبوع مع علي

12.4. Practice:

1. من أين أشتري الجريدة؟
2. متى / أي ساعة ستزورني الليلة؟
3. من أين أشتري صندوق حلوى؟
4. لماذا أنت متأخر؟
5. كنت مشغولا بالعمل و لذلك لم أعمل الواجب
6. أحتاج بعض الوقت لأستعد

12.5. Practice:

1. عثمان كان في الملعب
2. طارق كان يبحث عن عثمان
3. طارق يريد أن يدرس مع علي
4. عثمان و طارق سيدرسان في المكتبة
5. علي يريد أن يذهب الى المطعم

12.6. Practice:

Plural الجمع	Profession وظيفة
صحفيين / صحفيات	ssahafi صحفي
محاميين / محاميات	mohami محام
فنانين / فنانات	fannan فنان
سائقين / سائقات	sa'iq سائق
مساعدين / مساعدات	mosa'ed مساعد
مصممين / مصممات	mosamem مصمم

Plural الجمع	Profession وظيفة
مدرسين / مدرسات	moddares مدرس
مهندسين / مهندسات	mohandis مهندس
نجارين / نجارات	najjar نجار
معلمين / معلمات	moa'lim معلم
مديرين / مديرات	modeer مدير

12.7. Practice:

(7) فستان

(8) الخامسة الا الربع

(6) عطلة نهاية الأسبوع

(1) نهاية

(9) يوافق

(10) شركة

(4) رجل

(5) الساعة العاشرة مساء

(3) الدجاج مع الأرز

(2) عصير ليمون

Lesson 13

13.1. Practice:

Future Tense	Present Tense	Transliteration	Past tense	Meaning
سيشرب	يشرب	Shariba	شرب	Drank
سيدخل	يدخل	Dakhala	دخل	Entered
سيخرج	يخرج	Kharaja	خرج	Got out
سيطبخ	يطبخ	Tabakha	طبخ	Cooked
سيفعل	يفعل	Fa'ala	فعل	Did
سيرسم	يرسم	Rasama	رسم	Drew
سيشاهد	يشاهد	Shahada	شاهد	Watched
سيذهب	يذهب	Thahaba	ذهب	Went
سيأكل	يأكل	Akala	أكل	Ate
سيعمل	يعمل	Amila	عمل	Did
سيعرف	يعرف	A'rafa	عرف	Knew
سيقرأ	يقرأ	Qara'	قرأ	Read
سيدرس	يدرس	Darasa	درس	Studied
سيسكن	يسكن	Sakana	سكن	Inhabited
سيتكلم	يتكلم	Takkalama	تكلم	Spoke

Future Tense	Present Tense	Transliteration	Past tense	Meaning
سيسمع	يسمع	Samia'	سمع	Heard
سيساعد	يساعد	Sa'ada	ساعد	Helped
سيستأجر	يستأجر	Ista'jara	أستأجر	Rented
سيؤجر	يؤجر	ajjara	أجر	Rented someone

13.2. Practice:

2. ما هي أول كلمة تعلمتها من اللغة العربية؟

1. من أين أستأجر سيارة؟

4. ما هي هوايتك المفضلة؟

3. هل تحب مدرستك ؟ لماذا؟

6. ما هو الأفضل في رأيك : أشتري بيت أم أستأجر شقة؟

5. ما هو أجمل مكان زرته؟

13.3. Practice:

4. تقيمين - تعملين   3. يحققا.   2. تأخرت.   1. أغير

8. زاروا   7. نقرأه   6. نشعر   5. تحبين - تشاهدي

11. تنامون   10. تريد   9. جلسا

13.4. Practice:

4. اسم   3. ايمان   2. عشرة   1. أحمد

8. لوح   7. أخي   6. الأربعاء   5. جامعة

13.5. Practice:

1. المعلومة الخاطئة عن العالم العربي هي أن كل العالم العربي صحراء

2. نعم يوجد أنهار في العالم العربي

3. أطول نهر في العالم هو نهر النيل و يقع في مصر و السودان

4. جزر العالم العربي البحرين و جزيرة سقطرة في خليج عدن و جزيرة مصيرة في البحر العربي .

5. دول الخليج العربي تقع على الخليج العربي

Lesson 14

14.1. Practice:

5. العبن   4. غادروا / اتركوا   3. ادرسا   2. اكتب   1. اجلسوا

14.2. Practice:

3. ليس عندنا فصل اليوم   2. لا تعطي رقم تلفوني الى علي   1. لا تنسي حقيبتك

5. لا تركضي بسرعة   4. لا ترمي حذاؤك

14.3. Practice:

5. اشربوا   4. اشتريتما   3. تذهبي   2. نم   1. ابدأ

14.4. Practice:

5. لا تسبحن   4. لا تشربوا   3. لا تأكلي   2. لا تنتقلا   1. لا تذهبوا

14.5. Practice:

1. يوما   2. تريدين   3. خضراء   4. قررتا   5. عادوا

14.6. Practice:

1. ليس   2. ليست   3. ليسا   4. ليست   5. ليست

14.7. Practice:

1. بدأوا   2. ربح   3. ساروا   4. وقفوا   5. سيصبح

6. يساعدهما   7. أغلقت   8. استمعوا   9. يريدان   10. شاهدتا

14.8. Practice:

(4) صورة لشاطئ البحر   (3) عن الأسئلة

(5) رسالة في البريد   (1) الكتاب صفحة

(2) كلام الأستاذ   (6) التلفون داخل الفصل

14.9. Practice:

1. جلس الأصدقاء في النادي

2. قضى أحمد يوم الجمعة كلة في النادي يتدرب

3. أكل محمد طعام العشاء في مطعم صيني

4. جمال لعب مع أولاد الجيران كرة القدم

14.10. Practice:

1. تعالوا الى الفصل على الوقت

2. ضعوا تلفوناتكم في حقائبكم

3. لا تتكلموا مع الطلاب بجانبكم

4. حلوا التمارين لوحدكم

5. لا تنسوا أن تكتبوا التاريخ على أوراقكم

Lesson 15

15.1. Practice:

1. النوافذ التي في صفي كبيرة

2. كلية العلوم قريبة من بيتي

3. فقد مفاتيح سيارتة

4. دراجة أحمد في الموقف

5. الجريدة على مكتب الأستاذ

15.2. Practice:

1. correct   الحاسوب القديم على الطاولة   2. it should be: الأستاذة العربية في المكتب

3. it should be: المكتب الجديد واسع   4. it should be: عند أخي سيارة قديمة

5. correct   على الجدار صورة قديمة.   6. it should be: المفاتيح الصغيرة في الحقيبة

15.3. Practice:

Write whether the following is *idafa* or noun and adjective:

1. *Idafa*
2. noun and adjective
3. noun and adjective
4. *idafa*
5. *idafa*
6. noun and adjective
7. noun and adjective
8. *idafa*
9. *Idafa*
10. *idafa*

15.4. Practice:

5. الدرس	4. نحن	3. تعرف	2. يحبون	1. كثيرة
10. يقرأون	9. حملت	8. تشرب	7. الموسيقى	6. الا

15.5. Practice:

8. خليج العقبة	7. قارة أفريقيا	4. وادي النيل	3. نهر دجلة	2. جبل الشيخ

15.6. Practice:

3. السوق	2. محطة البنزين	1. مكتب السفريات
	5. مركز الشرطة	4. مكتب البريد

15.7. Practice:

1. عمي أحمد عمره ٥٦ سنة
2. في بيته طابقين
3. في الطابق الثاني يوجد ثلاث غرف نوم و حمامين و غرفة مكتب
4. تخرج أولاده و بناته من الجامعة و تزوجوا
5. عمي و زوجته يحبون أن يطبخوا طعام العشاء معا و يجلسون و يتحدثون عن أبنائهم دائما

15.8. Practice:

5. عندي ألم في رأسي	1. سيبدأ المشروع سنة 2020
6. هم يحبون الرياضة بجميع أنواعها	2. استمر الفيلم لمدة ساعتين و نصف
7. هو يعمل مدير شركة الكترونية	3. سيقضون في لبنان عشرة أيام
8. كلي الخضار و الفواكه و لا تكثري من الدهون	4. استعملي هذا الدواء و اشربي ماءً كثيراً

Lesson 16

16.1. Practice:

4. كانا	3. كنت	2. كانتا	1. كان
7. كان	6. كنا	5. كنّ	

16.2. Practice:

5. صرت	4. ظلت	3. أمسينا	2. أصبحوا	1. كنتم
10. ظلوا	9. أصبحنا	8. ما زالت	7. كنت	6. كنت

16.3. Practice:

1. هذا الشهر لا يلعب محمد مع الفريق لأنه مريض
2. عبدالله كان يقضي ساعات طويلة في صيد الطيور
3. تفضل جدتي العلاج الطبيعي
4. بعد الحادث أجريت له عملية ناجحة في المستشفى
5. هي تدرس الطب في أمريكا

16.4. Practice:

4. اشتريت   3. أريد   2. أخذت   1. جلست

8. التي   7. الذي   6. ستذهبين   5. يدرسون

16.5. Practice:

2. كانوا يقرأون الرواية   1. كنت تحب الأفلام العلمية

4. غادرا قبل أن نحضر   3. كنا نشاهد فيلم رعب

6. كان الشاي باردا لذلك لم أشربه   5. كنت أحب قراءة الشعر

8. كانت غرفتنا كبيرة جدا و باردة   7. كنت خائفا

10. كان عندها برد و لذلك ذهبت الى الطبيب   9. كانت الرياح قوية جدا

16.6. Practice:

4. أصغر   3. أطول   2. أكبر   1. أجمل

8. أحسن   7. أقدم   6. أكثر   5. أسهل

16.7. Practice:

5. ورقة   4. عدد   3. أخت   2. اسم   1. يوم

10. أمير   9. ابن   8. فنجان   7. سؤال   6. أسبوع

16.8. Practice:

1. أيام العمل الرسمية تبدأ يوم الأحد و حتى يوم الخميس

2. لجمعة و السبت هما يوما عطلة نهاية الأسبوع

3. يبدأ الدوام في الشركات من الساعة السابعة و النصف صباحا حتى الساعة الثانية عشرة

4. ينتهي الدوام في المؤسسات الحكومية الساعة الثانية ظهرا. ظهرا و ثم من الساعة الثالثة و النصف عصرا حتى الساعة السادسة و النصف مساء

5. قارن بين ساعات العمل في بلدك و بين ساعات العمل في الدول العربية!

16.9. Practice:

5. ذهبوا   4. الأسبوع   3. المقهى   2. على   1. أدرس

10. أصغر   9. هما   8. ماذا   7. تنسى   6. يقضيان

Lesson 17
17.1. Practice:

5. اسألهم لعل أفكارهم جديدة   1. انهما يكتبان كتابا جديدا

6. ان أبوهم رجل ناجح جدا   2. كأنه تعبان اليوم .

7. لا يوجد أحد هنا لعلهم ذهبوا الى مكان آخر.   3. قلت لهم أن يحضروا لكنهم اعتذروا

4. لم تحضر الى الحفل لأنها مريضة

17.2. Practice:

1. يذهب علاء مع أبيه الى السوق   2. كل يوم جمعة بعد صلاة الظهر

3. يذهب علاء و أبوه الى المكتبة لشراء مجلة "العربي" لأنهما   4. أبو علاء يحب الموز و البرتقال
يحبانها كثيرا

5. تذكر أبو علاء أنهم يحتاجون القهوة

17.3. Practice:

5. تريدون   4. سيسافر   3. تدرسين   2. يوما   1. أحمد

10. يحبون   9. هذه   8. مع   7. صغير   6. طويل

17.4. Practice:

1. الكراسي مريحة.

2. البنات طويلات.

3. غرف النوم كبيرة و فارغة.

4. يوجد حدائق جميلة.

5. هذه شقق صغيرة في عمارة كبيرة .

17.5. Practice:

5. الأخبار   4. مؤثرة   3. الأغاني   2. رسالة   1. الجريدة

17.6. Practice:

1. اشترى أحمد سيارة أمريكية ـ.

2. يذهب الناس الى البحر في الصيف .

3. هذا مفتاح مكتب الأستاذ

4. سافرت من تركيا الى أمريكا بالطائرة .

5. وصلت الى الأردن في شهر نوفمبر

17.7. Practice:

1. لماذا ذهبت الى المكتبة؟

2. لمن هذه الحقيبة؟

3. كم نافذة في منزلك؟

4. ما هو لونك المفضل ؟

5. كم قطة و كلب عندك ؟

6. ما اسم صديقتك؟

17.8. Practice:

To review your attached pronouns, attach the suitable pronoun for the following nouns:

1. طائرتها   2. سائقهم   3. والدتهما   4. قصتها   5. مدرستنا

6. نظارتي   7. دراجتهما   8. ساعتك   9. مخبزنا   10. مفتاحك

Lesson 18

18.1. Practice:

1. الذين   2. التي   3. اللذان   4. اللاتي   5. التي

6. اللتان   7. الذي   8. التي   9. الذي   10. الذين

18.2. Practice:

1. حليب   2. قلم   3. مسجد   4. نظارة   5. حقيبة

6. كأس   7. السوق   8. البنك   9. الجزائر   10. البحرين

18.3. Practice:

1. تحضر الأم طعام الغداء
2. الصور هناك على الحائط
3. تضع أمل الملابس في الحقيبة
4. يعمل أحمد القهوة في المطبخ
5. رجع الطلاب الى الكلية في شهر أغسطس
6. بيتي في هذه العمارة في الطابق الرابع :

18.4. Practice:

1. بارد - معتدل
2. درجة الحرارة
3. تنخفض
4. شهري
5. الهجرة
6. المرور

18.5. Practice:

- قررنا أنا و أصدقائي أن نذهب الى الأردن
- اشترينا تذاكر من مكتب السفريات
- أعددنا حقائبنا للسفر
- ركبنا سيارة الأجرة من بيتنا الى المطار
- ركبنا في الطيارة لمدة ست ساعات
- ذهبنا الى الأردن و زرنا الكثير من الأماكن السياحية و الآثار
- رجعنا و معنا الكثير من الهدايا لعائلاتنا
- استمتعنا بالرحلة كثيرا

18.6. Practice:

1. هل عندك وقت لنتقابل يوم الجمعة ؟
2. هل تريد أن تلعب كرة القدم أم تفضل ألعاب الالكترونية ؟
3. ممكن أن تساعدني في واجب اللغة العربية ؟
4. سيكون الطقس اليوم أبرد كثيرا من أمس
5. انتهيت من طباعة كتابي الأول
6. هل تعرف قانون الهجرة ؟
7. هذه هي العاصفة التي كنت أتحدث عنها
8. أين المركز الاجتماعي الذي كنت تتحدث عنه ؟
9. ما هو حيوانك المفضل ؟ هل عندك واحد في البيت ؟
10. ما هي درجة الحرارة اليوم ؟ هل يجب أن ألبس الجاكيت ؟

18.7. Practice:

1. حسن كان يفكر أن لطَّقْسُ أَصْبَحَ بَارِدًا وَ يحْتَاجَ إِلَى جَاكِيتٍ وَ حِذَاءٍ
2. لا يستطيع أن يذهب الى السوق لان سيارته لا تعمل
3. لا الطقس بارد عند حسن
4. نَعَمْ. يريدُ أَنْ يشْتَرِيَ بَنْطَالًا جَدِيدًا.

18.8. Practice:

1. الذي
2. التي
3. التي
4. التي
5. الذين
6. الذي
7. التي
8. التي
9. التي

18.9. Practice:

2. جامعة : مكتب – مكتبة – كلية

4. مطبخ : كوب – طبق – حليب

6. صيدلية : دواء – صيدلي

8. دولة : نهر – جبل – صحراء

10. رياضة : سباحة – كرة قدم – ملعب

1. شارع سيارة – بيت – عمارة

3. ملابس : فستان – بنطال – شورت

5. شقة : غرفة نوم – حمام – غرفة سفرة

7. عائلة : زوجة – أب – ابن عم – خالة

9. طعام : دجاج – لحم – تفاح – سمك

Lesson 19

19.1. Practice:

2. تُشرَب القهوة بعد الافطار.

4. اشتريت حلويات كثيرة.

1. قيل أن لبنان بلد جميل.

3. يُحتَفَل بعيد الفطر بعد رمضان.

5. يُصَلى خمس مرات في اليوم.

19.2. Practice:

1. active tense   2. passive tense   3. passive tense   4. passive tense
5. active tense.   6. active tense   7. active tense   8. passive tense

19.3. Practice:

1. ماذا يدرس أخوك في الجامعة؟

2. تسكن والدتي في مدينة دبي.

3. عندي أخت تعمل في واشنطن الآن

4. يأكل معظم العرب الجبن و الخبز في الصباح.

5. كان موعد وصول الطائرة في السادسة و النصف مساء.

6. العشاء – الأم – و جلسوا – أحضرت – حول – جميعا – الطاولة.

7. أريد أن أزور جميع البلاد العربية

8. هم يعملون من الصباح الى المساء .

9. هذان الضيفان الذان زارانا أمس

10. سأراك يوم الأربعاء الساعة الثامنة و النصف صباحا.

19.4. Practice:

2. يناير هو أول شهر في السنة

4. بلال هو خالي و عمره خمس و سبعين سنة

6. أنا أردنية و هو كويتي

8. أنا جائعة أريد فلافل و حمص

10. ماذا يأتي بعد يوم الأحد؟

1. هناك مقهى على الشارع الثاني

3. انها الثامنة و النصف يجب أن أذهب في الساعة التاسعة

5. هذه هي الهام صديقتي السورية

7. عمتي في البيت مع ابنها و ابنتها

9. ما أسم أقرب فندق الى المطار؟

19.5. Practice:

١. وصل الطلاب الى الحفلة ليتسلموا جوائزهم.

٢. المسافرون وصلوا الى المطار ليركبوا الطائرة.

٣. جاء الاعبون الى النادي ليسبحوا.

٤. المهندسون يذهبون الى الشركة كل يوم الساعة السابعة صباحا.

٥. المدرسات كتبن الأسئلة على اللوح.

٦. صديقاتي يحببن أن يشربوا الشاي في المقهى.

٧. الأولاد يأكلون الفلافل و الحمص مع أخواتهم.

٨. هل عملتم الواجب يا أخوتي؟

٩. من أين اشتريتم ساعاتكم؟

١٠. اشترينا تذاكر لنشاهد مباراة كرة القدم.

19.6. Practice:

٥. هل	٤. لست	٣. هذان	٢. أحمر	١. أحمر
١٠. يساعدوا	٩. قديمة	٨. بعد	٧. الثالث	٦. الثانية عشرة

19.7. Practice:

(٦) حزين	(٣) صباح
(٥) يوم	(١) ينسى
(٧) سعيد	(٤) أسود
(٩) شتاء	(٢) خرج
(٨) مقهى	(١٠) جواب

19.8. Practice:

١. تعتبر جمهورية مصر العربية أكبر دولة في أفريقيا

٢. تم بناء مدينة القاهرة في سنة ٩٦٩ قبل الميلاد

٣. أشهر الأماكن في القاهرة المتحف المصري و جامعة الأزهر و سوق خان الخليلي

٤. أقدم جامعة في العالم هي جامعة الأزهر

٥. أشهر المساجد فيها جامع السيدة زينب و جامع عمرو بن العاص و مسجد الحسين

19.9. Practice:

ذهبنا الى قرية . القرية ليس فيها فندق = ذهبنا الى القرية التي ليس فيها فندق

١. أين البنطال البني الذي غسلته أمس؟

٢. هل أكل الأولاد الذين كانوا في المطعم؟

٣. اشترت هدى لفستان الذي كان في الخزانة.

٤. اجتمع المدير مع الموظفين الذين طلبوا اجتماعا.

٥. زرت الأهرامات التي في مصر.

19.10. Practice:

4. محطات   3. أكواب   2. حمامات   1. أبناء

8. الهدايا   7. الأماكن   6. مراكز   5. مهندسين

19.11. Practice:

3. أين نسيت هاتفك؟   2. هل عندك سؤال؟   1. كم غرفة نوم في بيتك؟

6. أين تعمل؟   5. كم يوما أقمت في الفندق؟   4. هل تسكن مع أختك في أمريكا؟

9. هل عندك خالين؟   8. متى سنذهب الى المقهى؟   7. أين تدرس الرياضيات؟

10. ماذا تعمل أمك؟

Lesson 20

20.1. Practice:

5. كما   4. مثل   3. كأن   2. كفستانك   1. كما.

10. كأنه   9. كما   8. مثل   7. كما   6. كالقهوة

20.2. Practice:

1. أصغر بلد عربي هو البحرين

2. أكبر بلد عربي هو الجزائر

3. أطول نهر في العالم هو نهر النيل

4. أقدم جامعة في العالم هي جامعة الأزهر في القاهرة

5. يصوم المسلمون في شهر رمضان

6. ما هو الشهر السابع في السنة؟

7. هناك عشرة أيام فرق بين السنة الميلادية و السنة الهجرية

8. أحب أن أزور ..... من العالم العربي

9. يوم الأحد هو أول يوم في الأسبوع في العالم العربي

10. لا ليست جميع النساء العربيات محجبات

20.3. Practice:

2. المطبخ واسع و فيه شباك كبير.   1. شقته ضيقة و ايجارها غالي.

4. الطاولة و الكراسي قديمين.   3. غرفة النوم كبيرة و السرير جديد.

6. المكتبة مليئة بالكتب   5. الحمام وسخ.

8. الطقس بارد و السماء غائمة.   7. غرفة الجلوس قريبة عن المطبخ.

10. ليس عند أمل سيارة تويوتا.   9. غادر أحمد أمريكا.

20.4. Practice:

2. سبع	1. ثلاث
4. اثنا عشر شهرا	3. ستة و خمسين
6. عشرة	5. اسبوعين
8. الخامس عشر من أغسطس سنة ألفين و تسع عشر	7. السادسة
10. الف و مائتين و ستين	9. خمسة و عشرين

20.5. Practice:

5. المقهى	4. جامعة	3. درجة	2. أسبوع	1. أستاذ
10. الأمير	9. حديقة	8. تفاح	7. الأم	6. سيارة

20.6. Practice:

4. يقرأ	3. يشتري	2. يشرب	1. يأكل
8. يسكن	7. يلبس	6. يسافر / يطير	5. يكتب
12. يشاهد	11. يسمع	10. يجلس	9. يسوق

20.7. Practice:

5. يحبون	4. أ	3. ماذا	2. كيف	1. ماذا
10. ستبدأ	9. يستطيع	8. تشتري	7. مزدحم	6. سأتناول

20.8. Practice:

2. هل تحب الفلافل؟	1. من أين أنت؟
4. أين يدرسون التجارة ؟/ في أي جامعة يدرسون؟	3. أين يعمل؟
6. لماذا ذهبت الى الأردن؟	5. أين تسكن أمل؟
8. متى تسقط أوراق الشجر؟	7. ما هي عاصمة السعودية؟
10. هل عملت الواجب؟	9. هو أكبر ميناء في الهند؟

20.9. Practice:

1. التكنولوجيا الحديثة جعلت العالم قرية صغيرة

2. أشتري كتبي من الانترنت

3. نعم أذهب الى السوق لاشتري ملابسي / أشتري ملابسى من الانترنت

4. درست على الكمبيوتر ..... مواد

5. كيف تتوقع أن يصبح العالم بعد خمسين سنة؟

English–Arabic Dictionary

Notes: If a letter has a (') it means it is pronounced as ع. When a letter is doubled, then there is *shaddah* on it and it should be stressed.

gh stands for غ   *dh* stands for ض   *th-th* stands for ظ
q stands for ق   *kh* stands for خ   *tt* stands for ط
"ii" means long ee   *hh* stands for ح   *ss* stands for ص

A

English	Arabic	Transliteration
about	حوالي/تقريبا	*hawaaly / taqreeban*
above	فوق	*fawq*
abroad	في خارج البلاد	*fee al-kharij*
accident	حادث	*haadith*
adaptor	وصلة	*wasla*
add	يضيف	*yodheef*
address	عنوان	*onwaan*
admission	دخول	*dukhool*
adult	بالغ	*baaligh*
advice	نصيحة	*nasiiha*
airplane	طائرة	*taa'ira*
after	بعد	*ba'd*
aftershave	كولونيا	*kuloonya*
again	مرة اخرى	*marra ukhraa*
against	ضد	*dhid*
age	عمر	*'umr*
AIDS	أيدز	*aydiz*
air conditioning	مكيف	*mokayyef*
airmail	بريد جوي	*bariid jawwii*
airplane	طائرة	*taa'ira*
airport	مطار	*mataar*
alarm	إنذار	*inthaar*
alarm clock	منبه	*monabbeh*
alcohol	كحول/خمر	*khamr /kuhuul*
Allah	الله	*Allah*
all day	طوال اليوم	*ttiwal al-yawm*
allergy	حساسية	*hassasiyya*
alone	وحيد	*waheed*
altogether	جميعا	*jamee'an*
always	دائما	*daa'iman*
ambulance	سيارة إسعاف	*sayyaarat is'aaf*
America	امريكا	*amariikaa*
American (m.)	امريكي	*amareeki*
American (f.)	أمريكية	*amareekiyyah*

English	Arabic	Transliteration
amount	كمية	*kemmiyya*
anesthetic	تخدير	*takhdeer*
angry	غاضب	*ghadheb*
animal	حيوان	*hayawan*
ankle	كعب	*ka'ib*
answer	جواب/ رد	*jawab/rad*
ant	نمله	*namla*
antique	قديم	*qadeem*
apartment	شقه	*shaqqa*
apologies	اعتذار	*i'tithaar*
apple	تفاحة	*tuffaaha*
appointment	موعد	*maw'id*
April	ابريل	*ibreel*
architecture	هندسة معمارية	*handasa mi'maariya*
area	مساحة/منطقة	*masaaha/mintaqa*
area code	الرقم البريدي	*arraqam albareedi*
arm	ذراع	*thiraa'*
arrange	يرتب	*yuratib*
arrive	يصل	*yasil*
arrow	سهم	*sahm*
art	فن	*fan*
article	مقال	*maqaal*
ashtray	منفضة سجائر	*minfadat sajaa'ir*
ask (question)	يسال	*yas'al*
ask for	يطلب	*yattlub*
aspirin	اسبرين	*asbireen*
assault	اعتداء	*i'tidaa*
assorted	مصنف	*musannaf*
at home	في البيت	*fi al-bayt*
at night	في الليل	*fi al-layl*
at the back	في الخلف	*fi al-khalf*
at the front	في الامام	*fi al-amaam*
at least	على الاقل	*'alaa al-qal*
August	أغسطس	*oghostos*
Australia	استراليا	*ustiraaliyaa*

automatic	اوتوماتيكي/ألي	*utumaateeki/aali*
autumn	الخريف	*al-khareef*
awake	مستيقظ	*mustayqith*
awning	الظل	*ath-th-ill*

B

baby	طفل	*tifl*
babysitter	حاضنة	*hadhina*
back	خلف	*khalf*
backpack	حقيبة	*haqibah*
bad (rotten)	فاسد	*faasid*
baker	خباز	*khabbaz*
balcony	شرفة	*shurfa*
ball	كرة	*kura*
banana	موز	*mawz*
bandage	ضماد	*dhimaad*
bank	مصرف/بنك	*masraf/bank*
bank (river)	ضفة	*dhiffa*
barbecue	شواء	*shiwaa'*
basketball	كرة السلة	*korat as-salla*
bathroom	حمام	*hammaam*
battery	بطارية	*battaariya*
beach	شاطىء	*shatii'*
beans	فاصوليا	*fassoliya*
beautiful	جميل	*jameel*
because	لأنْ	*le'nna*
bed	فراش	*firash*
bedding	مفروشات السرير	*mafruushaat as-sariir*
bee	نحلة	*nahhla*
beef	لحم بقر	*lahhm baqar*
beer	بيرة	*beera*
begin	بيدأ	*yabda'*
behind	خلف	*khalf*
belt	حزام	*hizaam*
berth	رصيف الميناء	*raseef almeenaa'*
better	أحسن	*ahsan*
bicycle	دراجة	*darraja*
bill	فاتورة	*fatoora*
billiards	بليارد	*bilyaard*
birthday	عيد ميلاد	*eed meelad*
biscuit	بسكويت	*baskaweet*
bite	لدغه	*ladgha*

bitter	مر	*morr*
black	أسود	*aswad*
blanket	بطانية	*battaaniyya*
bleach	مبيض	*mubbayyidh*
bleed	ينزف	*yanzif*
blind (can't see)	اعمى	*a'maa*
blind (on window)	ستارة	*sitaara*
blond (m. & f.)	اشقر/شقراء	*ashqar/shaqraa*
blood	دم	*dam*
blouse	بلوزة	*blooza*
blue	أزرق	*azraq*
board	مَجلِس	*majlis*
boat	قارب	*qarib*
body	جسم	*jism*
boiled	مغلي	*maghli*
bone	عظم	*'athm*
book	كتاب	*kitaab*
booked (reserved)	محجوز	*mahjooz*
border	حدود	*hudood*
boring	ممل	*mumil*
born	مولود	*mawlood*
borrow	يستعير	*yasta'eer*
both	كلاهما	*kilahuma*
bottle	قنينة	*qinneena*⬚
box	صندوق	*ssondooq*
boy	ولد	*walad*
boyfriend	صديق	*ssadiiq*
bracelet	سوار	*siwaar*
brake	فرامل	*faramil*
bread	خبز	*khubz*
break	استراحة	*istiraha*
breakfast	فطور	*fotoor*
bridge	جسر	*jisr*
briefs	ملخص	*mulakhas*
bring	يجلب	*yajlib*
brochure	منشور	*manshoor*
broken	مكسور	*maksoor*
broth	حساء	*hisaa'*
brother	أخ	*akh*
brown	بني	*bunni*
bruise	رضوض	*rodhoodh*
brush	فرشاة	*furshaah*

English	Arabic	Transliteration
bucket	سطل	*ssatl*
buffet	خزانة	*khazana*
building	بناية	*binaayah*
burglary	سطو/سرقة	*sattw/sariqa*
burn (v.)	يحرق/يحترق	*yuhriq/yahtariq*
burnt	محروق	*mahrooq*
bus	باص/حافلة	*hafila/bass*
bus station	محطة الباص	*mahattat al-bass*
business card	بطاقة	*bittaqqa*
business trip	رحلة عمل	*rihlat 'amal*
busy (schedule)	مشغول	*mashghool*
busy (traffic)	ازدحام	*izdiham*
butcher	جزار/قصاب	*qassab/jazar*
butter	زبدة	*zobda*
button	زر	*zerr*
by (with)	بـ	*bi*
by phone	بالتليفون	*bit-tilifoon*

C

English	Arabic	Transliteration
cabin	كوخ	*kookh*
call (n.)	مكالمة	*mokalamah*
call (v.)	يتصل	*yattassil*
camera	كاميرا	*kamira*
camping	مخيم	*mukhayyam*
cancel	يلغي	*yolghi*
candle	شمعة	*sham'a*
candy	حلوى	*halwaa*
car	سيارة	*sayyaara*
careful	حذر	*hathir*
carpet	سجادة	*sijjaada*
carriage	عربة	*'araba*
carrot	جزر	*jazar*
cash	فلوس/نقدي	*naqdi/fuloos*
card	بطاقة	*bittaqah*
casino	كازينو	*kazeenu*
castle	قلعة	*qal'a*
cat	قطة	*qitta*
catalog	كتالوج	*katalug*
cause	سبب	*sabab*
cave	كهف	*kahf*
celebrate	يحتفل	*yahtafil*
cell phone	جوال/محمول	*mahmoul/jawwal*
cemetery	مقبرة	*maqbara*

English	Arabic	Transliteration
center (middle)	مركز	*markaz*
centimeter	سنتيميتر	*sentimeeter*
central	مركزي	*markazi*
certificate	شهادة/وثيقة	*shahada/watheeqa*
chair	كرسي	*kursi*
chambermaid	عاملة تنظيف	*a'amelat funduq*
champagne	شمبانيا	*shimbaniya*
change (n.)	تغير	*taghyeer*
change (v.)	يغير	*yughayyir*
charger	شاحن	*shahin*
chat	دردشة	*dardasha*
check (n.)	شيك	*shek*
check (v.)	فحص	*fahs*
check in	ينزل	*yanzil*
check out	يغادر	*yoghader*
cheers!	صحتين	*saheen*
cheese	جبن	*jobn*
chess	شطرنج	*shataranj*
chicken	دجاجة	*dajaja*
child	طفل	*ttifl*
chilled	مثلج/مجمد	*muthallaj/ mujammad*
China	الصين	*asseen*
chocolate	شوكلاتة	*shokolatta*
choose	يختار	*yakhtar*
chopsticks	أعواد	*a'waad*
church	كنيسة	*kaneesa*
cigar	سيجار	*siigaar*
cigarette	سيجارة	*sigaara*
circle	دائرة	*daa'ira*
circus	سيرك	*serk*
citizen	مواطن	*muwattin*
city	مدينة	*madeena*
clean (adj.)	نظيف	*nath-theef*
clean (v.)	ينظف	*yunath-thif*
clearance (sale)	تصفية	*tasfiya*
clock	ساعة	*saa'ah*
closed	مغلق	*mughlaq*
clothes	ملابس	*malaabis*
coat (jacket)	جاكيت/معطف	*jakiet/mi'taf*
cockroach	صرصور	*sarsoor*
cocoa	كاكاو	*kakaw*
coffee	قهوه	*qahwa*

English	Arabic	Transliteration
cold (not hot)	بارد	*barid*
cold (flu)	إنفلونزا	*influwanza*
collar	باقة	*baqa*
colleague	زميل	*zameel*
collision	تصادم	*tassadum*
cologne	عطر	*'itr*
color	لون	*lawn*
colored	ملون	*mulawwan*
comb	مشط	*musht*
come	تعال	*ta'aal*
come back	ارجع	*irja'*
committee	لَجنة	*lajna*
company	شَرِكة	*shareka*
compartment	جناح/ مقصورة	*maasoora/janaah*
complaint	شكوى	*shakwaa*
completely	تماما	*tamaman*
compliment (v.)	يمدح	*yamdahh*
computer	حاسوب/كمبيوتر	*kombyooter/ haasoob*
concert	حفلة موسيقية	*hafla muusiqiyya*
concierge	حارس	*haris*
concussion	ارتجاج	*irtijaj*
condensed	مكثف	*mukkath-thaf*
congratulations	مبروك/تهانينا!	*tahaaneena/ mabrook*
connection	وصلة	*waslah*
consulate	قنصلية	*qunsiliyya*
consultation	إستشارة	*istishaara*
contagious	معدي	*mu'dii*
cook (person)	طباخ	*tabbakh*
cook (v.)	يطبخ	*yatbukh*
cookie	بسكويت	*baskawiit*
copper	نحاس	*nuhaas*
copy	نسخة	*nuskha*
corkscrew	مفتاح	*miftaah*
corner	ركن	*rukn*
cornflower	دقيق الذرة	*daqiiq ath-thura*
correct	صحيح	*saheeh*
correspond	يراسل	*yurasil*
corridor	ممر	*mammar*
cosmetics	تجميل	*tajmeel*
costume	زي	*zay*
cotton	قطن	*qutn*
cough (n.)	سعال/كحة	*su'aal/kahha*
cough (v.)	يسعل/يكح	*yas'ul/yakuhh*
counter	عكس/ضد	*'aks/dhidh*
country (nation)	بلد	*balad*
course	دورة	*dawrah*
cousin	ابن عم/بنت عم	*ibn 'am/bint 'am*
crab	سرطان البحر	*sarataan al-bahr*
cracker	كسارة	*kassaara*
cream	قشطة	*qishta*
credit card	بطاقة اعتماد	*bitaaqat i'timaad*
crime	جريمة	*jareema*
crockery	ادوات فخارية	*adawaat fakhariyya*
cross (v.)	يقطع	*yaqta'*
crossroad	تقاطع طرق	*taqaatu'turuq*
crutch	عكاز	*'ukkaaz*
cry	بكاء	*bukaa'*
cubic	مكعب	*muka'ab*
cucumber	خيار	*khiyaar*
cuff	الكم	*al-kumm*
cup	كوب	*kuub*
curly	مجعد	*muja'ad*
current	حديث	*hadeeth*
curtains	ستائر	*sataa'ir*
cushion	وسادة	*wisaada*
custom	عادة	*'aada*
customs	جمارك	*jamaarik*
cut (n.)	جرح	*jurh*
cut (v.)	يقطع	*yaqta'*
cutlery	لوازم المائدة	*lawaazim al-maa'ida*
cycling	سباق الدراجات	*sibaaq ad- darraajaat*

D

English	Arabic	Transliteration
damage	ضرر/ خراب	*dharar kharaab*
dance (v.)	يرقص	*yarqus*
dance (n.)	رقص	*raqs*
dandruff	قشرة	*qishra*
danger	خطر	*khatar*
dangerous	خطير	*khatiir*
dark	ظلام	*zthklaam*
date	تاريخ	*taariikh*
date of birth	تاريخ الميلاد	*taariikh almiilaad*

daughter	بنت	*bint*
day	يوم	*yawm*
dead	ميت	*mayyit*
deaf	اطرش	*attrash*
December	ديسمبر	*desember*
declare	يصرح	*yussarrih*
deep	عميق	*'amiiq*
degree	درجة	*darajah*
delay	تأخير	*ta'khiir*
delicious	لذيذ	*latheeth*
dentist	طبيب أسنان	*ttabiib asnaan*
dentures	طقم اسنان	*ttaqm asnaan*
deodorant	معطر	*mu'attir*
department	قسم	*qism*
depart	يغادر	*yoghader*
departure	مغادرة	*mughaadara*
deposit (n.)	امانة/وديعة	*amaana/wadii'a*
deposit (v.)	يودع	*yuwdi'*
desert	صحراء	*sahraa'*
dessert	حلويات	*halawiyyaat*
destination	مقصد/مصير	*maqsad/maeeir*
detergent	مادة مطهرة	*maadda mutahhira*
develop (photo)	تحميض	*tahmeedh*
diabetic	سكري	*sukkari*
dial	يتصل	*yatassel*
diamond	ألماس	*almaas*
diarrhea	اسهال	*iss-haal*
dictionary	قاموس	*qaamoos*
diesel oil	زيت الديزل	*zayt ad-deezil*
diet	حمية	*hhimyyah*
difficulty	صعوبة	*ssu'ooba*
dinner	عشاء	*'ashaa'*
direction	إتجاه	*ittijaah*
direct	مباشر	*mubashir*
directly	مباشرة	*mubasharah*
dirty	وسخ	*wasikh*
disabled	معاق	*mu'aaq*
disco	ديسكو	*diskoo*
discount	تخفيض	*takhfeedh*
dish	صحن/طبق	*sahin/tabaq*
distance	مسافة	*masaafa*
disturb	يزعج	*yuz'ij*
disturbance	ازعاج	*iz'aaj*

dive	يغوص	*yaghoos*
diving	غطس	*ghatts*
divorced	مطلق	*muttallaq*
dizzy	دوار / دوخة	*duwar/dowkha*
do	يعمل	*ya'mal*
doctor	دكتور	*doctoor*
dog	كلب	*kalb*
doll	دمية / لعبة	*dumiya/loo'bah*
domestic	محلي	*mahallii*
done (cooked)	مطبوخ	*mattbuukh*
door	باب	*baab*
double	ضعف	*di'f*
down	اسفل	*asfal*
download	تحميل	*tahmeel*
drapes	ستائر	*sataa'ir*
draught	جفاف	*jafaf*
dream (v.)	يحلم	*yahlam*
dream (n.)	حلم	*helm*
dress (v.)	يلبس	*yalbas*
dress (n.)	فستان	*fostaan*
drink (n.)	شراب	*sharaab*
drink (v.)	يشرب	*yashrab*
drive	يسوق	*yasooq*
driver	سائق	*saa'iq*
driver's license	رخصة سياقة	*rukhsat siyaaqa*
drunk	سكران	*sakraan*
dry (n.)	جاف	*jaaf*
dry (v.)	يجف/يجفف	*yujaffif/yajuf*
dry clean	مصبغة الغسيل	*masbaghat ghaseel*
duck	بطة	*batta*
during	خلال	*khilaal*
duty (responsibility)	واجب	*wajib*
duty (tax)	رسم جمركي	*rasm jumrukii*
duty-free	غير خاضعة للرسم الجمركي	*ghayr khaadi'a lir-rasm al-jumrukii*

E

ear	أذن	*uthun*
earache	ألم في الأذن	*alam fii al-udhun*
ear drops	قطرة للأذن	*qatra lil-uthon*
early	مبكر	*mubakkir*
earrings	دخل	*dakhl*

earth	أرض	*ardh*
east	شرق	*sharq*
easy	سهل	*sahl*
eat	يأكل	*ya'kul*
economy	اقتصاد	*iqtissad*
eczema	اكزما	*akzima*
eel	سمكة الأنقليس	*samakat al-anqaliis*
egg	بيض	*baydh*
eggplant	باذنجان	*baathinjaan*
electric	كهربائي	*kahrabaa'i*
electricity	كهرباء	*kahrabaa'*
electronic	الكتروني	*ilekiooni*
elephant	فيل	*feel*
elevator	مصعد كهربائي	*miss'ad kahrabaa'ii*
email	بريد إلكتروني	*bariid iliktoronii*
embassy	سفارة	*safara*
embroidery	تطريز	*tattreez*
emergency	طوارئ	*ttawaari'*
emperor	امبراطور	*imbirattour*
empty	فارغ	*farigh*
engaged (to be married)	مخطوبة/مخطوب	*makhttooba/makhttoob*
England	انجلترا	*ingiltra*
English	انجليزي	*ingleezi*
enjoy	يتمتع	*yatamata'*
enquire (v.)	يستفسر	*yastafsir*
enquiry	استفسار	*istifsaar*
envelope	ظرف	*th-tharf*
escealate	يرفع	*yarfaa'*
escalator	درج متحرك	*daraj motaharrek*
escort	يرافق	*yurafiq*
essential	اساسي	*asaasi*
evening	مساء	*masaa'*
event	مناسبة/حدث	*munasaba/hadath*
everything	كل شيئ	*kol shay'*
everywhere	في كل مكان	*fii kol makan*
examine	يفحص	*yafhas*
excellent	ممتاز	*mumtaz*
exchange	يصرف/يبدل	*yubaddil /yusarrif*
excursion	رحلة	*rihla*
exhibition	معرض	*ma'rad*
exit	مخرج	*makhraj*

expenses	مصاريف/نفقات	*nafaqaat/masaariif*
expensive	غال	*ghaali*
explain	يشرح	*yashrah*
express	يعبر	*ya'bur*
external	خارجي	*khaariji*
eye	عين	*ayn*
eye-drops	قطرة للعين	*qatra lil-ayn*

F

fabric	قماش	*qimaash*
face	وجه	*wajh*
Facebook	فيس بوك	*feasbook*
factory	مصنع	*massna'*
fall (season)	خريف	*khareef*
fall (v.)	يسقط	*yasqut*
family	عائلة	*'aa'ila*
famous	مشهور	*mash-hoor*
fan	مروحة	*marwaha*
far	بعيد	*ba'eed*
farm	مزرعة	*mazra'a*
farmer	فلاح	*fallah*
fashion	زي	*zay*
fast	سريع	*saree'*
father	اب	*ab*
father-in-law	الحمو	*al-hamow*
fault	خطا	*khata'*
fax	فاكس	*faks*
February	فبراير	*febraayer*
feel	يشعر	*yash'ur*
feel like	يود	*yawwad*
fence	سور	*soor*
ferry	سفينة/عبارة	*safiina/'abbaara*
fever	حمي/حرارة	*hummaa/haraara*
fiancé	خطيب	*khateeb*
fiancée	خطيبة	*khateeba*
fill	يملأ	*yamla'*
filling	حشوة	*hashwa*
fill out (form)	يملأ	*yamla'*
film (movie)	فلم	*film*
film (v.)	يصور	*yossawer*
filter	مصفاة/ فلتر	*misfaa/filtar*
fine (good)	جيد / حسن	*jayyid /hasan*

English	Arabic	Transliteration
fine (money)	غرامة	gharaama
finger	إصبع	issbi'
finish (v.)	يَتَمُّ	yottem
fire	نار/حريق	naar/hreeq
fire alarm	منبه حريق	munabbih hariiq
first	اول	awwal
first aid	اسعافات اولية	is'aafaat awwaliyya
first class	درجة أولى	daraja owla
fish	سمك	samak
fish (v.)	يصطاد السمك	yassttaad as-samak
fit	يناسب	yonaseb
fitness	لياقة /تدريب	liyaaqa/tadriib
fitting room	غرفة القياس	ghurfat alqiyyas
fix	يصلح	yuslih
flag	علم	'alam
flashlight	مصباح يدوي	mosbah yadawee
flavor	نكهة	nak-ha
flea	برغوث	barghooth
flea market	سوق شعبي	sooq sha'abi
flight	رحلة طيران	rihlat tayaran
flood	فيضان	fayadhan
floor	طابق	tabiq
flour	طحين	tahiin
flu	إنفلونزا	influwanza
fly (insect)	ذبابة	dhubaaba
fly (v.)	يطير	yatteer
fog	ضباب	dhabab
folklore	فلكلور	fuliklor
follow	يتبع	yatba'
food	طعام/ غذاء	ta'aam /ghitha
foot	قدم	qadam
forbidden	يمنع/يحرم	yamna'/yuharrim
forehead	جبين	jabeen
foreign	غريب/أجنبي	ghareeb/ajnabi
forget	ينسى	yansaa
fork	شوكة	shawka
form	استمارة	istimara
founder	مُؤَسِّس	mo'sess
fountain	نافورة	nafoora
frame	أطار	ittar
free (no charge)	مجاني	majjani
free time	وقت فراغ	waqt faragh
freeze	تجمد	tajjamud
fresh	طازج	taazij
Friday	الجمعة	al-jumu'a
fried	مقلي	maqli
friend	صديق	sadeeq
friendly	ودي	woddi
frightened	مذعور	math'oor
frozen	مجمد	mujammad
fruit	فواكه	fawakih
full	شبعان/مملوء	shab'aan/mamluu'
fun	لهو/مرح	marah/lahw
funeral	جنازة	janaza

G

English	Arabic	Transliteration
gallery	صالة /بهو	bahw/saala
game	لعبة	lu'ba
hanger	علاقة	allaqa
garage	كراج	karaj
garbage	زبالة	zibala
garlic	ثوم	thoom
garden	حديقة	hadeeqa
garment	ثوب	thawb
gas	غاز	ghaz
gasoline	بنزين	banzeen
gas station	محطة وقود	mahattat waqood
gate	بوابة	bawwaba
gear (car)	التروس	at-turoos
gem	جوهرة	jawhara
gender	الجنس	al-jins
get off	ينزل/يخرج	yakhruj/yanzil
get on	يصعد	yass'ad
gift	هدية	hadiyya
ginger	زنجبيل	zanjabeel
girl	بنت	bint
girlfriend	صديقة	sadeeqa
glass (material)	زجاج	zujaj
glasses	نظارات	nathh-thharaat
glossy	لامع	laami'
gloves	قفازات	quffazat
glue	صمغ	samgh
gnat	بعوضة	ba'ooda
go	اذهب	ith-hab
goal	هَدَف	hadaf

go back	ارجع	*irji'*
go out	اخرج	*ukhroj*
gold	ذهب	*thahab*
golf	غولف	*gholf*
good	جيد	*jayyed*
goodbye	مع السلامة	*ma'a as-salaama*
goose	وزة	*wazza*
gram	غرام	*ghram*
grain	حبوب	*huboob*
grandchild	حفيد	*hafiid*
granddaughter	حفيدة	*hafeeda*
grandfather	جد	*jad*
grandmother	جدة	*jadda*
grapes	عنب	*'inab*
grave	مقبرة	*maqbara*
gray	رمادي	*ramaadi*
greasy	دهني	*dohnee*
green	أخضر	*akh-dhar*
greeting	تحية	*tahiyya*
grilled	مشوي	*mashwi*
grocer	بقال	*baqqaal*
groceries	بقالة	*biqala*
Groceries (food)	مواد غذائية	*mawaad ghithaa'iyya*
group	مجموعة	*majmoo'a*
guide (v.)	يوجه	*yowwajeh*
guide (book)	دليل	*daleel*
guide (person)	مرشد/موجه	*muwajjih/murshid*
guilt	ذنب/إثم	*thanb/ithm*
gulf	خَليج	*khaleej*
gym	صالة رياضة	*salat riyyadha*

H

hair	شعر	*sha'r*
hairbrush	مشط	*moshit*
haircut	قصة شعر	*qassat sha'r*
hairdresser	حلاق	*hallaaq*
hairdryer	مجفف شعر	*mujaffif sha'r*
hairspray	رشاش شعر	*rashash sha'r*
hairstyle	تسريحة شعر	*tasreehat sha'r*
half	نصف	*nissf*
hammer	مطرقة	*mitraqa*
hand	يد	*yad*

handbag	حقيبة يد	*haqeebat yad*
handkerchief	منديل	*mindeel*
handmade	صنع يدوي	*sun'yadawi*
happy	سعيد	*sa'eed*
harbor	ميناء	*minaa'*
hard (difficult)	صعب	*ssa'b*
hard (firm)	صلب/قاسي	*ssalb/qaasi*
hat	قبعة	*qubba'a*
head	رأس	*ra's*
headache	صداع	*sudaa'*
healthy	صحي	*sihhi*
hear	يسمع	*yasma'*
heart	قلب	*qalb*
heart attack	أزمة قلبية	*azma qalbiyya*
heat	حرارة	*harara*
heater	مدفأة	*midfa'a*
heavy	ثقيل	*thaqeel*
heel	كعب	*ka'b*
hello	اهلا	*ahlan*
help	مساعدة/النجدة	*musaa'ada/ an-najda*
helping	مساعدة	*musaa'ada*
hem	حافة	*hhaafat*
herbs	اعشاب	*'ashaab*
here	هنا	*hona*
high	عال	*'aali*
highway	طريق سريع	*tariiq sarii'*
hiking	سير على الاقدام	*sayr'alaa al-aqdaam*
hip	ورك	*werk*
hire	يستأجر	*yasta'jir*
hobby	هواية	*hiwaaya*
holiday	عطلة إجازة	*'utla /ijaaza*
homesick	الحنين إلى الوطن	*haniin- ila al watan*
honest	أمين	*amiin*
honey	عسل	*'asal*
hopefully	إن شاء الله	*in shaa'Allah*
horrible	كريه	*kareeh*
horse	حصان	*hissan*
hospital	مستشفى	*mustashfaa*
hospitality	ضيافة	*dhiyaafa*
hot	حار	*hhaar*

hotel	فندق	*fondoq*
hour	ساعة	*saa'a*
house	بيت	*bayt*
how?	كيف؟	*kayf*
hundred	مائة	*mi'ah*
hungry	جائع/ جوعان	*jaa'i'/jow'aan*
hurry	أسرع/بسرعة	*asri'/bisur'a*
husband	زوج	*zawj*
hut	كوخ	*kookh*

I

ice	ثلج	*thalj*
ice cream	بوظة	*boothha*
iced	مثلج	*muthallaj*
idea	فكرة	*fikra*
identification card	بطاقة شخصية	*bittaaqa shakhsiyya*
identify	يتعرف	*yuta'arraf*
ill	مريض	*mareedh*
illness	مرض	*maradh*
imagine	يتخيل	*yatakhayyal*
immediately	حالا	*haalan*
important	مهم	*muhim*
impossible	مستحيل	*mustaheel*
improve	يحسن/يطور	*yuhasin /yuttawir*
in	في	*fi*
indigestion	سوء هضم	*suu'hadhm*
in-laws	الأنساب	*al-ansaab*
included	مشمول	*mashmool*
indicate	يوضح	*yuwadhih*
inexpensive	رخيص	*rakhees*
infection	إلتهاب	*iltihaab*
infectious	معدي	*mu'di*
information	معلومات	*ma'luumaat*
injection	حقنة	*huqna*
injured	مجروح	*majrooh*
innocent	بريء	*barii'*
insect	حشرة	*hashara*
inside	داخل	*dakhil*
install	تثبيت	*tathbeet*
instructions	تعليمات	*ta'leemat*
insurance	تأمين/ضمان	*ta'meen /dhaman*
internal	داخلي	*dakhili*

international	دولي	*duwali*
Internet	إنترنت	*Internet*
interpreter	مترجم	*motarjim*
intersection	تقاطع	*taqaatu'*
introduce	يعرف / يقدم	*yuqaddim/yu'arrif*
invite	يدعو	*yad'u*
invoice	فاتورة	*fatoora*
iodine	اليود	*al-youd*
Ireland	ايرلندا	*erlanda*
iron (metal)	حديد	*hadiid*
iron (for clothes)	مكواة	*mikwaah*
iron (v.)	يكوي	*yakwii*
Islamic	إسلاميّ	*islaamee*
island	جزيرة	*jaziira*
itch	حكة	*hakka*

J

jack (for car)	رافعة	*raafi'a*
jam	مربى	*murabba*
January	يناير	*yanayer*
jaw	فك	*fak*
jeans	جينز	*jeanz*
jellyfish	قنديل البحر	*qandeel al-bahr*
jeweler	صائغ	*sayigh*
jewelry	مجوهرات	*mujawharat*
job	وظيفة/شغل	*shughl/watheefa*
jog	يركض	*yarkudh*
joke	نكتة	*nukta*
journey	رحلة	*rihla*
juice	عصير	*'aseer*
July	يوليو	*yolyo*
June	يونيو	*yunyo*
junk mail	البريد غير المرغوب فيه	*al-bareed ghair marghoub feeh*

K

kerosene	كيروسين	*kirooseen*
key	مفتاح	*miftah*
kidney	الكلى	*al-kila*
kilogram	كيلوغرام	*kiloghram*
king	ملك	*malik*
kingdom	مَملَكة	*mamlakah*
kiss	قبلة	*qubla*
kiss (v.)	يقبّل	*yuqabbil*

kitchen	مطبخ	*mattbakh*
knee	ركبة	*rukba*
knife	سكين	*sikeen*
knit	يحوك	*yahook*
know	يعرف	*ya'rif*

L

ladder	سلم	*sollam*
lake	بحيرة	*buhhayra*
lamb	خروف/ حمل	*kharoof/haml*
lamp	مصباح	*missbaah*
land (ground)	أرض	*ard*
land (v.)	يحط/ ينزل	*yahut /yanzil*
lane (of traffic)	مسار	*masar*
language	لغة	*lugha*
laptop	حاسوب محمول/ لاب توب	*hasoub mahmoul/ labtob*
large	كبير / واسع	*kabeer /waasi'*
last (final)	آخر	*akhir*
last night	الليلة الماضية	*al-layla al-madhiya*
late	متأخر	*muta'akhir*
later	فيما بعد	*feemaa ba'd*
laugh	يضحك	*yadhak*
law	قانون	*qaanoon*
lawyer	محامي	*muhamii*
laxative	ملين/ مسهل	*musahil/ mulayyin*
leak	تسرب	*tasarob*
leather	جلد	*jild*
leave	يغادر	*yughadir*
left	يسار	*yasar*
leg	ساق	*saaq*
leggings	غطاء الساقين	*ghitaa as-saaqayn*
leisure	وقت فراغ	*waqt faragh*
lemon	ليمون	*laymoon*
lend	يقرض	*yuqridh*
less	أقل	*aqal*
lesson	درس	*dars*
letter	رسالة/حرف	*risala/harf*
lettuce	خس	*khas*
library	مكتبة	*maktaba*
license	رخصة/إجارة	*rukhsa/ijaaza*

lie (be lying)	يكذب	*yakthib*
lie down	يستلقي	*yastalqii*
lift (elevator)	مصعد	*mis'ad*
lift (in car)	توصيلة	*tawsseela*
light (not dark)	مضيء	*mudhi'*
light (not heavy)	خفيف	*khafiif*
lighter	قداحة	*qaddaha*
lightning	برق	*barq*
like (v.)	يحب/ يرغب	*yuhib / yarghab*
line	خط	*khatt*
linen	كتان	*kittaan*
lining	بطانة	*bitaana*
listen	يستمع / يصغي	*yusghii / yastami'*
liter	لتر	*letr*
literature	ادب	*adab*
little (amount)	قليل	*qaleel*
little (small)	صغير	*sagheer*
live (alive)	يعيش	*ya'iish*
live (v.)	يسكن	*yaskun*
liver	الكبد	*al-kabid*
lobster	جراد البحر	*jarad al-bahr*
local	محلي	*mahhalli*
lock	يقفل/قفل	*qufl/yaqfil*
long	طويل	*taweel*
long-distance	مسافة بعيدة	*masafa ba'iida*
look at	ينظر الى	*yanthhur ilaa*
look for	يبحث عن	*yabhath 'an*
look up	يستطلع	*yastattle'*
lose	يفقد	*yafqid*
loss	فقدان /خسارة	*khasaara /fiqdaan*
lost (missing)	ضائع	*dhaa'i'*
lotion	كريم	*kreem*
loud	عال	*'aali*
love	حب	*hob*
love (v.)	يحب	*yohib*
low	منخفض	*munkhafid*
luck	خظ	*khatt*
luggage	امتعة/حقائب	*amti'a/haqaa'ib*
lumps (sugar)	مكعبات السكر	*moka'bat as-sukkar*
lunch	غداء	*ghidhaa'*
lungs	الرئتان	*ar-ri'ataan*

M

madam	مدام/ سيدة	*madam /sayyida*
magazine	مجلة	*majalla*
mail (letters)	بريد	*bareed*
mail (v.)	يرسل بالبريد	*yursil bilbareed*
main	رئيسي	*ra'isi*
make	يصنع	*yasna'*
makeup	مكياج	*mikyaaj*
man	رجل	*rajul*
manager	مدير	*mudeer*
mango	مانجا	*manga*
manicure	صبغ أظافر	*ath-thafir*
many	كثير	*katheer*
map	خارطة	*kharita*
marble	مرمر	*marmar*
March	مارس	*maris*
margarine	زبدة	*zubda*
marina	مرسى	*marsa*
market	سوق	*suuq*
married	متزوج	*mutazawwij*
mass	كتلة	*kutla*
mat	سجادة	*sijjadda*
match	يوافق /يناسب	*yuwaafiq/ yunaasib*
matches (fire starter)	كبريت	*kabreet*
May	مايو	*mayoo*
maybe	ربما	*rubbamaa*
mayonnaise	مايونيز	*maayuuneez*
mayor	محافظ	*mohaafiz*
meal	وجبة غذائية	*wajba ghidhaa'iyya*
mean (v.)	يعني	*ya'nee*
mean (not nice)	لئيم	*laieem*
mean (average)	معدل	*mo'addaal*
measure	يقيس	*yaqees*
meat	لحم	*lahm*
medication	علاج	*'ilaaj*
medicine	دواء	*dawaa'*
meet	يلتقي	*yaltaqi*
melon	شمام	*shimmaam*
member	عضو	*'udw*
mend	يصلح/تصليح	*yuslih/tasleeh*

menu	قائمة المأكولات	*qaa'imat al-ma'kuulaat*
message	رسالة	*risaala*
metal	معدن	*ma'dan*
meter	متر	*metr*
meter (in taxi)	عداد	*addad*
migraine	صداع الشقيقة	*sudaa'ashshaqeeqa*
mild (taste)	لطيف	*lateef*
milk	حليب	*haleeb*
millimeter	مليمتر	*millimitr*
minister	وَزير	*wazeer*
minute	دقيقة	*daqeeqa*
mirror	مراة	*mir'aah*
miss (loved one)	يشتاق	*yashtaaq*
missing	مفقود	*mafqood*
mist	ضباب	*dhabaab*
misty	غامض	*ghamidh*
mistake	خطأ/ غلطة	*khata'/ghaltta*
mistaken	مخطيء	*mukhti'*
misunderstanding	سوء فهم	*soo'fahm*
mixed	ممزوج	*mamzooj*
moment	لحظة	*lahh-tha*
Monday	الاثنين	*al-ithnayn*
money	نقود/ فلوس	*nuqood/fuloos*
monkey	قرد	*qird*
month	شهر	*shahr*
moon	قمر	*qamar*
mosquito	بعوضة	*ba'oodha*
motel	فندق صغير	*fundiq sagheer*
mother	ام	*um*
mother-in-law	الحماة	*al-hamaa*
motorbike	دراجة نارية	*darraaja naariyya*
mountain	جبل	*jabal*
mouse	فأر	*fa'r*
mouth	فم	*fam*
much	كثير	*katheer*
mud	طين	*tteen*
muscle	عضلة	*'adala*
museum	متحف	*mat-haf*
mushrooms	الفطر	*al-fetr*
music	موسيقى	*moseeqaa*

N

nail (finger)	ظفر	*thhifr*
nail (metal)	مسمار	*mismaar*
naked	عاري	*'aaree*
nation	أُمّة	*ommah*
national	وَطَنيّ	*wattane*
nationality	جنسية	*jinsiyya*
natural	طبيعي	*tabee'ee*
nature	طبيعة	*tabii'a*
near	قرب	*qurb*
nearby	قريب	*qareeb*
necessary	ضروري	*dhooroee*
neck	رقبة	*raqaba*
necklace	قلادة/عقد	*qilaada/e'qd*
necktie	ربطة عنق	*rabtat 'unuq*
needle	إبرة	*ibra*
neighbor	جار	*jaar*
nephew	ابن الاخت/ ابن الاخ	*ibn al-akh/ ibn al-ukht*
never	أبداً	*abadan*
new	جديد	*jadiid*
news	أخبار	*akhbaar*
newspaper	صحيفة/جريدة	*jariida/saheefa*
next	القادم/اللاحق	*al-laahiq/al-qaadim*
nice (person)	طيب	*tayyib*
nice (pleasant)	ممتع	*mumti'*
niece	بنت الاخت/بنت الاخ	*bint al-ukht /bint al-akh*
night	ليل	*layl*
no	كلا/لا	*laa/kallaa*
noise	ضوضاء	*dhawdhaa'*
nonstop	دون توقف	*doon tawaqquf*
noodles	معكرونة	*ma'karuuna*
normal	طبيعي	*tabii'ii*
north	شمال	*shamaal*
nose	انف	*anf*
notebook	دفتر ملاحظات	*daftar mulaahath-that*
nothing	لا شيء	*laa shay'*
November	نوفمبر	*november*
nowhere	ليس في أي مكان	*laysa fee ay makan*

| nurse | ممرضة | *mumarridha* |
| nuts | مكسرات | *mokasarat* |

O

occupation	شغل/وظيفة	*wathheefa /shughl*
October	اكتوبر	*octoober*
off (turned off)	يغلق/ يطفيء	*yughliq /yutfi'*
offer	عرض	*ardh*
office	مكتب	*maktab*
oil	زيت	*zayt*
ointment	مرهم	*marham*
okay	حسنا	*hhasanan*
onion	بصل	*basal*
open	مفتوح	*maftuuh*
open (v.)	يفتح	*yaftah*
only	فَقَط	*faqatt*
opposite	عكس/مقابل	*'aks/muqaabul*
orange (color)	برتقالي	*burtuqali*
orange (fruit)	برتقال	*butuqaal*
order	طلب/أمر	*ttalab/amr*
order (v.)	يأمر	*ya'mur*
other	آخر	*aakhar*
outside	خارج	*kharij*
overseas	في الخارج	*fii al-khaarij*
oyster	محار	*mahhaar*

P

page	صفحة	*safha*
pain	ألم	*alam*
painkiller	مسكن ألم	*musakkin alam*
paint	دهان/صبغ	*sabgh/dihaan*
painting	يصبغ	*yasbogh*
pajamas	بيجامة	*bijaama*
palace	مكان	*makaan*
pan	مقلاة	*miqlah*
pants	بنطلون	*bantaloon*
paper	ورقة	*waraqah*
parcel	رزمة/طرد	*ruzma/tard*
pardon	عفوا	*'afwan*
parents	والدان	*waalidaan*
park	حديقة	*hadiiqa*
park (v.)	يوقف	*yuqif*
parliament	مَجلِس الشَّعْب	*majlis ash-sha'ab*

part	جزء	juz'	pipe (plumbing)	انبوب	unbuub
partner	شريك	shareek	pipe (smoking)	غليون	ghalyoon
party	حفلة	hafla	pity	شفقة	shafaqa
passenger	مسافر	musaafir	plain (simple)	صريح/بسيط	baseet/ sariih
passport	جواز سفر	jawaaz safar	plain (unflavored)	بدون نكهة	bidoon nakha
password	كلمة السر	kalimat al-ser	plan (intention)	خطة/برنامج	khetta /barnamej
patient	صابر	ssabir	plane	طائرة	taa'ira
patient (sick)	مريض	mareedh	plant	نبات	nabat
pay	يدفع	yadfa'	plastic	بلاستك	blastik
peach	خوخ/دراق	khawkh/durraaq	platform	منصة	manassa
peanut	فستق	fustuq	play (drama)	مسرحية	masrahiyya
pear	إجاص	ajass	play (v.)	يلعب	yal'ab
pearl	لؤلؤ	lu'lu'	playground	منطقة لعب	mintaqat la'ib
peas	بازلاء	bazilla		للأطفال	lil-atfaal
pen	قلم	qalam	please	من فضلك	min fadlik
pencil	قلم رصاص	qalam rassaas	pleasure	متعة	mut'a
people	ناس	naas	pocket	جيب	jayb
performance	أداء	adaa'	poisonous	سام	saam
perfume	عطر	'itr	police	شرطة	shurta
perhaps	ربما	robama	politics	سياسة	siyasa
permit	رخصة	rokhsa	pond	بركة	birka
person	شخص	shakhs	pony	حصان صغير	hisaan saghiir
personal	شخصي	shakhsi	population	الكثافة السكانية	al-kathaafa as-
pet	حيوان اليف	hayawaan aleef			sukkaaniyya
petrol	وقود	waqood	pork	لحم خنزير	lahm khinziir
pharmacy	صيدلي	saydaliyya	port	ميناء	miinaa'
phone	تلفون/هاتف	tilifun/haatif	porter (concierge)	بواب	bawwab
phone (v.)	يتصل	yatassil	possible	ممكن	momkin
phone call	مكالمة	mukalama	post (v.)	يرسل بالبريد	yursil bilbarid
photo	صورة	ssoura	postage	اجرة البريد	ujrat al-barid
photocopier	آلة النسخ	aalat an-nasikh	postbox	صندوق بريد	sundooq barid
photocopy	نسخة	nuskha	postcode	رمز بريدي	ramz baridi
photocopy (v.)	يصور	yussawwir	post office	مكتب بريد	maktab bareed
phrasebook	كتاب عبارات	kitaab 'ibaaraat	postpone	يؤجل	yu'ajjl
pick up	يتسلم/ياخذ	yatasallam /	potato	بطاطس	batatis
		ya'khudh	poultry	دواجن	dawajin
picnic	رحلة	rihla	precious	ثمين	thameen
contraceptive	حبوب منع الحمل	huboob man'	prefer	يفضل	yufadhil
(pill)		al-hamal	preference	مفضل	mufaddal
pills (tablets)	حبوب	huboob	pregnant	حامل	hhaamil
pillow	مخدة	mikhadda	prescription	وصفة	wasfa
pin	دبوس	dabboos	present (gift)	هدية	hadiyya
pineapple	اناناس	ananas	present (here)	موجود	mawjood

press (v.)	يضغط	*yadghat*
pressure	ضغط	*daght*
pray	يُصَلّي	*yossali*
price	سعر	*si'r*
print (v.)	يطبع	*yattba'*
printer	طابعة	*ttabi'a*
probably	محتمل	*muhtamal*
problem	مشكلة	*moshkila*
profession	مهنة/ حرفة	*mihna /herfa*
profit	فائدة/ مصلحة	*faa'ida /maslaha*
program	برنامج	*barnamej*
project	مَشروع	*mashroo'*
pronounce	يتلفظ	*yatalaffath*
prophet	رسول	*rasool*
pull	يسحب	*yas-hab*
pulse	نبض	*nabdh*
pure	نقي	*naqi*
purple	بنفسجي	*banafsaji*
purse (handbag)	حقيبة	*haqeeba*
push	يدفع	*yadfa'*
puzzle	لغز	*lughz*
pyramids	أهرام	*ahraam*
pyjamas	بيجامة	*bijaama*

Q

quarter	ربع	*rub'*
queen	ملكة	*malika*
question	سؤال	*so'aal*
quick	سريع	*sarii'*
quiet	هاديء	*haadi'*

R

radio	مذياع/ راديو	*mithyaa'/radyo*
railroad, railway	سكة القطار	*sikkat al-qitaar*
rain (n.)	مطر	*matar*
rain (v.)	تمطر	*tomtter*
rape	اغتصاب	*ightisaab*
rapid	سريع	*sarii'*
rash	متهور	*mutahawwir*
rat	جرذ	*jurth*
raw	خام	*kham*
read	يقرأ	*yaqra'*
ready	جاهز	*jahiz*

really	حقا	*haqqan*
reason	سبب	*sabab*
receipt	وصل	*wasl*
reception	استقبال	*istiqbal*
recipe	وصفة	*wasfa*
recommend	ينصح	*yunssah*
rectangle	مستطيل	*mustatteel*
red	احمر	*ahmar*
reduction	إنخفاض	*inkhifadh*
refrigerator	ثلاجة	*thallaja*
refund	إعادة مال	*i'aadat al-maal*
regards	تحيات	*tahiyat*
registered	مسجل	*musajjal*
relatives	أقارب	*aqaarib*
reliable	موثوق	*mawthooq*
religion	دين	*deen*
rent	يستأجر	*yasta'jir*
repair	يصلح	*yuslih*
repairs	ترميم	*tarmeem*
repeat	يعيد	*yu'iid*
repeatedly	مِراراً	*mirarran*
reserve	يحجر	*yahjiz*
responsible	مسؤول	*mas'ool*
rest	يرتاح	*yartah*
restaurant	مطعم	*mat'am*
restroom	حمام	*hammaam*
result	نتيجة	*natiija*
retired	متقاعد	*mutaqaa'id*
reverse	يرجع	*yurji'*
rheumatism	الم المفاصل	*alam al-mafaasil*
ribbon	شريط	*shareett*
rice	أرز	*aruz*
ridiculous	سخيف	*sakheef*
riding	راكب	*rakib*
right (correct)	صحيح	*saheeh*
right (side)	يمين	*yamiin*
rinse	يشطف	*yashtuf*
ripe	ناضج	*naadij*
risk	خطر	*khatar*
river	نهر	*nahr*
road	طريق	*tariiq*
roasted	محمص	*muhammas*
rock (stone)	صخرة	*sakhra*

roof	سقف	*saqf*
room	غرفة	*ghurfa*
rope	حبل	*habl*
route	طريق	*tareeq*
rubber	مطاط	*mattat*
rude	غير مهذب	*ghayr muhathab*
ruins	خراب	*kharaab*
run	يركض	*yarkud*

S

sad	حزين	*hazeen*
safe	آمن	*aamin*
salad	سلطة	*salata*
sale	بيع	*bay'*
salt	ملح	*milh*
same	مشابه/نفس	*mushaabih/nafs*
sandals	صندل	*sandal*
satisfied	راض	*radi*
Saturday	السبت	*as-sabt*
sauce	مرق	*maraq*
saucepan	مقلاة	*miqlaah*
say	يقول	*yaqool*
scales	ميزان	*meezaan*
scarf	منديل	*mandeel*
school	مدرسة	*madrasa*
scissors	مقص	*miqas*
Scotland	اسكتلندا	*iskutlanda*
screw	برغي	*burghi*
sculpture	فن النحت	*fann an-naht*
sea	بحر	*bahr*
search	بحث	*bahth*
seat	مقعد	*maq'ad*
second (in line)	ثاني	*thaani*
second (instant)	ثانية	*thaaniya*
second-hand	مستعمل	*musta'mal*
sedative	مسكن	*musakkin*
see	يرى	*yara*
send	يرسل	*yursil*
sentence	جملة	*jumla*
separate	يفصل/منفصل	*yafsil/munfasil*
September	سبتمبر	*sebtember*
serious	خطير	*khateer*
service	خدمة	*khidma*

set	مجموعة/رزمة	*majmuua'/ruzma*
sew	يخيط	*yakheet*
shade	ظل	*thhil*
shallow	ضحل	*dhahl*
shame	عار	*'aar*
shampoo	شامبو	*shamboo*
shark	قرش	*qirsh*
sheet	شرشف	*sharshaf*
shirt	قميص	*qamees*
shoe	حذاء	*hithaa'*
shop (store)	مخزن/متجر	*makhzan/ matjar*
shop (v.)	يتسوق	*yatasawwaq*
short	قصير	*qaseer*
shoulder	كتف	*katif*
show	يعرض	*ya'redh*
shower	دش	*dush*
shrimp	ربيان	*robyan*
sightseeing	التنزه	*at-tanazzuh*
sign (road)	اشارة	*esharah*
sign (v.)	يوقع	*yuwwaqqi'*
signature	توقيع	*tawqii'*
silence	صمت	*ssamt*
silk	حرير	*hareer*
silver	فضة	*fidda*
simple	بسيط/سهل	*baseett/sahl*
similar	مِثْل	*mithla*
single (only one)	واحد/واحدة	*waahid /waahida*
single (unmarried)	أعزب	*a'zab*
sir	سيد	*sayyid*
sister	أخت	*ukht*
sit	يجلس	*yajlis*
size	حجم	*hajm*
skiing	تزلج	*tazalluj*
skin	جلد	*jild*
skirt	تنورة	*tannoora*
sleep	ينام	*yanaam*
sleeve	كم	*kum*
slip	ينزلق	*yanzaliq*
slippers	نعال خفيف	*nu'aal khafiif*
slow	بطيء	*batii'*
small	صغير	*sagheer*
smartphone	هاتف ذكي	*hatif dhakii*

English	Arabic	Transliteration
smell	رائحة	raa'iha
smoke	دخان/تدخين	dukhan/tadkhiin
smoked (adj.)	مدخن	mudakhan
snake	حية	hayya
snorkel	أنبوب تنفس مائي	unboob tanaffus maa'ii
snow	ثلج	thalj
snow (v.)	تثلج	tuthlij
soap	صابون	saabuun
soccer	كرة القدم	kurat al-qadam
socks	جوارب	jawaarib
someone	شخص	shakhs
sometimes	أحيانا	ahyaanan
somewhere	في مكان ما	fee makaanin ma
son	إبن	ibn
soon	قريبا	qareeban
sore	ملتهب	moltaheb
sorry	آسف	aasif
soup	شوربة/حساء	shuurba/hisaa'
sour	حامض	haamidh
south	جنوب	janoob
souvenir	تذكار	tithkaar
spare	اضافي/احتياطي	ihtiyatii/idhafi
speak	يتكلم	yatkallam
special	خاص	khass
specialist	اخصائي	akhissaa'i
spell	يتلفظ	yatalaffath
spices	توابل	tawaabil
spicy	حار	haar
spoon	ملعقة	mil'aqa
sport	رياضة	riyaadha
spring (season)	ربيع	rabii'
square (shape)	مربع	murabba'
stadium	ملعب	mal'ab
stain	بقعة	buq'a
stairs	سلم/درج	sullam/daraj
stamp	طابع	ttabe'
stand up	قم	qom
star	نجمة	najma
start	يبدا	yabda'
station	محطة	mahatta
statue	تمثال	timthal
stay (remain)	يبقى	yabqa
steal	يسرق	yasriq
steam	بخار	bukhar
steel	فولاذ	foolath
stepfather	زوج الام	zawj al-um
stepmother	زوجة الاب	zawjat al-ab
steps	خطوات/درجات	khutuwat /darajat
sterilize	يعقم	yu'aqqim
stitches	غرز	ghuraz
stomach (abdomen)	بطن	batn
stop (cease)	يتوقف	yatawaqqaf
store (shop)	مخزن	makhzan
storey	طابق	ttabeq
storm	عاصفة	'aasifa
straight	مستقيم	mustaqiim
strange	غَريب	ghareeb
straw	مصاصة	massaasah
street	شارع	shaari'
strike (work stoppage)	إضراب	idhraab
string	خيط/حبل	khayt/habl
strong	قوي	qawi
study	دراسة/يدرس	diraasa/yadrus
stuffing	الحشو	al-hashuu
subway	قطار الأنفاق	qitar al-anfaaq
succeed	ينجح	yanjah
sugar	سكر	sukkar
suit	بدلة	badla
suitcase	حقيبة	haqiiba
summer	الصيف	as-sayf
success	نَجاح	najahh
sun	شمس	shams
sunbathe	حمام شمسي	hammaam shamsii
Sunday	الاحد	al-ahad
sunglasses	نظارات شمسية	nathhaaraat shamsiyya
sunrise	شروق الشمس	shuruuq ashshams
sunset	غروب الشمس	ghuroob
sunstroke	ضربة شمس	dharbat shams
supermarket	سوق مركزي	sooq markazi
surf	أمواج متكسرة	amwaaj mutakassira
surname	لقب	laqab

surprise	مفاجأة	*mufaaja'a*
swallow (v.)	يبلع	*yabla'*
swamp	مستنقع	*mustanqa'*
sweat	عرق	*'araq*
sweet	حلو	*hhelo*
swim	يسبح	*yasbahh*
swindle	خداع/يخدع	*khedaa'/yakhda'*
switch	مفتاح	*miftah*
synagogue	معبد	*ma'bad*
syrup	دواء شرب	*dawaa'shorb*

T

table	منضدة / طاولة	*mindada/ ttawelah*
tablespoon	ملعقة	*milaqa'a*
tablets	حبوب	*hubuub*
tableware	أدوات المائدة	*adawaat al-maa'ida*
take (pick up)	يأخذ	*ya'khudh*
take (photo)	يلتقط صورة	*yaltaqit ssoorah*
talk	حديث/يتحدث	*yatahhadath/ hadeeth*
tall	طويل	*taweel*
tap	حنفية	*hhanafiyya*
taste (n.)	طعم	*tta'am*
taste (v.)	يذوق	*yathooq*
tax	ضريبة	*dhareeba*
taxi	تاكسي/سيارة اجرة	*taksi/sayyarat ojra*
tea	شاي	*shay*
team	فَريق	*fareeq*
teapot	أبريق شاي	*ibriiq shaay*
teaspoon	ملعقة شاي	*mil'aqat shaay*
television	تلفزيون	*telefizyoon*
temple	معبد	*ma'bad*
tennis	تنس	*tenis*
ten	عشرة	*a'shara*
tent	خيمة	*kkayma*
terrace	سطح	*satt-h*
terribly	بفظاعة	*bifathha'aa*
thank (v.)	يشكر	*yashkur*
thank you, thanks	شكرا	*shokran*
thaw	ذوبان	*thawaban*
theater	مسرح	*masrahh*
theft	سرقة	*sariqa*

there	هناك	*honak*
thermometer	ميزان الحرارة	*mezan al-harara*
thick	سميك	*sameek*
thief	لص	*liss*
thigh	فخذ	*fakhidh*
thin (not fat)	نحيف	*nahheef*
think	يظن	*yathhun*
third	ثلث	*tholuth*
thirsty	عطشان	*'atshaan*
this	هذا	*hatha*
thread	خيط	*khayt*
throat	حنجرة	*honjara*
thunderstorm	عاصفة رعدية	*assifa 'ra'diyya*
Thursday	الخميس	*al-khamees*
ticket (admission)	بطاقة دخول	*bitaaqat dukhuul*
ticket (travel)	تذكرة سفر	*tathkirat safar*
tidy	يرتب/ينظم	*yuratib / yunaththim*
tie (v.)	يربط	*yarbit*
time	وقت	*waqt*
timetable	جدول	*jadwal*
tin (can)	علبة	*ulba*
tip	بقشيش/إكرامية	*ikraamiyya/ baqsheesh*
tire	إطار	*itaar*
tissues	محارم	*mahaarim*
to	إلى	*ila*
tobacco	تبغ	*tibgh*
toddler	طفل	*ttifl*
toe	إصبع القدم	*isbi'al-qadam*
together	مع بعض	*maa'ba'dh*
toilet	المرحاض/التواليت	*al-mirhadh/ at-tuwaleet*
tomorrow	غدا	*ghadan*
tongue	لسان	*lisan*
tonight	هذه الليلة	*haathihi al-layla*
tool	أداة	*adah*
tooth	سن	*sin*
toothache	ألم أسنان	*alam asnan*
toothbrush	فرشاة أسنان	*forshat asnan*
toothpaste	معجون أسنان	*ma'joon asnan*
top	قمة	*qimma*
topic	مَوْضوع	*mawdhoo'*

total	مجموع	*majmoo'*
tough	خشن	*khashin*
tour	رحلة سياحية	*rihla siyahiyya*
tow	يسحب/ يجر	*yashab /yajor*
towards	نَحوَ	*nahhwa*
towel	منشفة	*minshafa*
tower	برج	*burj*
town	بلدة	*balda*
toy	دمية / لعبة	*lu'ba /dumya*
traffic	حركة المرور	*harakat al-muroor*
train	قطار	*qitar*
translate	يترجم	*yutarjim*
travel	سفر	*safar*
traveler	مسافر	*musafir*
treatment	معاملة	*mu'aamala*
triangle	مثلث	*muth-thallath*
trim	يقص	*yaqus*
trip	رحلة	*rihla*
truck	شاحنة	*shaahina*
trustworthy	موثوق	*mawthuuq*
Tuesday	الثلاثاء	*ath-thulaathaa'*
tunnel	نفق	*nafaq*
TV	تلفزيون	*tilifizyoon*
twitter	تويتر	*twitter*
typhoon	إعصار	*i'saar*

U

ugly	قبيح	*qabeeh*
ulcer	قرحة	*qurha*
umbrella	مظلة	*mithhalla*
under	تحت	*tahta*
understand	يفهم	*yafham*
undress	اخلع/يخلع	*ikhla'/yakhla'*
unemployed	عاطل عن العمل	*'atil 'an al-'amal*
uneven	متعرج	*mut'arrij*
united	مُتَّحِد	*mattahed*
university	جامعة	*jaami'a*
unleaded	بدون رصاص	*bidoon rasas*
up	أعلى/ فوق	*a'la /fawq*
upright	منتصب	*muntasib*
urgent	ملح/ عاجل	*mullih /aajel*
urine	بول	*bawl*
usually	عادة	*'aadatan*

V

vacate	يترك	*yatruk*
vacation	عطلة/ إجازة	*'utla /ijaza*
valid	قانوني	*qanooni*
valley	وادي	*waadi*
valuable	ثمين	*thameen*
van	شاحنة صغيرة	*shahina sagheerah*
vase	مزهرية	*mazhariyyah*
vegetable	خضروات	*khudrawaat*
vegetarian	نباتي	*nabaati*
vein	وريد	*wareed*
velvet	مخمل	*mokhmal*
venomous	سام	*saam*
vertical	عمودي	*'amoodi*
view	منظر	*manthar*
village	قرية	*qarya*
voice	صَوْت	*ssawt*
virus	فيروس	*fayroos*
visa	فيزا/تأشيرة	*ta'sheera (visa)*
visit (v.)	يزور	*yazoor*
visit (n.)	زيارة	*ziyaaa*
vitamins	فيتامينات	*vitameenat*
volcano	بركان	*burkaan*
volleyball	كرة الطائرة	*kurat at-taa'ira*

W

wait	إنتظر /ينتظر	*intathhir/ yantathhir*
waiter	نادل	*nadil*
waitress	نادلة	*nadilah*
wake up	ينهض	*yanhadh*
walk (n.)	مشي	*mashy*
walk (v.)	يمشي	*yamshi*
wall	حائط/ جدار	*haa'it /jidar*
wallet	محفظة نقود	*mihfathat nuqood*
warm	دافيء	*daafi*
warn	يحذر	*yuhathir*
warning	تحذير	*tah-theer*
wash	يغسل	*yaghsil*
watch (v.)	يشاهد	*yushahid*
watch	ساعة	*sa'aa*
water	ماء	*maa'*

English	Arabic	Transliteration
watermelon	بطيخ	*batteekh*
waterproof	ضد الماء	*dhidh al-maa'*
way (direction)	طريق	*tariiq*
we	نحن	*nahnu*
weak	ضعيف	*da'iif*
wear	يلبس	*yalbas*
weather	الطقس	*at-taqs*
webcam	كاميرا	*kamira*
wedding	حفل زفاف	*hafl zafaf*
Wednesday	الاربعاء	*al-arbi'aa'*
week	أسبوع	*usboo'*
weekend	عطلة نهاية الأسبوع	*'utlat nihaayat al-usboo'*
weigh	يزن	*yazin*
welcome	اهلا وسهلا	*ahlan wa sahlan*
well (good)	جيد	*jayyid*
west	غرب	*gharb*
wet	مبلل /رطب	*rattib/muballal*
what	ماذا	*matha*
wheel	عجل	*'ajal*
wheelchair	كرسي متحرك	*kursii mattaharrik*
when	متى	*mata*
where	أين	*ayna*
which	أي	*ayy*
white	أبيض	*abyadh*
who	من	*man*
why	لماذا	*limatha*
widow	أرملة	*armala*
widower	ارمل	*armal*
wife	زوجة	*zawja*
wind	ريح (p: رياح)	*riih/riyaah*
window	شباك	*shubbak*
winter	شتاء	*shitaa'*
wire	سلك	*silk*
with	مع	*maa'*
without	مِن دَونَ/بِدونَ	*bedoon/men doon*
witness	شاهد	*shahid*
woman	أمرأة	*imra'a*

English	Arabic	Transliteration
wonderful	رائع /جميل	*jameel/raa'i'*
wood	خشب	*khashab*
wool	صوف	*soaf*
word	كلمة	*kalima*
world	عالَم	*alam*
work	شغل /عمل	*'amal/shughl*
worn	ممزق /بالي	*baali/mumazzaq*
worried	قلق	*qaliq*
wound	جرح	*jurh*
wrap	يغلف /يلف	*yaluf/yughallif*
wrist	رسغ	*risgh*
write	يكتب	*yaktub*
wrong	غلط /خطأ	*khata'/ghalt*

Y

English	Arabic	Transliteration
yarn	خيط	*khayt*
yawn	يتثاءب	*yatatha'ab*
year	سنة	*sana*
yellow	اصفر	*asfar*
yes	نعم	*na'am*
yesterday	أمس	*ams*
you	أنت	*anta* (M)/*anti* (F)
young	شَبّ / فَتاة	*shabb / fatah*
youth	صِغَر	*ssighar*

Z

English	Arabic	Transliteration
zakat (alms giving in Islam)	زَكاة	*zakah*
zero	صفر	*sifr*
zip	رمز	*ramz*
zodiac	بُرج	*borj*
zone	مِنطَقة	*minttaqa*
zionist	صَهْيونيّ	*sahyyooni*
zoo	حديقة الحيوانات	*hadeeqat al-haywanat*
zucchini (courgette)	كوسة	*koosa*

Arabic-English Dictionary

A

a'maa	اعمى	blind (can't see)
'aa'ila	عائلة	family
'aada	عادة	custom
'aadatan	عادة	usually
'aali	عال	high
'aar	عار	shame
'aaree	عاري	naked
'aasifa	عاصفة	storm
'adala	عضلة	muscle
'afwan	عفوا	pardon
'ajal	عجل	wheel
'aks/dhidh	عكس/ضد	counter
'aks/muqaabul	عكس/مقابل	opposite
'alaa al-qal	على الاقل	at least
'alam	علم	flag
'amal/shughl	شغل /عمل	work
'amiiq	عميق	deep
'amoodi	عمودي	vertical
'araba	عربة	carriage
'araq	عرق	sweat
'asal	عسل	honey
'aseer	عصير	juice
'ashaa'	عشاء	dinner
'ashaab	اعشاب	herbs
'athm	عظم	bone
'atshaan	عطشان	thirsty
a'amelat funduq	عاملة تنظيف	chambermaid
a'shara	عشرة	ten
a'la /fawq	أعلى/ فوق	up
a'waad	أعواد	chopsticks
a'zab	أعزب	single (unmarried)
aakhar	آخر	other
aalat an-nasikh	آلة النسخ	photocopier
aali	عال	loud
aamin	آمن	safe
aasif	آسف	sorry
ab	اب	father
abadan	أبداً	never

abyadh	أبيض	white
adaa'	أداء	performance
adab	ادب	literature
adah	أداة	tool
adawaat al-maa'ida	أدوات المائدة	tableware
adawaat fakhariyya	ادوات فخارية	crockery
addad	عداد	meter (in taxi)
ahlan	اهلا	hello
ahlan wa sahlan	اهلا وسهلا	welcome
ahmar	احمر	red
ahraam	أهرام	pyramids
ahsan	أحسن	better
ahyaanan	أحيانا	sometimes
ajass	إجاص	pear
akh	أخ	brother
akh-dhar	أخضر	green
akhbaar	أخبار	news
akhir	آخر	last (final)
akhissaa'i	اخصائي	specialist
akzima	اكزما	eczema
al-ahad	الاحد	Sunday
al-ansaab	الأنساب	in-laws
al-arbi'aa'	الاربعاء	Wednesday
al-bareed ghair marghoub feeh	البريد غير المرغوب فيه	junk mail
al-fetr	الفطر	mushrooms
al-hamaa	الحماة	mother-in-law
al-hamow	الحمو	father-in-law
al-hashuu	الحشو	stuffing
al-ithnayn	الاثنين	Monday
al-jins	الجنس	gender
al-jumu'a	الجمعة	Friday
al-kabid	الكبد	liver
al-kathaafa as-sukkkaaniyya	الكثافة السكانية	population
al-khamees	الخميس	Thursday
al-khareef	الخريف	autumn
al-kila	الكلى	kidney
al-kumm	الكم	cuff

al-laahiq/ al-qaadim	القادم/اللاحق	next
al-layla al-madhiya	الليلة الماضية	last night
al-mirhadh/ at-tuwaleet	المرحاض/ التواليت	toilet
al-youd	اليود	iodine
alam	ألم	pain
alam	عالَم	world
alam al-mafaasil	ألم المفاصل	rheumatism
alam asnan	ألم أسنان	toothache
alam fii al-udhun	ألم في الأذن	earache
Allah	الله	Allah
allaqa	علاقة	hanger
almaas	ألماس	diamond
amaana/wadii'a	امانة/وديعة	deposit (n.)
amareeki	امريكي	American (m.)
amareekiyyah	أمريكية	American (f.)
amariikaa	امريكا	America
amiin	أمين	honest
ams	أمس	yesterday
amti'a/haqaa'ib	امتعة/حقائب	luggage
amwaaj mutakassira	أمواج متكسرة	surf
ananas	اناناس	pineapple
anf	انف	nose
anta (M)/anti (F)	أنت	you
aqaarib	أقارب	relatives
aqal	أقل	less
ar-ri'ataan	الرئتان	lungs
ard	أرض	land (ground)
ardh	أرض	earth
ardh	عرض	offer
armal	ارمل	widower
armala	أرملة	widow
arraqam albareedi	الرقم البريدي	area code
aruz	أرز	rice
as-sabt	السبت	Saturday
as-sayf	الصيف	summer
asaasi	اساسي	essential
asbireen	اسبرين	aspirin
asfal	اسفل	down
asfar	اصفر	yellow

ashqar / shaqraa	اشقر / شقراء	blond (m. & f.)
asri'/bisur'a	أسرع/بسرعة	hurry
asseen	الصين	China
assifa 'ra'diyya	عاصفة رعدية	thunderstorm
aswad	أسود	black
at-tanazzuh	التنزه	sightseeing
at-taqs	الطقس	weather
at-turoos	التروس	gear (car)
ath-th-ill	الظل	awning
ath-thafir	صبغ أظافر	manicure
ath-thulaathaa'	الثلاثاء	Tuesday
atil 'an al-'amal	عاطل عن العمل	unemployed
attrash	اطرش	deaf
awwal	اول	first
aydiz	أيدز	AIDS
ayn	عين	eye
ayna	أين	where
ayy	أي	which
azma qalbiyya	أزمة قلبية	heart attack
azraq	أزرق	blue

B

ba'eed	بعيد	far
ba'd	بعد	after
ba'ooda	بعوضة	gnat
ba'oodha	بعوضة	mosquito
baab	باب	door
baali /mumazzaq	ممزق /بالي	worn
baaligh	بالغ	adult
baathinjaan	باذنجان	eggplant
badla	بدلة	suit
bahr	بحر	sea
bahth	بحث	search
bahw/saala	صالة /بهو	gallery
balad	بلد	country (nation)
balda	بلدة	town
banafsaji	بنفسجي	purple
bantaloon	بنطلون	pants
banzeen	بنزين	gasoline
baqa	باقة	collar
baqqaal	بقال	grocer
bareed	بريد	mail (letters)
barghooth	برغوث	flea

barid	بارد	cold (not hot)
barii'	بريء	innocent
bariid iliktoronii	بريد إلكتروني	email
bariid jawwii	بريد جوي	airmail
barnamej	برنامج	program
barq	برق	lightning
basal	بصل	onion
baseet/ sariih	صريح/بسيط	plain (simple)
baseett / sahl	بسيط / سهل	simple
baskaweet	بسكويت	biscuit
baskawiit	بسكويت	cookie
batatis	بطاطس	potato
batii'	بطيء	slow
batn	بطن	stomach (abdomen)
batta	بطة	duck
battaaniyya	بطانية	blanket
battaariya	بطارية	battery
batteekh	بطيخ	watermelon
bawl	بول	urine
bawwab	بواب	porter (concierge)
bawwaba	بوابة	gate
bay'	بيع	sale
baydh	بيض	egg
bayt	بيت	house
bazilla	بازلاء	peas
bedoon / men doon	مِن دَونَ/بِدونَ	without
beera	بيرة	beer
bi	بـ	by (with)
bidoon nakha	بدون نكهة	plain (unflavored)
bidoon rasas	بدون رصاص	unleaded
bifathha'aa	بفظاعة	terribly
bijaama	بيجامة	pajamas
bilyaard	بلياردو	billiards
binaayah	بناية	building
bint	بنت	daughter
bint	بنت	girl
bint al-ukht / bint al- akh	بنت الاخت/بنت الاخ	niece
biqala	بقالة	groceries
birka	بركة	pond
bit-tilifoon	بالتليفون	by-phone

bitaana	بطانة	lining
bitaaqat dukhuul	بطاقة دخول	ticket (admission)
bitaaqat i'timaad	بطاقة اعتماد	credit card
bittaaqa shakhsiyya	بطاقة شخصية	identification card
bittaqah	بطاقة	card
bittaqqa	بطاقة	business card
blastik	بلاستك	plastic
blooza	بلوزة	blouse
boothha	بوظة	ice cream
borj	بُرج	zodiac
buhhayra	بحيرة	lake
bukaa'	بكاء	cry
bukhar	بخار	steam
bunni	بني	brown
buq'a	بقعة	stain
burghi	برغي	screw
burj	برج	tower
burkaan	بركان	volcano
burtuqali	برتقالي	orange (color)
butuqaal	برتقال	orange (fruit)

D

da'iif	ضعيف	weak
daa'iman	دائما	always
daa'ira	دائرة	circle
daafi	دافيء	warm
dabboos	دبوس	pin
daftar mulaahath-that	دفتر ملاحظات	notebook
daght	ضغط	pressure
dajaja	دجاجة	chicken
dakhil	داخل	inside
dakhili	داخلي	internal
dakhl	دخل	earrings
daleel	دليل	guide (book)
dam	دم	blood
daqeeqa	دقيقة	minute
daqiiq ath-thura	دقيق الذرة	cornflower
daraj motaharrek	درج متحرك	escalator
daraja owla	درجة أولى	first class
darajah	درجة	degree
dardasha	دردشة	chat

darraaja naariyya	دراجة نارية	motorbike
darraja	دراجة	bicycle
dars	درس	lesson
dawaa'	دواء	medicine
dawaa' shorb	دواء شرب	syrup
dawajin	دواجن	poultry
dawrah	دورة	course
deen	دين	religion
desember	ديسمبر	December
dhaa'i'	ضائع	lost (missing)
dhabaab	ضباب	mist
dhabab	ضباب	fog
dhahl	ضحل	shallow
dhaooree	ضروري	necessary
dharar /kharaab	ضرر/خراب	damage
dharbat shams	ضربة شمس	sunstroke
dhareeba	ضريبة	tax
dhawdhaa'	ضوضاء	noise
dhid	ضد	against
dhidh al-maa'	ضد الماء	waterproof
dhiffa	ضفة	bank (river)
dhimaad	ضماد	bandage
dhiyaafa	ضيافة	hospitality
dhubaaba	ذبابة	fly (insect)
di'f	ضعف	double
diraasa/yadrus	دراسة/يدرس	study
diskoo	ديسكو	disco
doctoor	دكتور	doctor
dohnee	دهني	greasy
doon tawaqquf	دون توقف	nonstop
dukhan/ tadkhiin	دخان/تدخين	smoke
dukhool	دخول	admission
dumiya/ loo'bah	دمية / لعبة	doll
dush	دش	shower
duwali	دولي	international
duwar/dowkha	دوار / دوخة	dizzy

E

eed meelad	عيد ميلاد	birthday
erlanda	ايرلندا	Ireland
esharah	اشارة	sign (road)

F

faa'ida/maslaha	فائدة/ مصلحة	profit
faasid	فاسد	bad (rotten)
fahs	فحص	check (v.)
fak	فاك	jaw
fakhidh	فخذ	thigh
faks	فاكس	fax
fallah	فلاح	farmer
fam	فم	mouth
fan	فن	art
fann an-naht	فن النحت	sculpture
faqatt	فَقَط	only
fa'r	فأر	mouse
faramil	فرامل	brake
fareeq	فَريق	team
farigh	فارغ	empty
fassoliya	فاصوليا	beans
fatoora	فاتورة	bill
fatoora	فاتورة	invoice
fawakih	فواكه	fruit
fawq	فوق	above
fayadhan	فيضان	flood
fayroos	فيروس	virus
feasbook	فيس بوك	Facebook
febraayer	فبراير	February
fee al-kharij	في خارج البلاد	abroad
fee makaanin ma	في مكان ما	somewhere
feel	فيل	elephant
feemaa ba'd	فيما بعد	later
fi	في	in
fi al-amaam	في الامام	at the front
fi al-bayt	في البيت	at home
fi al-khalf	في الخلف	at the back
fi al-layl	في الليل	at night
fidda	فضة	silver
fii al-khaarij	في الخارج	overseas
fii kol makan	في كل مكان	everywhere
fikra	فكرة	idea
film	فلم	film (movie)
firash	فراش	bed
fondoq	فندق	hotel
foolath	فولاذ	steel
forshat asnan	فرشاة أسنان	toothbrush

fostaan	فستان	dress (n.)
fotoor	فطور	breakfast
fuliklor	فلكلور	folklore
fundiq sagheer	فندق صغير	motel
furshaah	فرشاة	brush
fustuq	فستق	peanut

G

ghaali	غال	expensive
ghadan	غدا	tomorrow
ghadheb	غاضب	angry
ghalyoon	غليون	pipe (smoking)
ghamidh	غامض	misty
gharaama	غرامة	fine (money)
gharb	غرب	west
ghareeb	غَريب	strange
ghareeb/ajnabi	غريب/أجنبي	foreign
ghatts	غطس	diving
ghayr khaadi'a lir-rasm al-jumrukii	غير خاضعة للرسم الجمركي	duty-free
ghayr muhathab	غير مهذب	rude
ghaz	غاز	gas
ghidhaa'	غداء	lunch
ghitaa as-saaqayn	غطاء الساقين	leggings
gholf	غولف	golf
ghram	غرام	gram
ghuraz	غرز	stitches
ghurfa	غرفة	room
ghurfat alqiyyas	غرفة القياس	fitting room
ghuroob	غروب الشمس	sunset

H

haa'it /jidar	حائط/ جدار	wall
haadi'	هاديء	quiet
haadith	حادث	accident
haalan	حالا	immediately
haamidh	حامض	sour
haar	حار	spicy
haathihi al-layla	هذه الليلة	tonight
habl	حبل	rope
hadaf	هَدَف	goal
hadeeqa	حديقة	garden

hadeeqat al-haywanat	حديقة الحيوانات	zoo
hadeeth	حديث	current
hadhina	حاضنة	babysitter
hadiid	حديد	iron (metal)
hadiiqa	حديقة	park
hadiyya	هدية	gift
hadiyya	هدية	present (gift)
hafeeda	حفيدة	granddaughter
hafiid	حفيد	grandchild
hafila /bass	باص /حافلة	bus
hafl zafaf	حفل زفاف	wedding
hafla	حفلة	party
hafla muusiqiyya	حفلة موسيقية	concert
hajm	حجم	size
hakka	حكة	itch
halawiyyaat	حلويات	dessert
haleeb	حليب	milk
hallaaq	حلاق	hairdresser
halwaa	حلوى	candy
hammaam	حمام	bathroom/ restroom
hammaam shamsii	حمام شمسي	sunbathe
handasa mi'maariya	هندسة معمارية	architecture
haniin-ila al watan	الحنين إلى الوطن	homesick
haqeeba	حقيبة	purse (handbag)
haqeebat yad	حقيبة يد	handbag
haqibah	حقيبة	backpack
haqiiba	حقيبة	suitcase
haqqan	حقا	really
harakat al-muroor	حركة المرور	traffic
harara	حرارة	heat
hareer	حرير	silk
haris	حارس	concierge
hashara	حشرة	insect
hashwa	حشوة	filling
hasoub mahmoul/ labtob	حاسوب محمول/ لاب توب	laptop
hassasiyya	حساسية	allergy
hatha	هذا	this
hathir	حذر	careful

hatif dhakii	هاتف ذكي	smartphone
hawaaly / taqreeban	حوالي/تقريبا	about
hayawaan aleef	حيوان اليف	pet
hayawan	حيوان	animal
hayya	حية	snake
hazeen	حزين	sad
helm	حلم	dream (n.)
hhaafat	حافة	hem
hhaamil	حامل	pregnant
hhaar	حار	hot
hhanafiyya	حنفية	tap
hhasanan	حسنا	okay
hhelo	حلو	sweet
hhimyyah	حمية	diet
hisaa'	حساء	broth
hisaan saghiir	حصان صغير	pony
hissan	حصان	horse
hithaa'	حذاء	shoe
hiwaaya	هواية	hobby
hizaam	حزام	belt
hob	حب	love
hona	هنا	here
honak	هناك	there
honjara	حنجرة	throat
huboob	حبوب	grain
huboob	حبوب	pills (tablets)
huboob man' al-hamal	حبوب منع الحمل	contraceptive (pill)
hubuub	حبوب	tablets
hudood	حدود	border
hummaa / haraara	حمي/حرارة	fever
huqna	حقنة	injection

I

i'aadat al-maal	إعادة مال	refund
ibn	إبن	son
ibn al-akh/ibn al-ukht	ابن الاخت/ابن الاخ	nephew
ibn 'am / bint 'am	ابن عم/بنت عم	cousin
ibra	إبرة	needle
ibreel	ابريل	April

ibriiq shaay	أبريق شاي	teapot
idhraab	إضراب	strike (work stoppage)
ightisaab	اغتصاب	rape
ihtiyatii/idhafi	اضافي/احتياطي	spare
ikhla'/yakhla'	اخلع/يخلع	undress
ikraamiyya/ baqsheesh	بقشيش/إكرامية	tip
ila	إلى	to
ilekiooni	الكتروني	electronic
iltihaab	إلتهاب	infection
imbirattour	امبراطور	emperor
imra'a	أمرأة	woman
in shaa'Allah	إنْ شاء الله	hopefully
influwanza	إنفلونزا	cold (flu)
influwanza	إنفلونزا	flu
ingiltra	انجلترا	England
ingleezi	انجليزي	English
inkhifadh	إنخفاض	reduction
intathhir/ yantathhir	إنتظر/ينتظر	wait
Internet	إنترنت	Internet
inthaar	إنذار	alarm
iqtissad	اقتصاد	economy
irja'	ارجع	come back
irji'	ارجع	go back
irtijaj	ارتجاج	concussion
is'aafaat awwaliyya	اسعافات اولية	first aid
i'saar	إعصار	typhoon
isbi'al-qadam	إصبع القدم	toe
iskutlanda	اسكتلندا	Scotland
islaamee	إسلاميّ	Islamic
iss-haal	اسهال	diarrhea
issbi'	إصبع	finger
istifsaar	استفسار	enquiry
istimara	استمارة	form
istiqbal	استقبال	reception
istiraha	استراحة	break
istishaara	إستشارة	consultation
itaar	إطار	tire
ith-hab	اذهب	go
i'tidaa	اعتداء	assault

i'tithaar	اعتذار	apologies
ittar	أطار	frame
ittijaah	إتجاه	direction
iz'aaj	ازعاج	disturbance
izdiham	ازدحام	busy (traffic)

J

jaa'i'/jow'aan	جائع/ جوعان	hungry
jaaf	جاف	dry (n.)
jaami'a	جامعة	university
jaar	جار	neighbor
jabal	جبل	mountain
jabeen	جبين	forehead
jad	جد	grandfather
jadda	جدة	grandmother
jadiid	جديد	new
jadwal	جدول	timetable
jafaf	جفاف	draught
jahiz	جاهز	ready
jakiet/mi'taf	جاكيت/معطف	coat (jacket)
jamaarik	جمارك	customs
jamee'an	جميعا	altogether
jameel	جميل	beautiful
jameel /raa'i'	رائع /جميل	wonderful
janaza	جنازة	funeral
janoob	جنوب	south
jarad al-bahr	جراد البحر	lobster
jareema	جريمة	crime
jariida/saheefa	صحيفة/جريدة	newspaper
jawaarib	جوارب	socks
jawaaz safar	جواز سفر	passport
jawab/ rad	جواب/ رد	answer
jawhara	جوهرة	gem
jayb	جيب	pocket
jayyed	جيد	good
jayyid	جيد	well (good)
jayyid /hasan	جيد/ حسن	fine (good)
jazar	جزر	carrot
jaziira	جزيرة	island
jeanz	جينز	jeans
jild	جلد	leather
jild	جلد	skin
jinsiyya	جنسية	nationality

jism	جسم	body
jisr	جسر	bridge
jobn	جبن	cheese
jumla	جملة	sentence
jurh	جرح	cut (n.)
jurh	جرح	wound
jurth	جرذ	rat
juz'	جزء	part

K

ka'b	كعب	heel
ka'ib	كعب	ankle
kabeer /waasi'	كبير/واسع	large
kabreet	كبريت	matches (fire starter)
kahf	كهف	cave
kahrabaa'	كهرباء	electricity
kahrabaa'i	كهربائي	electric
kakaw	كاكاو	cocoa
kalb	كلب	dog
kalima	كلمة	word
kalimat al-ser	كلمة السر	password
kamira	كاميرا	camera
kamira	كاميرا	webcam
kaneesa	كنيسة	church
karaj	كراج	garage
kareeh	كريه	horrible
kassaara	كسارة	cracker
katalug	كتالوج	catalog
katheer	كثير	many
katheer	كثير	much
katif	كتف	shoulder
kayf	كيف؟	how?
kazeenu	كازينو	casino
kemmiyya	كمية	amount
khaariji	خارجي	external
khabbaz	خباز	baker
khafiif	خفيف	light (not heavy)
khaleej	خَليج	gulf
khalf	خلف	back
khalf	خلف	behind
kham	خام	raw
khamr /kuhuul	كحول/خمر	alcohol
kharaab	خراب	ruins

khareef	خريف	fall (season)
kharij	خارج	outside
kharita	خارطة	map
kharoof/haml	خروف/ حمل	lamb
khas	خس	lettuce
khasaara /fiqdaan	فقدان /خسارة	loss
khashab	خشب	wood
khashin	خشن	tough
khass	خاص	special
khata'	خطا	fault
khata'/ghalt	غلط /خطأ	wrong
khata'/ghaltta	خطا/ غلطة	mistake
khatar	خطر	danger
khatar	خطر	risk
khateeb	خطيب	fiancé
khateeba	خطيبة	fiancée
khateer	خطير	serious
khatiir	خطير	dangerous
khatt	خط	line
khatt	خظ	luck
khawkh/durraaq	خوخ/دراق	peach
khayt	خيط	thread
khayt	خيط	yarn
khayt/habl	خيط/حبل	string
khazana	خزانة	buffet
khedaa'/yakhda'	خداع/يخدع	swindle
khetta /barnamej	خطة /برنامج	plan (intention)
khidma	خدمة	service
khilaal	خلال	during
khiyaar	خيار	cucumber
khubz	خبز	bread
khudrawaat	خضروات	vegetable
khutuwat /darajat	خطوات/درجات	steps
kilahuma	كلاهما	both
kiloghram	كيلوغرام	kilogram
kirooseen	كيروسين	kerosene
kitaab	كتاب	book
kitaab 'ibaaraat	كتاب عبارات	phrasebook
kittaan	كتان	linen
kkayma	خيمة	tent
kol shay'	كل شيئ	everything
kombyooter/ haasoob	حاسوب/كمبيوتر	computer

kookh	كوخ	cabin
kookh	كوخ	hut
koosa	كوسة	zucchini (courgette)
korat as-salla	كرة السلة	basketball
kreem	كريم	lotion
kuloonya	كولونيا	aftershave
kum	كم	sleeve
kura	كرة	ball
kurat al-qadam	كرة القدم	soccer
kurat at-taa'ira	كرة الطائرة	volleyball
kursi	كرسي	chair
kursii mattaharrik	كرسي متحرك	wheelchair
kutla	كتلة	mass
kuub	كوب	cup

L

laa/kallaa	كلا/لا	no
laa shay'	لا شيء	nothing
ladgha	لدغه	bite
lahh-tha	لحظة	moment
lahhm baqar	لحم بقر	beef
lahm	لحم	meat
lahm khinziir	لحم خنزير	pork
laami'	لامع	glossy
laieem	لئيم	mean (not nice)
lajna	لَجنة	committee
laqab	لقب	surname
lateef	لطيف	mild (taste)
latheeth	لذيذ	delicious
lawaazim al-maa'ida	لوازم المائدة	cutlery
lawn	لون	color
layl	ليل	night
laymoon	ليمون	lemon
laysa fee ay makan	ليس في أي مكان	nowhere
le'nna	لأنْ	because
letr	لتر	liter
limatha	لماذا	why
lisan	لسان	tongue
liss	لص	thief
liyaaqa/tadriib	لياقة /تدريب	fitness
lu'ba	لعبة	game

lu'ba /dumya	دمية / لعبة	toy
lu'lu'	لؤلؤ	pearl
lugha	لغة	language
lughz	لغز	puzzle

M

ma'a as-salaama	مع السلامة	goodbye
ma'bad	معبد	synagogue
ma'bad	معبد	temple
ma'dan	معدن	metal
ma'joon asnan	معجون أسنان	toothpaste
ma'karuuna	معكرونة	noodles
ma'luumaat	معلومات	information
ma'rad	معرض	exhibition
maa'	مع	with
maa'	ماء	water
maa'ba'dh	مع بعض	together
maadda mutahhira	مادة مطهرة	detergent
maasoora/janaah	جناح/مقصورة	compartment
maayuuneez	مايونيز	mayonnaise
madam/sayyida	مدام/ سيدة	madam
madeena	مدينة	city
madrasa	مدرسة	school
mafqood	مفقود	missing
mafruushaat as-sariir	مفروشات السرير	bedding
maftuuh	مفتوح	open
maghli	مغلي	boiled
mahaarim	محارم	tissues
mahallii	محلي	domestic
mahatta	محطة	station
mahattat al-bass	محطة الباص	bus-station
mahattat waqood	محطة وقود	gas station
mahhaar	محار	oyster
mahhalli	محلي	local
mahjooz	محجوز	booked (reserved)
mahmoul/jawwal	جوال/محمول	cell phone
mahrooq	محروق	burnt
majalla	مجلة	magazine
majjani	مجاني	free (no charge)
majlis	مَجلِس	board
majlis ash-sha'ab	مَجلِس الشَّعْب	parliament
majmoo'	مجموع	total
majmoo'a	مجموعة	group
majmuua'/ruzma	مجموعة/رزمة	set
majrooh	مجروح	injured
makaan	مكان	palace
makhraj	مخرج	exit
makhttooba/ makhttoob	مخطوبة/مخطوب	engaged (to be married)
makhzan/matjar	مخزن/متجر	shop (store)
maksoor	مكسور	broken
maktab	مكتب	office
maktab al-breed	مكتب البريد	post office
maktab bareed	مكتب بريد	post office
maktaba	مكتبة	library
mal'ab	ملعب	stadium
malaabis	ملابس	clothes
malik	ملك	king
malika	ملكة	queen
mamlakah	مَملَكة	kingdom
mammar	ممر	corridor
mamzooj	ممزوج	mixed
man	من	who
manassa	منصة	platform
mandeel	منديل	scarf
manga	مانجا	mango
manshoor	منشور	brochure
manthar	منظر	view
maq'ad	مقعد	seat
maqaal	مقال	article
maqbara	مقبرة	cemetery
maqbara	مقبرة	grave
maqli	مقلي	fried
maqsad/maeeir	مقصد/مصير	destination
maradh	مرض	illness
marah/lahw	لهو/مرح	fun
maraq	مرق	sauce
mareedh	مريض	ill
mareedh	مريض	patient (sick)
marham	مرهم	ointment
maris	مارس	March
markaz	مركز	center (middle)
markazi	مركزي	central

marmar	مرمر	marble
marra ukhraa	مرة اخرى	again
marsa	مرسى	marina
marwaha	مروحة	fan
mas'ool	مسؤول	responsible
masaa'	مساء	evening
masaafa	مسافة	distance
masaaha/ mintaqa	مساحة/منطقة	area
masafa ba'iida	مسافة بعيدة	long-distance
masar	مسار	lane (of traffic)
masbaghat ghaseel	مصبغة الغسيل	dry clean
mash-hoor	مشهور	famous
mashghool	مشغول	busy (schedule)
mashmool	مشمول	included
mashroo'	مَشروع	project
mashwi	مشوي	grilled
mashy	مشي	walk (n.)
masraf/ bank	مصرف/بنك	bank
masrahh	مسرح	theatre
masrahiyya	مسرحية	play (drama)
massa	مساء	afternoon
massaasah	مصاصة	straw
massna'	مصنع	factory
mat-haf	متحف	museum
mat'am	مطعم	restaurant
mata	متى	when
mataar	مطار	airport
matar	مطر	rain (n.)
math'oor	مذعور	frightened
matha	ماذا	what
mattahed	مُتَّحِد	united
mattat	مطاط	rubber
mattbakh	مطبخ	kitchen
mattbuukh	مطبوخ	done (cooked)
maw'id	موعد	appointment
mawaad ghithaa'iyya	مواد غذائية	groceries (food)
mawdhoo'	مَوْضوع	topic
mawjood	موجود	present (here)
mawlood	مولود	born
mawthooq	موثوق	reliable

mawthuuq	موثوق	trustworthy
mawz	موز	banana
mayoo	مايو	May
mayyit	ميت	dead
mazhariyyah	مزهرية	vase
mazra'a	مزرعة	farm
meezaan	ميزان	scales
metr	متر	meter
mezan al-harara	ميزان الحرارة	thermometer
mi'ah	مائة	hundred
midfa'a	مدفأة	heater
miftaah	مفتاح	corkscrew
miftah	مفتاح	key
miftah	مفتاح	switch
mihfathat nuqood	محفظة نقود	wallet
mihna /herfa	مهنة/حرفة	profession
miinaa'	ميناء	port
mikhadda	مخدة	pillow
mikwaah	مكواة	iron (for clothes)
mikyaaj	مكياج	makeup
mil'aqa	ملعقة	spoon
mil'aqat shaay	ملعقة شاي	teaspoon
milaqa'a	ملعقة	tablespoon
milh	ملح	salt
millimitr	مليمتر	millimeter
min fadlik	من فضلك	please
minaa'	ميناء	harbor
mindada/ ttawelah	منضدة/طاولة	table
mindeel	منديل	handkerchief
minfadat sajaa'ir	منفضة سجائر	ashtray
minshafa	منشفة	towel
mintaqat la'ib lil-atfaal	منطقة لعب للأطفال	playground
minttaqa	مِنطقة	zone
miqas	مقص	scissors
miqlaah	مقلاة	saucepan
miqlah	مقلاة	pan
mir'aah	مراة	mirror
mirrarran	مِراراً	repeatedly
mis'ad	مصعد	lift (elevator)
misfaa/filtar	مصفاة/فلتر	filter
mismaar	مسمار	nail (metal)

miss'ad kahrabaa'ii	مصعد كهربائي	elevator
missbaah	مصباح	lamp
mithhalla	مظلة	umbrella
mithla	مِثْل	similar
mithyaa'/radyo	مذياع/ راديو	radio
mitraqa	مطرقة	hammer
mo'addaal	معدل	mean (average)
mo'sess	مُؤَسِّس	founder
mohaafiz	محافظ	mayor
moka'bat as-sukkar	مكعبات السكر	lumps (sugar)
mokalamah	مكالمة	call (n.)
mokasarat	مكسرات	nuts
mokayyef	مكيف	air conditioning
mokhmal	مخمل	velvet
moltaheb	ملتهب	sore
momkin	ممكن	possible
monabbeh	منبه	alarm clock
morr	مر	bitter
mosbah yadawee	مصباح يدوي	flashlight
moseeqaa	موسيقى	music
moshit	مشط	hairbrush
moshkila	مشكلة	problem
motarjim	مترجم	interpreter
mu'aamala	معاملة	treatment
mu'aaq	معاق	disabled
mu'attir	معطر	deodorant
mu'di	معدي	infectious
mu'dii	معدي	contagious
mubakkir	مبكر	early
mubasharah	مباشرة	directly
mubashir	مباشر	direct
mubbayyidh	مبيض	bleach
mudakhan	مدخن	smoked (adj.)
mudeer	مدير	manager
mudhi'	مضيء	light (not dark)
mufaaja'a	مفاجأة	surprise
mufaddal	مفضل	preference
mughaadara	مغادرة	departure
mughlaq	مغلق	closed
muhamii	محامي	lawyer
muhammas	محمص	roasted

muhim	مهم	important
muhtamal	محتمل	probably
muja'ad	مجعد	curly
mujaffif sha'r	مجفف شعر	hairdryer
mujammad	مجمد	frozen
mujawharat	مجوهرات	jewelry
muka'ab	مكعب	cubic
mukalama	مكالمة	phone call
mukhayyam	مخيم	camping
mukhti'	مخطيء	mistaken
mukkath-thaf	مكثف	condensed
mulakhas	ملخص	briefs
mulawwan	ملون	colored
mullih/'aajel	ملح/ عاجل	urgent
mumarridha	ممرضة	nurse
mumil	ممل	boring
mumtaz	ممتاز	excellent
mumti'	ممتع	nice (pleasant)
munabbih hariiq	منبه حريق	fire alarm
munasaba/hadath	مناسبة/حدث	event
munkhafid	منخفض	low
muntasib	منتصب	upright
murabba	مربى	jam
murabba'	مربع	square (shape)
musaa'ada	مساعدة	helping
musaa'ada/an-najda	مساعدة/النجدة	help
musaafir	مسافر	passenger
musafir	مسافر	traveler
musahil/mulayyin	ملين/مسهل	laxative
musajjal	مسجل	registered
musakkin	مسكن	sedative
musakkin alam	مسكن ألم	painkiller
musannaf	مصنف	assorted
mushaabih/nafs	مشابه/نفس	same
musht	مشط	comb
musta'mal	مستعمل	second-hand
mustaheel	مستحيل	impossible
mustanqa'	مستنقع	swamp
mustaqiim	مستقيم	straight
mustashfaa	مستشفى	hospital

mustatteel	مستطيل	rectangle
mustayqith	مستيقظ	awake
mut'a	متعة	pleasure
mut'arrij	متعرج	uneven
muta'akhir	متأخر	late
mutahawwir	متهور	rash
mutaqaa'id	متقاعد	retired
mutazawwij	متزوج	married
muth-thallath	مثلث	triangle
muthallaj	مثلج	iced
muthallaj/ mujammad	مثلج/مجمد	chilled
muttallaq	مطلق	divorced
muwajjih/ murshid	مرشد/موجه	guide (person)
muwattin	مواطن	citizen

N

na'am	نعم	yes
naadij	ناضج	ripe
naar/hreeq	نار/حريق	fire
naas	ناس	people
nabaati	نباتي	vegetarian
nabat	نبات	plant
nabdh	نبض	pulse
nadil	نادل	waiter
nadilah	نادلة	waitress
nafaq	نفق	tunnel
nafaqaat/ masaariif	مصاريف/نفقات	expenses
nafoora	نافورة	fountain
nahheef	نحيف	thin (not fat)
nahhla	نحلة	bee
nahhwa	نَحوَ	towards
nahnu	نحن	we
nahr	نهر	river
najahh	نَجاح	success
najma	نجمة	star
nak-ha	نكهة	flavor
namla	نمله	ant
naqdi/fuloos	فلوس/نقدي	cash
naqi	نقي	pure
nasiiha	نصيحة	advice

nath-theef	نظيف	clean (adj.)
nathh-thharaat	نظارات	glasses
nathhaaraat shamsiyya	نظارات شمسية	sunglasses
natiija	نتيجة	result
nissf	نصف	half
november	نوفمبر	November
nu'aal khafiif	نعال خفيف	slippers
nuhaas	نحاس	copper
nukta	نكتة	joke
nuqood/fuloos	نقود/ فلوس	money
nuskha	نسخة	copy
nuskha	نسخة	photocopy

O

octoober	اكتوبر	October
oghostos	أغسطس	August
ommah	أُمّة	nation
onwaan	عنوان	address

Q

qaamoos	قاموس	dictionary
qaanoon	قانون	law
qabeeh	قبيح	ugly
qadam	قدم	foot
qaddaha	قداحة	lighter
qadeem	قديم	antique
qahwa	قهوه	coffee
qaa'imat al-ma'kuulaat	قائمة المأكولات	menu
qal'a	قلعة	castle
qalam	قلم	pen
qalam rassaas	قلم رصاص	pencil
qalb	قلب	heart
qaleel	قليل	little (amount)
qaliq	قلق	worried
qamar	قمر	moon
qamees	قميص	shirt
qandeel al-bahr	قنديل البحر	jellyfish
qanooni	قانوني	valid
qareeb	قريب	nearby
qareeban	قريبا	soon
qarib	قارب	boat

qarya	قرية	village
qaseer	قصير	short
qassab/jazar	جزار/قصاب	butcher
qassat sha'r	قصة شعر	haircut
qatra lil-ayn	قطرة للعين	eye-drops
qatra lil–uthon	قطرة للأذن	ear drops
qawi	قوي	strong
qilaada/e'qd	قلادة/عقد	necklace
qimaash	قماش	fabric
qimma	قمة	top
qinneena	قنينة	bottle
qird	قرد	monkey
qirsh	قرش	shark
qishra	قشرة	dandruff
qishta	قشطة	cream
qism	قسم	department
qitar	قطار	train
qitar al-anfaaq	قطار الأنفاق	subway
qitta	قطة	cat
qom	قم	stand up
qubba'a	قبعة	hat
qubla	قبلة	kiss
quffazat	قفازات	gloves
qufl/yaqfil	يقفل/قفل	lock
qunsiliyya	قنصلية	consulate
qurb	قرب	near
qurha	قرحة	ulcer
qutn	قطن	cotton

R

ra'isi	رئيسي	main
ra's	رأس	head
raa'iha	رائحة	smell
raafi'a	رافعة	jack (for car)
rabii'	ربيع	spring (season)
rabtat 'unuq	ربطة عنق	necktie
radi	راض	satisfied
rajul	رجل	man
rakhees	رخيص	inexpensive
rakib	راكب	riding
ramaadi	رمادي	gray
ramz	رمز	zip
ramz baridi	رمز بريدي	postcode

raqaba	رقبة	neck
raqs	رقص	dance (n.)
raseef almeenaa'	رصيف الميناء	berth
rashash sha'r	رشاش شعر	hairspray
rasm jumrukii	رسم جمركي	duty (tax)
rasool	رسول	prophet
rattib/muballal	مبلل /رطب	wet
rihla	رحلة	excursion
rihla	رحلة	journey
rihla	رحلة	picnic
rihla	رحلة	trip
rihla siyahiyya	رحلة سياحية	tour
rihlat 'amal	رحلة عمل	business trip
rihlat tayaran	رحلة طيران	flight
riih/riyaah	ريح (lp: رياح)	wind
risaala	رسالة	message
risala/harf	رسالة/حرف	letter
risgh	رسغ	wrist
riyaadha	رياضة	sport
robama	ربما	perhaps
robyan	ربيان	shrimp
rodhoodh	رضوض	bruise
rokhsa	رخصة	permit
rub'	ربع	quarter
rubbamaa	ربما	maybe
rukba	ركبة	knee
rukhsa/ ijaaza	رخصة/إجارة	license
rukhsat siyaaqa	رخصة سياقة	driver's license
rukn	ركن	corner
ruzma/tard	رزمة/طرد	parcel

S

sa'aa	ساعة	watch
sa'eed	سعيد	happy
saa'a	ساعة	hour
saa'ah	ساعة	clock
saa'iq	سائق	driver
saabuun	صابون	soap
saam	سام	poisonous, venemous
saaq	ساق	leg
sabab	سبب	cause

sabab	سبب	reason
sabgh/dihaan	دهان/صبغ	paint
sadeeq	صديق	friend
sadeeqa	صديقة	girlfriend
safar	سفر	travel
safara	سفارة	embassy
safha	صفحة	page
safiina/'abbaara	سفينة/عبارة	ferry
sagheer	صغير	little (small)
sagheer	صغير	small
saheeh	صحيح	correct
saheeh	صحيح	right (correct)
saheen	صحتين	cheers!
sahin/tabaq	صحن/طبق	dish
sahl	سهل	easy
sahm	سهم	arrow
sahraa'	صحراء	desert
sahyyooni	صَهْيونيّ	zionist
sakheef	سخيف	ridiculous
sakhra	صخرة	rock (stone)
sakraan	سكران	drunk
salat riyyadha	صالة رياضة	gym
salata	سلطة	salad
samak	سمك	fish
samakat al-anqaliis	سمكة الأنقليس	eel
sameek	سميك	thick
samgh	صمغ	glue
sana	سنة	year
sandal	صندل	sandals
saqf	سقف	roof
sarataan al-bahr	سرطان البحر	crab
saree'	سريع	fast
sarii'	سريع	quick
sarii'	سريع	rapid
sariqa	سرقة	theft
sarsoor	صرصور	cockroach
sataa'ir	ستائر	curtains
sataa'ir	ستائر	drapes
satt-h	سطح	terrace
sattw/sariqa	سطو/سرقة	burglary
saydaliyya	صيدلي	pharmacy
sayigh	صائغ	jeweler
sayr 'alaa al-aqdaam	سير على الاقدام	hiking
sayyaara	سيارة	car
sayyaarat is'aaf	سيارة إسعاف	ambulance
sayyid	سيد	sir
sebtember	سبتمبر	September
sentimeeter	سنتيميتر	centimeter
serk	سيرك	circus
sha'r	شعر	hair
shaahina	شاحنة	truck
shaari'	شارع	street
shab'aan/ mamluu'	شبعان/مملوء	full
shabb/fatah	شَبّ / فَتاة	young
shafaqa	شفقة	pity
shahada/ watheeqa	شهادة/وثيقة	certificate
shahid	شاهد	witness
shahin	شاحن	charger
shahina sagheerah	شاحنة صغيرة	van
shahr	شهر	month
shakhs	شخص	person
shakhs	شخص	someone
shakhsi	شخصي	personal
shakwaa	شكوى	complaint
sham'a	شمعة	candle
shamaal	شمال	north
shamboo	شامبو	shampoo
shams	شمس	sun
shaqqa	شقه	apartment
sharaab	شراب	drink (n.)
shareek	شريك	partner
shareett	شريط	ribbon
shareka	شَرِكة	company
sharq	شرق	east
sharshaf	شرشف	sheet
shataranj	شطرنج	chess
shatii'	شاطئ	beach
shawka	شوكة	fork
shay	شاي	tea
shek	شيك	check (n.)

shimbaniya	شمبانيا	champagne
shimmaam	شمام	melon
shitaa'	شتاء	winter
shiwaa'	شواء	barbecue
shokolatta	شوكلاتة	chocolate
shokran	شكرا	thank you, thanks
shubbak	شباك	window
shughl/watheefa	وظيفة/شغل	job
shurfa	شرفة	balcony
shurta	شرطة	police
shuruuq ashshams	شروق الشمس	sunrise
shuurba/hisaa'	شوربة/حساء	soup
si'r	سعر	price
sibaaq ad-darraajaat	سباق الدراجات	cycling
sifr	صفر	zero
sigaara	سيجارة	cigarette
sihhi	صحي	healthy
siigaar	سيجار	cigar
sijjaada	سجادة	carpet
sijjadda	سجادة	mat
sikeen	سكين	knife
sikkat al-qitaar	سكة القطار	railroad, railway
silk	سلك	wire
sin	سن	tooth
sitaara	ستارة	blind (on window)
siwaar	سوار	bracelet
siyasa	سِياسة	politics
so'aal	سؤال	question
soaf	صوف	wool
sollam	سلم	ladder
soo'fahm	سوء فهم	misunderstanding
sooq markazi	سوق مركزي	supermarket
sooq sha'abi	سوق شعبي	flea market
soor	سور	fence
ssa'b	صعب	hard (difficult)
ssabir	صابر	patient
ssadiiq	صديق	boyfriend
ssalb/qaasi	صلب/قاسي	hard (firm)
ssamt	صمت	silence
ssatl	سطل	bucket

ssawt	صَوْت	voice
ssighar	صِغَر	youth
ssondooq	صندوق	box
ssoura	صورة	photo
ssu'ooba	صعوبة	difficulty
su'aal/kahha	سعال/كحة	cough (n.)
sudaa'	صداع	headache
sudaa' ashshaqeeqa	صداع الشقيقة	migraine
sukkar	سكر	sugar
sukkari	سكري	diabetic
sullam/daraj	سلم/درج	stairs
sun'yadawi	صنع يدوي	handmade
sundooq barid	صندوق بريد	postbox
suu'hadhm	سوء هضم	indigestion
suuq	سوق	market

T

ta'aal	تعال	come
ta'aam /ghitha	طعام/ غذاء	food
ta'khiir	تأخير	delay
ta'leemat	تعليمات	instructions
ta'meen/dhaman	تأمين/ضمان	insurance
ta'sheera (visa)	فيزا/تأشيرة	visa
taa'ira	طائرة	airplane
taa'ira	طائرة	plane
taariikh	تاريخ	date
taariikh almiilaad	تاريخ الميلاد	date of birth
taazij	طازج	fresh
tabbakh	طباخ	cook (person)
tabee'ee	طبيعي	natural
tabii'a	طبيعة	nature
tabii'ii	طبيعي	normal
tabiq	طابق	floor
taghyeer	تغير	change (n.)
tah-theer	تحذير	warning
tahaaneena/ mabrook	مبروك/تهانينا!	congratulations
tahiin	طحين	flour
tahiyat	تحيات	regards
tahiyya	تحية	greeting
tahmeedh	تحميض	develop (photo)

tahmeel	تحميل	download
tahta	تحت	under
tajjamud	تجمد	freeze
tajmeel	تجميل	cosmetics
takhdeer	تخدير	anesthetic
takhfeedh	تخفيض	discount
taksi/sayyarat ojra	تاكسي/ سيارة اجرة	taxi
tamaman	تماما	completely
tannoora	تنورة	skirt
taqaatu'	تقاطع	intersection
taqaatu' turuq	تقاطع طرق	crossroad
tareeq	طريق	route
tariiq	طريق	road
tariiq	طريق	way (direction)
tariiq sarii'	طريق سريع	highway
tarmeem	ترميم	repairs
tasarob	تسرب	leak
tasfiya	تصفية	clearance (sale)
tasreehat sha'r	تسريحة شعر	hairstyle
tassadum	تصادم	collision
tathbeet	تثبيت	install
tathkirat safar	تذكرة سفر	ticket (travel)
tattreez	تطريز	embroidery
tawaabil	توابل	spices
taweel	طويل	long
taweel	طويل	tall
tawqii'	توقيع	signature
tawsseela	توصيلة	lift (in car)
tayyib	طيب	nice (person)
tazalluj	تزلج	skiing
telefizyoon	تلفزيون	television
tenis	تنس	tennis
th-tharf	ظرف	envelope
thaani	ثاني	second (in line)
thaaniya	ثانية	second (instant)
thahab	ذهب	gold
thalj	ثلج	ice
thalj	ثلج	snow
thallaja	ثلاجة	refrigerator
thameen	ثمين	precious
thameen	ثمين	valuable
thanb/ithm	ذنب/إثم	guilt

thaqeel	ثقيل	heavy
thawaban	ذوبان	thaw
thawb	ثوب	garment
thhifr	ظفر	nail (finger)
thhil	ظل	shade
thiraa'	ذراع	arm
tholuth	ثلث	third
thoom	ثوم	garlic
tibgh	تبغ	tobacco
tifl	طفل	baby
tilifizyoon	تلفزيون	TV
tilifun/haatif	تلفون/ هاتف	phone
timthal	تمثال	statue
tithkaar	تذكار	souvenir
tomtter	تمطر	rain (v.)
tta'am	طعم	taste (n.)
ttabe'	طابع	stamp
ttabeq	طابق	storey
ttabi'a	طابعة	printer
ttabiib asnaan	طبيب أسنان	dentist
ttalab/amr	طلب/ أمر	order
ttaqm asnaan	طقم اسنان	dentures
ttawaari'	طوارىء	emergency
tteen	طين	mud
ttifl	طفل	child
ttifl	طفل	toddler
ttiwal al-yawm	طوال اليوم	all day
tuffaaha	تفاحة	apple
tuthlij	تثلج	snow (v.)
twitter	تويتر	twitter

U

ujrat al-barid	اجرة البريد	postage
ukhroj	اخرج	go out
ukht	أخت	sister
ulba	علبة	tin (can)
um	ام	mother
unboob tanaffus maa'ii	أنبوب تنفس مائي	snorkel
unbuub	انبوب	pipe (plumbing)
usboo'	أسبوع	week
ustiraaliyaa	استراليا	Australia
uthun	أذن	ear

utlat nihaayat al-usboo'	عطلة نهاية الأسبوع	weekend
utumaateeki/aali	اوتوماتيكي/ألي	automatic

V

vitameenat	فيتامينات	vitamins

W

waadi	وادي	valley
waahid/waahida	واحد/واحدة	single (only one)
waalidaan	والدان	parents
waheed	وحيد	alone
wajba ghidhaa'iyya	وجبة غذائية	meal
wajh	وجه	face
wajib	واجب	duty (responsibility)
walad	ولد	boy
waqood	وقود	petrol
waqt	وقت	time
waqt faragh	وقت فراغ	free time
waqt faragh	وقت فراغ	leisure
waraqah	ورقة	paper
wareed	وريد	vein
wasfa	وصفة	prescription
wasfa	وصفة	recipe
wasikh	وسخ	dirty
wasl	وصل	receipt
wasla	وصلة	adaptor
waslah	وصلة	connection
wathheefa/shughl	شغل/وظيفة	occupation
wattane	وَطَنيّ	national
wazeer	وَزير	minister
wazza	وزة	goose
werk	ورك	hip
wisaada	وسادة	cushion
woddi	ودي	friendly

Y

ya'bur	يعبر	express
ya'iish	يعيش	live (alive)
ya'khudh	يأخذ	take (pick up)
ya'kul	يأكل	eat

ya'mal	يعمل	do
ya'mur	يأمر	order (v.)
ya'nee	يعني	mean (v.)
ya'redh	يعرض	show
ya'rif	يعرف	know
yabda'	بيدأ	begin
yabda'	بيدا	start
yabhath 'an	يبحث عن	look for
yabla'	يبلع	swallow
yabqa	يبقى	stay (remain)
yad	يد	hand
yad'u	يدعو	invite
yadfa'	يدفع	pay
yadfa'	يدفع	push
yadghat	يضغط	press (v.)
yadhak	يضحك	laugh
yafham	يفهم	understand
yafhas	يفحص	examine
yafqid	يفقد	lose
yafsil/munfasil	يفصل/منفصل	separate
yaftah	يفتح	open (v.)
yaghoos	يغوص	dive
yaghsil	يغسل	wash
yahjiz	يحجر	reserve
yahlam	يحلم	dream (v.)
yahook	يحوك	knit
yahtafil	يحتفل	celebrate
yahut/yanzil	يحط/ينزل	land (v.)
yajlib	يجلب	bring
yajlis	يجلس	sit
yakheet	يخيط	sew
yakhruj/yanzil	ينزل/يخرج	get off
yakhtar	يختار	choose
yakthib	يكذب	lie (be lying)
yaktub	يكتب	write
yakwii	يكوي	iron (v.)
yal'ab	يلعب	play (v.)
yalbas	يلبس	dress (v.)
yalbas	يلبس	wear
yaltaqi	يلتقي	meet
yaltaqit ssoorah	يلتقط صورة	take (photo)
yaluf/yughallif	يغلف/يلف	wrap
yamdahh	يمدح	compliment (v.)

yamiin	يمين	right (side)
yamla'	يملأ	fill
yamla'	يملأ	fill out (form)
yamna'/ yuharrim	يمنع/يحرم	forbidden
yamshi	يمشي	walk (verb)
yanaam	ينام	sleep
yanayer	يناير	January
yanhadh	ينهض	wake up
yanjah	ينجح	succeed
yansaa	ينسى	forget
yanthhur ilaa	ينظر الى	look at
yanzaliq	ينزلق	slip
yanzif	ينزف	bleed
yanzil	ينزل	check in
yaqees	يقيس	measure
yaqool	يقول	say
yaqra'	يقرأ	read
yaqta'	يقطع	cross (v.)
yaqta'	يقطع	cut (v.)
yaqus	يقص	trim
yara	يرى	see
yarbit	يربط	tie (v.)
yarfaa'	يرفع	escelate
yarkud	يركض	run
yarkudh	يركض	jog
yarqus	يرقص	dance (v.)
yartah	يرتاح	rest
yas-hab	يسحب	pull
yas'al	يسأل	ask (question)
yas'ul/yakuhh	يسعل/يكح	cough (v.)
yasar	يسار	left
yasbahh	يسبح	swim
yasbogh	يصبغ	painting
yash'ur	يشعر	feel
yashab/yajor	يسحب/يجر	tow
yashkur	يشكر	thank (v.)
yashrab	يشرب	drink (v.)
yashrah	يشرح	explain
yashtaaq	يشتاق	miss (loved one)
yashtuf	يشطف	rinse
yasil	يصل	arrive
yaskun	يسكن	live (v)
yasma'	يسمع	hear
yasna'	يصنع	make
yasooq	يسوق	drive
yasqut	يسقط	fall (v.)
yasriq	يسرق	steal
yass'ad	يصعد	get on
yassttaad as-samak	يصطاد السمك	fish (v.)
yasta'eer	يستعير	borrow
yasta'jir	يستأجر	hire
yasta'jir	يستأجر	rent
yastafsir	يستفسر	enquire (v.)
yastalqii	يستلقي	lie down
yastattle'	يستطلع	look up
yatahhadath/ hadeeth	حديث/يتحدث	talk
yatakhayyal	يتخيل	imagine
yatalaffath	يتلفظ	pronounce
yatalaffath	يتلفظ	spell
yatamata'	يتمتع	enjoy
yatasallam/ ya'khudh	يتسلم/ياخذ	pick up
yatasawwaq	يتسوق	shop (v.)
yatassel	يتصل	dial
yatassil	يتصل	phone (v.)
yatatha'ab	يتثاءب	yawn
yatawaqqaf	يتوقف	stop (cease)
yatba'	يتبع	follow
yatbukh	يطبخ	cook (v.)
yathhun	يظن	think
yathooq	يذوق	taste (v.)
yatkallam	يتكلم	speak
yatruk	يترك	vacate
yattassil	يتصل	call (v.)
yattba'	يطبع	print (v.)
yatteer	يطير	fly (v.)
yattlub	يطلب	ask for
yawm	يوم	day
yawwad	يود	feel like
yazin	يزن	weigh
yazoor	يزور	visit (v.)
yodheef	يضيف	add
yoghader	يغادر	check out

yoghader	يغادر	depart
yohib	يحب	love (v.)
yolghi	يلغي	cancel
yolyo	يوليو	July
yonaseb	يناسب	fit
yossali	يُصَلّي	pray
yossawer	يصور	film (v.)
yottem	يَتِمُّ	finish (v.)
yowwajeh	يوجه	guide (v.)
yu'ajjl	يؤجل	postpone
yu'aqqim	يعقم	sterilize
yu'iid	يعيد	repeat
yubaddil/yusarrif	يصرف/يبدل	exchange
yufadhil	يفضل	prefer
yughadir	يغادر	leave
yughayyir	يغير	change (v.)
yughliq/yutfi'	يغلق/ يطفيء	off (turned off)
yuhasin/yuttawir	يحسن/يطور	improve
yuhathir	يحذر	warn
yuhib/yarghab	يحب / يرغب	like (v.)
yuhriq/yahtariq	يحرق/يحترق	burn (v.)
yujaffif/yajuf	يجف /يجفف	dry (v.)
yunath-thif	ينظف	clean (v.)
yunssah	ينصح	recommend
yunyo	يونيو	June
yuqabbil	يقبل	kiss (v.)
yuqaddim/yu'arrif	يعرف/ يقدم	introduce
yuqif	يوقف	park (v.)
yuqridh	يقرض	lend
yurafiq	يرافق	escort
yurasil	يراسل	correspond
yuratib	يرتب	arrange
yuratib/ yunathhim	يرتب/ينظم	tidy
yurji'	يرجع	reverse
yursil	يرسل	send
yursil bilbareed	يرسل بالبريد	mail (v.)

yursil bilbarid	يرسل بالبريد	post (v.)
yusghii / yastami'	يستمع/ يصغي	listen
yushahid	يشاهد	watch (v.)
yuslih	يصلح	fix
yuslih	يصلح	repair
yuslih/tasleeh	يصلح/تصليح	mend
yussarrih	يصرح	declare
yussawwir	يصور	photocopy (v.)
yuta'arraf	يتعرف	identify
yutarjim	يترجم	translate
yuwaafiq /yunaasib	يوافق /يناسب	match (sports)
yuwadhih	يوضح	indicate
yuwdi'	يودع	deposit (v.)
yuwwaqqi'	يوقع	sign (v.)
yuz'ij	يزعج	disturb

Z

zakah	زَكاة	*zakat* (alms giving in Islam)
zameel	زميل	colleague
zanjabeel	زنجبيل	ginger
zawj	زوج	husband
zawj al-um	زوج الام	stepfather
zawja	زوجة	wife
zawjat al-ab	زوجة الاب	stepmother
zay	زي	costume
zay	زي	fashion
zayt	زيت	oil
zayt ad-deezil	زيت الديزل	diesel oil
zerr	زر	button
zibala	زبالة	garbage
ziyaaa	زيارة	visit (N.)
zobda	زبدة	butter
zthklaam	ظلام	dark
zubda	زبدة	margarine
zujaj	زجاج	glass (material)

PHOTO CREDITS